THE
REFERENCE
SHELF

THE BREAKUP OF

COMMUNISM:

The Soviet Union and

Eastern Europe

Edited by MATTHEW A. KRALJIC

THE REFERENCE SHELF

Volume 65, Number 1

THE H.W. WILSON COMPANY

New York   1993

THE REFERENCE SHELF

The books in this series contain reprints of articles, excerpts from books, and addresses on current issues and social trends in the United States and other countries. There are six separately bound numbers in each volume, all of which are generally published in the same calendar year. One number is a collection of recent speeches; each of the others is devoted to a single subject and gives background information and discussion from various points of view, concluding with a comprehensive bibliography that contains books and pamphlets and abstracts of additional articles on the subject. Books in the series may be purchased individually or on subscription.

Library of Congress Cataloging-in-Publication Data

The breakup of Communism : the Soviet Union and Eastern Europe / edited by Matthew A. Kraljic.
    p.   cm. – (The reference shelf : v. 65, no. 2).
   Includes bibliographical references (p.   ).
   ISBN 0-8242-0840-4
   1. Communism—Europe, Eastern—History—20th century. 2. Europe, Eastern—Politics and government—1989– I. Kraljic, Matthew A.
   II. Series.
   HX240.7.A6B73   1993
   320.947—dc20   92-42466
                                               CIP

Cover: Demonstrators burn the flag of the Romanian Communist party during a commeration for the victims of the revolution in Bucharest.
Photo: AP/Wide World Photos

Printed in the United States of America

CONTENTS

PREFACE

When the founders of European and Soviet communism envisioned what Karl Marx called *the withering away of the state,* it is doubtful they had in mind the events that have come to shape Eastern Europe and the Soviet Union since 1989. Leninist-Stalinist models of Marxism have been abandoned, though it is not clear what sort of political systems will replace them. Rather than a retreat from capitalism, these recently independent countries have begun a return to market economies.

Ironically, these events were, for the most part, fashioned and implemented in true Marxist style by the masses or common people—a shipyard worker, a writer, dissidents huddled in a church, protesters facing down an army and winning it over. While in most cases little or no blood was shed in ousting communist regimes, the aftermath has not been as peaceful.

World War II, which ended in 1945, was quickly followed by the Cold War. The latter ended with the demise of the Soviet Union and its hold on satellite nations, particularly those of eastern Europe. Section One of this compilation examines the global, bipolar nature of the Cold War and provides theories on why the Soviet system failed.

Political and social transitions in the post-Cold War period have been difficult. Section Two addresses some of the changes that have occurred since the 1989 collapse of the Berlin Wall. Uncertainty has become a hallmark of even the more stable systems in Eastern Europe. The monolith that was the Soviet Union has been shattered. Most of its former republics have joined to form a loose confederation—the Commonwealth of Independent States (CIS)—but ancient nationalistic and ethnic rivalries have resurfaced, not only threatening the CIS, but also leading to wars of secession in various republics and triggering a bloody genocide in what was Yugoslavia.

Although many theories exist for the shift from capitalism to socialism, few of them take into account the immense challenges facing those countries that wish to move from a planned to a free-market economy. Some of the problems and hardships created by the economic reforms in Eastern Europe and the former Soviet republics are dealt with in Section Three.

The passing of communism and of the Soviet Union as a superpower has left a void in world politics. The articles in Section Four consider what the "new world order" is or might be in the wake of the changes. Some of the authors note that the death of communism does not necessarily portend the birth of democracy. The rise of totalitarian or fundamentalist religious regimes in some countries is not only possible but even likely. Some articles also examine the possible roles of Russia, the Commonwealth of Independent States, Germany, the European Community, the countries of central Asia, and the United States, among other entities within the framework of various regional and global scenarios.

The editor is indebted to the authors and publishers who have granted permission for these materials to be reprinted herein. In addition, special thanks are due to the reference and circulation staffs of the Patchogue-Medford Library, and to my wife and family for their patience and understanding.

Matthew A. Kraljic

December 1992

I. THE ASH HEAP OF HISTORY

EDITOR'S INTRODUCTION

As National Security Advisor to President Jimmy Carter, Zbigniew Brzezinski became intimately involved in the dynamics of the Cold War. In a recent paper written for *Foreign Affairs*, Brzezinski opens this section with an assessment of the history of the Cold War and its impact on the participants. He defines the victory of the West over communism as a victory of ideology reinforced by NATO arms initiatives and a U.S. policy stressing human rights. He also maintains that economically and politically the Soviet Union was ripe for a collapse, particularly after the strategic miscalculations of its leadership during the 1980s. In Brzezinski's view, the Western nations must now act with clear-headed geopolitical aims if they are to bring about the peaceful end to the Russian empire and the stable consolidation of the newly independent non-Russian states.

An article published in *The American Spectator,* the second selection, details the events leading to the final ouster of Soviet President Mikhail Gorbachev and the formation of the Commonwealth of Independent States under the skillful maneuvering of Russian President Boris Yeltsin and President Leonid Kravchuk of Ukraine. The author, Adrian Karatnycky, views the breakup of the Soviet Union optimistically and discusses the possible alliances that may ultimately shape the former Soviet Republics.

Marxism-Leninism, according to George Weigel writing in the *National Review,* was a false doctrine from its onset, and it was the heretical nature of communism that led to the revolutions of 1989 in Eastern Europe and in the 1991 revolution in Russia. The author further argues that the collapse of these regimes demonstrates that the true roots of politics are a function of culture and, ultimately, of religion.

THE COLD WAR AND ITS AFTERMATH[1]

Karl von Clausewitz defined war as the continuation of policy by other means. By extension the Cold War can be defined as warfare by other (non-lethal) means. Nonetheless, warfare it was. And the stakes were monumental. Geopolitically the struggle, in the first instance, was for control over the Eurasian landmass and, eventually, even for global preponderance. Each side understood that either the successful ejection of the one from the western and eastern fringes of Eurasia or the effective containment of the other would ultimately determine the geostrategic outcome of the contest.

Also fueling the conflict were sharply conflicting, ideologically motivated conceptions of social organization and even of the human being itself. Not only geopolitics but philosophy—in the deepest sense of the self-definition of mankind—were very much at issue.

After some forty-five years of political combat, including some secondary military skirmishes, the Cold War did indeed come to a final end. And, given its designation as a form of war, it is appropriate to begin with an assessment deliberately expressed in terminology derived from the usual outcomes of wars, that is, in terms of victory and defeat, capitulation and postwar settlement. The Cold War did end in the victory of one side and in the defeat of the other. This reality cannot be denied, despite the understandable sensitivities that such a conclusion provokes among the tenderhearted in the West and some of the former leaders of the defeated side.

A simple test reinforces the above assertion. Suppose at some stage of the Cold War—say, ten years ago [around 1982] or even earlier—one were to have asked: What might be a reasonable but also substantive definition of a Western or American victory? Or, alternatively, what might a communist or Soviet victory look like? The answers are revealing, for they indicate that the final outcome was even more one-sided than most dared to expect.

Until 1956 some in the West might have defined victory as the

[1]Article by Zbigniew Brzezinski, counselor at the Center for Strategic and International Studies and professor of American foreign policy at the Johns Hopkins University, from *Foreign Affairs* 71:31–49 Fall '92. Copyright © 1992 by the Council on Foreign Relations, Inc. Reprinted with permission.

liberation of central Europe from Soviet domination. Western passivity during the Hungarian uprising, however, indicated that the Western, and especially the American, commitment to a policy of liberation was largely rhetorical. Thereafter most serious Westerners probably would have defined victory as involving primarily a combination of the following arrangements: German reunification by mutual agreement, with at least the former East Germany neutralized and with many in the West (and especially in Germany itself) even willing to accept German neutrality in exchange for unity; a mutual NATO-Warsaw Pact treaty, providing for significant troop reductions on both sides but also for the retention of some political-military links between Moscow and the central European states; genuine liberalization of the Soviet-imposed regimes, but with many liberal Westerners quite happy to settle for Kadar-type versions; a comprehensive strategic and conventional arms reduction agreement; and the termination of ideological hostility.

In brief, victory would have been defined largely as an accommodation in some respects consistent with the Western understanding of the Yalta agreement: de facto acceptance of a somewhat benign Soviet sphere of influence in central Europe, in return for Soviet acceptance of America's ties to Western Europe (and also to Japan and South Korea). To be sure, a more militant Western minority would have viewed the above as inadequate, while liberal progressives were in general inclined to accept the status quo as the basis for terminating the Cold War.

A Soviet definition of victory is somewhat more difficult to delineate, given the universalist aspirations of communist ideology and the more limited scope of actual Soviet power. Moreover one can also differentiate in the Soviet case between the radicals and the conservatives. The former favored the energetic pursuit of world revolution, exploiting what they perceived to be the general postwar crisis of capitalism. Others warned that caution dictated first consolidating the postwar Soviet gains. One can also deduce to some extent the basic geostrategic assumptions of the Soviet leadership from the top-level and confidential Soviet-Nazi exchanges in late 1940 regarding the postwar division of spoils in the event of the then anticipated Nazi victory. Both Hitler and Stalin agreed that America should be excluded from any role whatsoever in Eurasia, and that appears to have been the continuing Soviet goal during the Cold War.

Thus it seems reasonable to conclude that a working definition of a Soviet strategic victory in the Cold War would have entailed the submissive neutralization of both Western Europe (through the dismantling of NATO) and Japan, and the withdrawal of U.S. political and military presence across the oceans. Moreover, following adoption of the 1962 program of the Communist Party of the Soviet Union (CPSU), victory was also defined as attaining the worldwide economic supremacy of communism over capitalism, said to be inevitable by 1980. In the meantime anti-Western "national liberation" struggles would isolate "the imperialist camp," with the rest being only a global mop-up operation.

It is a useful exercise to ponder these two alternative notions of victory. Not only did the Soviet victory not come to pass (whether it could have ever been attained is discussed later), but the most likely conventional Western scenario of victory has been exceeded to a degree that is truly staggering. Germany is reunited and already wholly in NATO, with Soviet forces to be withdrawn altogether by 1994; the Warsaw Pact has been abolished, and Soviet forces have been evicted from Hungary and Czechoslovakia and are in process of their final departure from Poland; the Soviet-imposed regimes in central Europe have not only been overthrown but Poland, Hungary and Czechoslovakia are moving toward joining the European Community (EC) and even knocking at the doors of NATO.

Most important of all, the Soviet Union itself has crumbled and central Eurasia is now a geopolitical vacuum. The former Soviet army is being demobilized and is already demoralized. The Baltic states are free, Ukraine is consolidating its independent statehood and so are the Central Asian republics. Russia's own unity may soon also be at stake, with perhaps the Far Eastern provinces tempted before too long to set up a separate Siberian-Far Eastern republic of their own. Indeed the economic and even the political destiny of what was not long ago a threatening superpower is now increasingly passing into de facto Western receivership. Instead of the once acclaimed theory of "convergence" of the two competing systems, the reality is that of one-sided conversion.

This is an outcome historically no less decisive and no less one-sided than the defeat of Napoleonic France in 1815, or of Imperial Germany in 1918, or of Nazi Germany and Imperial Japan in 1945. Unlike the Peace of Westphalia, which ended the Thirty Years War in a grand religious compromise, *cuius regio, cuius religio* does not apply here. Rather, from a doctrinal point of view, the outcome is more similar to 1815 or 1945: the ideology of the losing side has itself been repudiated. Geopolitically the outcome is also suggestive of 1918: the defeated empire is in the process of dismantlement.

As in previous terminations of war there was a discernible moment of capitulation, followed by postwar political upheavals in the losing state. That moment came most probably in Paris on November 19, 1990. At a conclave marked by ostentatious displays of amity designed to mask the underlying reality, the erstwhile Soviet leader, Mikhail Gorbachev, who had led the Soviet Union during the final stages of the Cold War, accepted the conditions of the victors by describing in veiled and elegant language the unification of Germany that had taken place entirely on Western terms as "a major event." This was the functional equivalent of the act of capitulation in the railroad car in Compiègne in 1918 [ending World War I] or on the U.S.S. *Missouri* in August 1945 [ending the Japanese role in World War II] even though the key message was subtly couched in "friendship."

Defeats tend to be politically unsettling. Not only do warlosing regimes tend to be overthrown, but the leaders who accept the necessity of capitulation also tend to pay the political price. The kaiser's regime collapsed within days after November 11, 1918—Armistice Day. Within a year the Soviet leader who had accepted the thinly disguised defeat of the Soviet Union was himself overthrown. More than that: the doctrinal past was also formally condemned, the red flag was officially lowered, the ideology and systemic features of the victorious side were henceforth to be formally imitated. The Cold War was, indeed, over.

The critical question on history's agenda now is this: What kind of peace? To what end? On what models of previous postwar settlements? But before those issues are addressed, a second set of major, as well as some subordinate, questions still need to be examined:

—How was the Cold War actually played? More specifically, were there discernible phases to it? Which side was on the offensive and which on the defensive, and when?

—Was the outcome foreordained? Was an earlier Western victory possible? Could there have been a compromise outcome? And, finally, could the Soviet Union have won and, if so, when?

Both sets of questions are not only of historical interest. There are lessons to be learned for the kind of relations that should now be fostered in the new postwar settlement era, both from the mistakes as well as the accomplishments of the past, and from the very nature of the grand contest itself.

It now seems clear that in the Cold War's initial phase, which lasted until after Stalin's death in March 1953, both sides were motivated more by fear than by aggressive designs, but each also perceived the other as, indeed, intent on aggression. In fact *both* significantly demobilized their forces, though the traditional Stalinist secrecy that masked the Soviet demobilization fed Western fears of a possible Soviet conventional sweep westward by a huge Soviet land army that actually no longer existed.

It is now evident that for Stalin the central concern then was to keep and to digest his principal war gain—control over central Europe—while avoiding a premature collision with the ascending Western power, America. He was no doubt motivated also by the hope that America would eventually disengage from Europe. He thus counseled caution and restraint to his more radical and impatient revolutionary allies, notably Yugoslavia's Marshal Tito and China's Mao Zedong.

Stalin was also convinced that the West would seek to contest his primacy in central Europe. He interpreted the Western demands for democratic elections as an effort to inject Trojan horses into his domain. He saw in the introduction of the new West German currency a deliberate effort to undermine his own occupation of East Germany. As the Cold War heated up, he became increasingly paranoid, prompting massive purges of his own satellite communist elites and witch-hunts against any and all manifestations of independent political thinking.

This does not mean that Stalin's intentions were altogether defensive. Rather one can argue that Stalin had a realistic appreciation of the correlation of forces, that he knew how to bide his time and that he wanted first to consolidate his gains before moving forward. Eventually he did expect that with the hoped-for American disengagement from Europe, continental domination (and thus ideological victory) would be his. In a revealing exchange at Potsdam, Stalin responded to Churchill's congratulations on the Russian capture of Berlin by noting wistfully that in 1815 Alexander I had triumphantly marched into Paris.

During this first phase the West also maintained a defensive posture. The West condemned the Soviet subjugation of central Europe but did not contest it. Then the Berlin blockade in 1947 was perceived as the beginning of a Soviet westward push, meant to force the West not only out of Berlin itself but also out of Germany. The Korean War was viewed at a minimum as a diversionary offensive tactic, preliminary to the central showdown in Europe, but also as a part of the effort to complete the expulsion of America from the mainland of Asia and an effort to intimidate Japan.

The Western, and especially the American, response remained cautious throughout. Preventive war against the Soviet Union was not seriously contemplated, despite the U.S. nuclear monopoly. "Massive retaliation," based on U.S. strategic superiority, was in effect a defensive doctrine. The Berlin blockade was contested only indirectly. China was not attacked, despite its massive intervention in the Korean War. The West, instead, placed increased emphasis on the political integration of its slowly recovering former enemies, Germany and Japan, and America undertook explicit commitments to remain militarily present both in the western and eastern extremities of Eurasia. The Korean War demonstrated the American resolve to remain in shattered Korea and Japan, while the creation of NATO in 1949 represented a binding security marriage between America and the still weak Western Europe. The lines were thus clearly drawn. They endured for some forty years.

Stalin's death brought this first phase of the Cold War to an end. Not only were both sides ready for a respite, but the West seemed poised for an offensive. American self-restraint in the Korean War was becoming increasingly strained, and the new Republican administration was broadly hinting that nuclear weapons might be employed. More important, the new U.S. secretary of state, John Foster Dulles, had publicly committed the United States to a policy of "liberation" of central Europe from Soviet domination. With NATO in existence, with German rearmament under active consideration, and with the United States assertively proclaiming a forward strategy of its own, the proclamation of the policy of liberation appeared to foreshadow a comprehensive Western offensive on the central front, boldly directed at the enemy's weakest sector.

The offensive never materialized. The reasons were basically twofold. The first is that the American side never fully meant it. The policy of liberation was a strategic sham, designed to a significant degree for domestic political reasons. To the extent that it was taken seriously by U.S. policymakers, it prompted more intensified Radio Free Europe broadcasts to the satellite nations, more financial support for émigré political activities, and larger-scale efforts to support anti-Soviet undergrounds behind the Iron Curtain. The policy was basically rhetorical, at most tactical.

America's European allies, in any case, not only had never embraced the concept but in fact had been basically against it. The strategic hollowness of the liberation policy was fully exposed during the dramatic months of October and November 1956, when the communist regimes in Hungary and Poland were teetering and when the post-Stalin regime in Moscow was torn by fear and uncertainty. America did nothing to deter the eventual Soviet intervention in Hungary, while the Anglo-French invasion of Egypt signaled that America's principal allies had other priorities.

The other reason the offensive never emerged was that the post-Stalin Soviet leadership was so fearful that the West might actually attempt to exploit the consequences of the tyrant's death that it promptly moved in the direction of diffusing the more dangerous facets of the ongoing Cold War. One of the principal contenders for Stalin's mantle, the secret police boss Lavrenti Beria, even explored the notion of German reunification (in exchange for neutrality). If implemented it would have meant an unprecedented pullback of Soviet power. The other Soviet leaders were not prepared to go quite that far, but they did strive to facilitate the end of the Korean War and, lead by the comical duo of Nikita Khrushchev and Nikolai Bulganin, they eagerly embraced "the spirit of Geneva" that the British and French (fearful of the new American rhetoric) were promoting.

The interlude did not last long. The American-led Western offensive that the post-Stalin leadership so feared never materialized, while before long the spirit of Geneva fizzled out as well. In the meantime the new Soviet leadership, increasingly consolidated under Khrushchev, gradually regained self-confidence and began to craft a new and comprehensive strategy, designed to break out of the Eurasian containment that the West had fashioned. That strategy was to be based on three elements: growing Soviet strategic power, which was beginning to neutralize the U.S. deterrent; Soviet economic vitality, which Moscow hoped would before long match the industrial might of the United States and become an ideological magnet for the developing countries; and the promotion of "national liberation" struggles around the world, thereby forging a de facto alliance between the newly emancipated Third World and the Soviet-led bloc.

The Soviet Union now moved to the offensive. Eurasia was still the central stake but no longer the central front. Containment was to be defeated by encirclement. Since it could not be pierced without a central war, it would be enveloped. Victory would come somewhere around 1980. This target date was postulated with extraordinary optimism—and supported by massive statistics—in the new CPSU platform proclaimed by Khrushchev in 1962. By that date not only was the Soviet Union to surpass the United States economically but the communist world as a whole was to become economically stronger than the capitalist world. At that point the scales of history would tip.

This second major phase, with its various ups and downs, including some temporary Soviet setbacks, lasted almost twenty years, from the late 1950s to the late 1970s. Although there were brief periods of Western tactical assertiveness as well as occasional "ceasefires," the Cold War on the geostrategic level during this phase was characterized by an offensive Soviet posture. It was marked by boastful assertions of Soviet rocket superiority, by the expansion of Soviet political-military influence into the Middle East and by the successful acquisition of the highly symbolic but potentially geostrategically important base in Cuba. It even involved two brief but dangerous U.S.-Soviet confrontations, one in Berlin and the other in Cuba, both precipitated by Soviet assertiveness.

Despite the prevailing view of the time that these two dangerous clashes ended as American victories, the U.S. successes were largely tactical while the Soviet gains were more strategic. The uncontested Soviet construction of the Berlin Wall [in 1961] consolidated Soviet control over East Germany—thereby terminating Soviet fears of Western subversion of its domination over central Europe—while the withdrawal of Soviet missiles from Cuba was purchased by the Kennedy administration throughout a blanket guarantee of the continued existence of a pro-Soviet regime. In effect, immunity was successfully extorted for a geopolitically important Soviet forward base in defiance of the line drawn by the once inviolable Monroe Doctrine.

Despite the fall of Khrushchev in 1964 the basic thrust of the Soviet strategy was sustained under the less colorful and more bureaucratic Brezhnev regime. The strategic buildup continued

for the next two decades, imposing such enormous strains on the
Soviet economy that, in the end, they vitiated the (in any case,
unrealistic) goal of surpassing the United States in the economic
domain. The efforts to expand the Soviet role in the Third
World, thereby piercing Western containment within Eurasia,
were likewise sustained, despite tactical accommodations with the
Johnson and Nixon administrations, both of them burdened by
the Vietnam War and eager for some respite in the Cold War.

The resulting U.S.-Soviet accommodations were, however,
confined to only two areas: some modest progress in arms control
negotiations and some relaxation of tensions in Europe. But
though the Soviet expansion into the Third World and the Soviet
strategic buildup continued, even that limited progress on several
occasions led the West to proclaim the premature end of the Cold
War. In the late 1960s and early 1970s "détente" became a fashionable concept, "beyond the Cold War" a frequent title for op-ed
pieces, and a U.S. president even announced in the early 1970s
that "a generation of peace" had been attained.

During this phase of the contest America's European allies,
fully recovered and protected by containment based on American
power, tended to act as if they were increasingly neutral in the
global Cold War and ready to negotiate separate ceasefires in
Europe itself. While this posture was not formally opposed by the
United States, it did tend to create tensions in the alliance as well
as openings for Soviet diplomacy. To many people the slogan
"Europe to the Urals" or the term "Ostpolitik" were code words
for a separate European posture on the critical East-West issues.
The unpopularity of the Vietnam War tended to contribute to a
sense of American isolation, and that in turn fed into U.S. slogans
advocating "Come home, America."

The Soviet offensive thrust reached its apogee in the 1970s.
Soviet momentum interacted with America's post-Vietnam fa-
tigue and with the widespread Western eagerness for détente to
a degree that America seemed ready to settle the Cold War even
on the basis of accepting strategic inferiority. President Nixon's
brilliant coup in opening the U.S.-Chinese relationship altered
the geostrategic context, but it could not compensate for internal American dissension and demoralization. That condition
prompted Secretary of State Henry Kissinger—himself inclined
toward historical pessimism—to diligently seek an accommodation modeled on the Peace of Westphalia: each side was to retain
its geopolitical and ideological realms. It would be stabilized by a

new emphasis on arms control, thereby slowing down the massive Soviet buildup but at the price even of accepting (in SALT I) Soviet strategic superiority.

The Soviet global offensive continued unabated into the second half of the 1970s. No longer politically deterred by American strategic power, Soviet troops were deployed in Vietnam, Ethiopia, Yemen, Cuba, not to mention the geopolitically vital Middle East, while Soviet military surrogates were active in Mozambique, Angola and elsewhere. The Soviet military buildup reached unprecedented and truly threatening proportions. The SS-20 deployments aimed at Western Europe and Japan were specifically designed for intimidation. For the first time during the entire Cold War the Soviet Union seemed to be genuinely preparing to dictate the outcome, both by encirclement and perhaps even on the central front.

Yet self-delusion lingered in the Western capitals and in Washington. French and German leaders competed in courting Brezhnev and in extolling his virtues. President Carter was counseled by some of his own top associates that he and Brezhnev "shared the same aspirations" and they urged the elevation of arms control into a Holy Grail, the solution to the overall ideological and geopolitical struggle. Indeed, in that view, not only was any linkage between arms control negotiations and Soviet misconduct dogmatically excluded, but the Soviets were even seen as entitled to exercise "negative" linkage, that is, they had the right to view as an obstruction to arms control those American policies they did not like (such as any strategic enhancement of the U.S.-Chinese relationship). Détente came to be viewed as an end in itself.

The moment seemed ripe for a historical turning point, but it did not occur. Instead the dramatic reversal only gradually took shape, mushroomed, and eventually produced an outcome beyond the wildest expectations even of the few historical optimists who persisted in the conviction that the Soviet drive, if confronted, could be stopped; and once stopped, that it could be reversed. As often in history, this happened for a variety of reasons, ranging from human folly to fortune. Most important perhaps were the errors and miscalculations of the Soviets themselves. Misjudging the historical situation, they pushed their forward thrust beyond the limits of toleration of even the most accommodationist elements in the West, while at the same time they strained Soviet internal resources to a point that the inherent weaknesses and corruption of the Soviet system assumed dynamic dimensions. Their conduct, in brief, fitted well Paul Kennedy's concept of "imperial overstretch."

The result was the final phase of the Cold War, roughly from 1979 until 1991. It was marked by the West's gradual recapture of the ideological initiative, by the eruption of a philosophical and political crisis in the adversary's camp and by the final and decisive push by the United States in the arms race. This phase lasted slightly more than a decade. Its outcome was victory.

The historically dramatic turnabout was precipitated by three critical cases of Soviet overstretch. Geopolitically the Soviet invasion of Afghanistan in December 1979—apparently taken on the assumption that the United States would not react—propelled the United States to adopt, for the first time ever during the entire Cold War, a policy of directly supporting actions aimed at killing Soviet troops. The Carter administration not only undertook immediately to support the Mujahedeen, but it also quietly put together a coalition embracing Pakistan, China, Saudi Arabia, Egypt and Britain on behalf of the Afghan resistance. Equally important was the American public guarantee of Pakistan's security against any major Soviet military attack, thereby creating a sanctuary for the guerillas. The scale and quality of U.S. support steadily expanded during the 1980s under the subsequent Reagan administration. America—along with Pakistan, which played a courageous and decisive role in the effort—thus succeeded in bogging down the Soviet Union in its own equivalent of Vietnam.

Moreover, with the influence of the accommodationist school of thought undercut by Soviet assertiveness, the United States qualitatively expanded its relationship with China. As early as 1980 U.S.-Chinese cooperation assumed a more direct strategic dimension, with sensitive undertakings not only toward Afghanistan but also on other matters. Thus the Soviet Union faced the growing geopolitical menace of a counter encirclement.

In addition, the Carter administration initiated the creation of a Rapid Deployment Force, and, most important, the decision was made together with key NATO allies to match the Soviet SS-20 deployments with new and highly accurate American intermediate-range missiles positioned on European soil. The latter prompted a vigorous Soviet campaign of intimidation directed at Europe, with Europe explicitly warned (in the words of Foreign Minister Andrei Gromyko) that it might suffer the fate of

Pompeii unless the Atlantic security link was significantly loos-
ened. However, America's European allies held firm—encouraged by the increasingly assertive tones emanating from Washington and by the acceleration of the U.S. defense buildup adopted
by the Reagan administration.

The massive U.S. defense buildup of the early 1980s—
including the decision to proceed with the Strategic Defense
Initiative—both shocked the Soviets and then strained their resources. Its scale, momentum and technological daring had been
totally unexpected in Moscow. By 1983 a genuine war scare began
to develop in the Kremlin, with the United States seen as bent
perhaps even on a military solution. And then by the middle of
the decade it dawned on Soviet leaders that they could neither
match nor even keep up with the American efforts.

This realization interacted dynamically with the third reversal, on the ideological and social planes. In the second half of the
1970s President Carter launched his human rights campaign.
Within Soviet-controlled Eastern Europe and then within the Soviet Union itself, it first encouraged a few individuals, then larger
groups, to pick up the standard of human rights, counting on
Western moral and even political support. The struggle for human rights mushroomed, especially in Poland, galvanized by the
election of the first Polish pope in Rome. By the late 1970s Solidarity's mass movement was beginning to threaten the communist
regime of the Soviet Union's most important European satellite.

The Soviets were poised to intervene militarily in Poland, once
in December 1980 and then again in March 1981. In both cases
two successive U.S. administrations made clear, through direct
and indirect signals, that such intervention would produce grave
consequences, a message in the meantime made more credible by
U.S. support for the Afghan resistance. Under these circumstances the Kremlin leaders chose to rely on an only partially
effective imposition of martial law by the Polish communists
themselves. As a result the Polish crisis festered through the decade, progressively undermining not only the Polish communist
regime but gradually infecting other East European states.

The human rights campaign and the arms buildup thus became the mutually reinforcing central prongs of a U.S. response
that not only blunted the Soviet offensive but also intensified the
crisis of the Soviet political and socioeconomic system itself. Power
and principle combined to reverse the Soviet momentum. Neither
one alone would have sufficed.

By the mid-1980s a new and younger Soviet leadership had come to power. Imbued with the realization that Soviet policies, both internal and external, were a failure, Moscow was determined to repair the communist system through energetic reforms and to place its satellite regimes on a more domestically acceptable basis. To do that it needed a period of respite. These Soviet leaders thus eagerly seized the olive branch extended by the Reagan administration in 1985—especially in connection with the December 1985 Geneva summit—in the hope of gaining relief from the arms race.

The recent past is still fresh in memory. The domestic reforms, conducted pell-mell, did not revitalize the Soviet system but merely brought to the surface its hypocrisies and weaknesses. The arms race had exhausted the Soviet economy, while refuting its ideological expectations. Failure to crush the Solidarity underground in Poland gradually forced the Polish communist regime into a compromise that rapidly turned into a progressive concession of power, with contagious effects in the neighboring satellites. Gorbachev's willingness to tolerate what he thought would be limited change in east-central Europe—in order to gain a breathing spell for his own domestic reforms—precipitated not the emergence of more popularly endorsed and reformist communist leadership but eventually the collapse of the communist systems as a whole.

By 1989 the choice left to Moscow was either a last-gasp effort to reimpose its rule through massive bloodshed—which not only could have precipitated violent domestic or external explosions but in all probability an intensification of the arms race and hostility with America—or to acquiesce. The reformist Gorbachev leadership—flattered, courted, even bribed by the West, and in the final phases skillfully manipulated personally by President Bush and German Chancellor Helmut Kohl—chose the second course. The result was chaos in east-central Europe and then capitulation.

Could the outcome have been different? And what of the future, given the past?

The West perhaps might have won sooner, but at a higher cost and with a greater risk of war. The key opportunity for the West came in the period 1953–56. Greater Western elasticity in 1953 might have facilitated a Soviet pullback from Germany. But the Kremlin almost certainly would have used the Soviet army to maintain its grip on Warsaw and Prague, while in the West the neutralization of Germany might have precluded the establishment of binding NATO links between America and Europe. In contrast greater Western toughness in 1956—still a time of decisive U.S. strategic superiority—might have resulted in forcing the Soviet Union out of Hungary and Poland. The communist regimes in these countries were crumbling, and the Soviet leadership itself was in a state of panic.

The Cold War, however, would not have ended. Communism was not ripe for a collapse within Russia itself, and on the global scale the ideological momentum of communism was far from spent. Communist movements were strong even in Western Europe, and the communist wave in the Far East was still cresting. Thus any respite in the Cold War would have been just temporary. Moreover one cannot exclude the possibility that in these circumstances at least a conventional war might have broken out in central Europe.

The only other opportunity for ending the Cold War may have existed in the early 1970s, on the basis of what might be called "the Peace of Westphalia formula." But both sides would have had then to accept the status quo in Europe as fixed. The West seemed ready to do so. However, by the mid-1970s, the Soviets saw themselves as being on a historical roll. Hence Moscow wanted the status quo in Europe as well as American acquiescence to continued Soviet global expansion and to a gradual shift in "the correlation of forces." In effect any acceptance of the European status quo would have been for the Soviets merely a temporary expedient.

This is why it is historically important to reiterate here the fact that the Kremlin was in no mood to be propitiated either through arms control or an acceptance by the West of the existing division of Europe. The Cold War eventually ended because the West succeeded in combining firm containment with an active offensive on human rights and a strategic buildup of its own, while aiding the resistance of Afghanistan and Poland.

A more plausible case can be made for the proposition that the West could have spared itself a decade or so by adopting earlier an offensive ideological and strategic posture. But in real life democracies are not able to adopt a forward strategy that requires philosophical and military mobilization without overwhelming and truly threatening provocation from the other side. That provocation was apparent to some in the 1970s; to most

Americans and Europeans it became evident only in the early 1980s, in the wake of the blatant Soviet SS-20 threats, the invasion of Afghanistan and the suppression of Poland's Solidarity movement.

Throughout the Cold War it was America that bore most of the burden and displayed the strongest will to persist. America's allies were generally steadfast in critical moments, but otherwise they were more tempted to settle for a compromise. It was America that sustained large scale efforts—especially by means of radio—to pierce the Iron Curtain, and it was America that in the later phases of the Cold War most directly supported the resistance in Afghanistan and the underground in Poland while intimidating Moscow through its crash strategic buildup. And it was America that throughout the Cold War deterred Soviet power with a posture and a leadership that was on the whole remarkably consistent.

In that regard the historical credit for fashioning the winning strategy and for forging the victorious coalition must go to one man above all: Harry Truman. He committed America because he understood the stakes. Eisenhower then built on Truman regarding NATO; Carter built on Nixon regarding China; Bush built on Reagan regarding the arms race. American policy may not have been brilliant and, at times, it was overly defensive, but it was steady. It also remained tactically focused on the weakest link in the Soviet "front": east-central Europe. From the 1960s onward the United States consistently sought, overtly and covertly, to soften Soviet control over the region by a policy of peaceful engagement, with the payoff coming finally in the 1980s.

In contrast Soviet policy lacked consistency. With the exception of Stalin himself the Soviet leadership proved to be less steady and operationally inferior to America's. Stalin was the Great Calculator, carefully husbanding his resources, devouring his enemies, while cautiously bluffing in order to obscure his system's weaknesses. But even he made a basic and historically decisive error: his brutal policies in east-central Europe united the West, and that unity precluded America's disengagement from Europe. Once that became clear a conclusive Soviet victory was no longer possible.

Stalin's successors were second rate. Khrushchev was the Master Bumbler, pressing and posturing, creating the illusion of historical momentum at a time of Western indecision. But he could not achieve a breakthrough, even though he brought both sides dangerously close to a military collision at a time of still relative Soviet strategic inferiority. Brezhnev, the Gray Plodder, posed more of a threat, with his steady buildup of Soviet strategic might, but he did not know when to exploit that might for political gain. Had Brezhnev proved more imaginative, he might have taken advantage of Nixon's realism to reach an advantageous peace of Westphalia or the goodwill of the American president in the latter 1970s, and of the naïvete of some of his advisers, to conclude an even more beneficial accommodation. Instead, Brezhnev pursued the policy of global encirclement, with some peripheral successes but no breakthrough on the central front.

The last Soviet leader, Gorbachev, can be considered operationally the Grand Miscalculator and historically a tragic figure. He thought he could revitalize the Soviet economy that Brezhnev, through his military spending, had ruined, but he did not know how. He thought he could reach a broad détente with the West, but he underestimated the corrosive effects of the war in Afghanistan and of the survival of the Solidarity movement in Poland. Attempts at East-West accommodation, instead of stabilizing Soviet rule in east-central Europe, exploded in his face, especially once the fear of Soviet intervention had been dissipated by Gorbachev's cultivation of the West and by the Soviet military's failures in Afghanistan.

Could the Soviets have won the Cold War? The final outcome was the product of objective and subjective factors, and on both scores the Soviet side turned out to have been at a disadvantage. The Western socioeconomic system proved much stronger and its underlying ideas ultimately much more appealing. In effect, despite some illusions propagated by Khrushchev and entertained by Brezhnev, the Soviet Union was forced to play "catch-up ball" throughout the Cold War.

The bottom line thus has to be that a full-blown Soviet victory was never in the cards, except very briefly right after World War II. Had America disengaged, the outcome would have been quite different. But that alternative was foreclosed early on. Thereafter the Kremlin could have sought and perhaps obtained favorable settlements that could have served as launchpads for later offensives, but its leaders failed to exploit the occasional opportunities. These knocked on history's doors early in the 1950s and even more so in the 1970s. Finally, the grand scale of the final defeat in the late 1980s could also have been minimized, if the Gorbachev leadership had been more skillful in handling its domestic reforms and had moved more rapidly in the mid-1980s to resolve the Afghan and Polish problems.

What should now be the West's central strategic objective toward its former Cold War rival?

The point of departure for a meaningful answer is to recognize that, from a historical point of view, the collapse of the Soviet Union, which endured for some seventy years, is more than overshadowed by the disintegration of the great Russian empire, which lasted for more than three hundred years. This is an event of truly historic magnitude, pregnant with geopolitical uncertainties. It will be many years before the dust finally settles, but it is already clear that the postcommunist transition in the former empire will be more difficult and much more prolonged than the democratic reconstruction of either Germany or Japan after 1945.

The West must support that transition with the same commitment and magnanimity with which America acted after the victory in 1945. That commitment, however, must be guided by a longer-range geopolitical vision that goes beyond the West's currently one-sided concentration on facilitating Russia's socioeconomic recovery. While that recovery is desirable, its attainment should be seen as part of a broader effort designed to accomplish two interrelated objectives: the emergence of a truly postimperial Russia that can assume its proper place in the concert of the world's leading democratic nations; and the stable consolidation of the newly independent non-Russian states, some of which are only in the early stages of their own nation building, in order to create an enduring geopolitical context that by itself reinforces Russia's transformation into a post-imperial state. Each of the foregoing is dependent on the other, and hence both must be deliberately sought.

Any Western ambiguity on this matter could prove historically shortsighted. Just as it would have been a historic mistake to settle for less than the liberation of east-central Europe from Moscow's domination, so now too a recovery program for the Russian economy that does not at the same time seek to transform Russia into a post-imperial state could prove to be ephemeral. Accordingly any Russian efforts to isolate and eventually again to subordinate Ukraine through the maintenance of a Moscow-controlled outpost in Crimea, for example, or to delay the evacuation of Russian troops from the Baltic republics should be unambiguously viewed as obstacles to effective financial and economic assistance.

However it is also essential to provide the Russians with a meaningful alternative to their longstanding imperial status, and that has to be the offer of partnership with the West. The West is correct in stressing that it sees Russia's eventual destiny as a major player in the European concert of nations and as one of America's partners in dealing with the world's wider problems. But to become such a player the transformation of Russia requires—as earlier in the cases of Germany and Japan—the shedding of its imperial aspirations.

Since as a practical matter any formal association of Russia with Europe is still a long way off, some thought should now be given to the creation of intermediary forms of involvement with Europe. One such step might involve Western support for a Baltic Sea/Black Sea zone of enhanced cooperation. This would engage the central European states that are already becoming associated with the EC in a common effort with Russia, the Baltic states, Ukraine and Belarus to enhance their communications, transport and eventually free trade. Kaliningrad, while remaining Russian politically, could also become a European free-trade zone. The recent agreement between Belarus and Poland for Belarussian use of the Polish port of Gdynia is a sign that central European regional cooperation can extend eastward. Russia should not be made to feel that a new *cordon sanitaire* separates it from the West.

The above must be matched by sustained Western efforts to promote nation building in the former Soviet empire. Above all it is geopolitically essential that Ukraine succeed in stabilizing itself as a secure and independent state. That will automatically increase the chances of Russia's evolution as a democratizing and increasingly European post-imperial state. Accordingly a critical component of Western strategy has to be the deliberate effort—not only economic but also political—to consolidate a stable and sovereign Ukraine. Elsewhere in the former empire the process of nation building is likely to be even more complex than in Ukraine, and yet it too will have to be supported simultaneously with the postcommunist socioeconomic transformation itself.

That socioeconomic transformation will be long and painful. The West, in proffering aid and advice, must be careful not to replace old communist slogans with new dogmas of its own regarding the application of capitalist practices. Any attempt to create simultaneously a free-market economy and a political democracy that does not carefully seek to minimize the social pains of the needed transition could precipitate a destructive collision between these two objectives. This collision could then discredit both goals in the eyes of the affected peoples and enhance the appeal of some new escapist doctrines.

The aftermath of the Cold War thus poses an agenda for the West that is truly daunting. Its essence is to make certain that the disintegration of the Soviet Union becomes the peaceful and enduring end of the Russian empire, and that the collapse of communism truly means the end of the utopian phase in modern political history. But these grand goals will come to pass only if the West again demonstrates strategic staying power, focused on clearheaded geopolitical—and not just on narrow socioeconomic or vaguely idealistic—aims.

MINSK MEET[2]

On December 8, [1991,] President Boris Yeltsin of Russia and President Leonid Kravchuk of Ukraine, with the concurrence of Stanislav Shushkevich of Belarus (formerly Byelorussia), met in Minsk to sign the obituary of the last empire: "The Union of Soviet Socialist Republics, as a subject of international law and a geopolitical reality, is ceasing its existence." Their declaration was a call upon the world community to withdraw diplomatic recognition from the Soviet Union and to confer it upon the newly sovereign republics of the Commonwealth of Independent States. If their action was driven by urgency and necessity, it was also calmly reasoned and well thought out. In dispensing with the USSR, the leaders of Europe's three newest nation-states were not opting for anarchy and civil war. Indeed, as events showed, Yeltsin, Kravchuk, and Shushkevich would not have acted without at least some assurance from the military that it would back their gambit. These were not three reckless, irrational men.

The urgency of their undertaking was clear: a worsening economic crisis, institutional paralysis, an almost willfully destructive central state, and a military uncertain whom it should serve. As early as October 1991, the USSR had been replaced by a loose

[2]Article by Adrian Karatnycky, author and special assistant to the president of the AFL-CIO, from *The American Spectator* 23:27–33 F'92. Copyright © 1992 by The American Spectator. Reprinted with permission.

economic community. After the [August 1991] coup, fewer than half of the old USSR's fifteen republics—Russia, Belarus, Kazakhstan, Uzbekistan, Kirgizstan, Turkmenistan, and Tajikistan—were participating in the reorganized Supreme Soviet. Yet even this parliamentary structure, which underwent a facelift following the August coup, could not survive. Its only significant legislative initiative came on November 19[, 1991]—a law guaranteeing deputies six months' severance pay in the event of the dissolution of the parliament. By December 11 [1991] the Supreme Soviet of the USSR—with Russia and Belarus no longer participating—could not even muster a quorum. The new Commonwealth was proof that democratic nationalism was the central political engine in the collapse of Communism and the unraveling of empire.

Mikhail Gorbachev's myth of a unitary Soviet state was accepted to the bitter end only by President Bush, whose man in Moscow Robert Strauss initially questioned the viability of the new Slavic-led Commonwealth. But since the failed coup, Gorbachev's central state had been taking a daily beating. In Azerbaijan, all USSR government offices were ordered closed as of October 19[, 1991]. By late November, Yeltsin had taken control of the economic levers of central state power. Then he announced that Russia would cease payments to seventy central ministries, leaving 100,000 of Mikhail Gorbachev's apparatchiks headed for the unemployment line. When conflicts arose among the republics, it was Boris Yeltsin and Nursultan Nazarbayev who plunged into action, as when they brokered a temporary respite to the Armenian-Azerbaijani conflict in early October. When economic issues such as dividing the Soviet debt were at stake, Kiev—not Moscow—was the venue for deliberations and Ukrainian leader Kravchuk—not Gorbachev—hosted them. Gorbachev was deliberately excluded when ministers and presidents of the republics gathered in Alma-Ata, Kazakhstan, to discuss the post-Soviet economic community. And it was Minsk, the Slavic USSR's westernmost capital, that became the venue of the empire's iron curtain call.

There were other signs of imperial collapse. In Ukraine, troops patrolling the republic's western border with Czechoslovakia, Hungary, Romania, and Poland were taking down the red Soviet flag and raising the blue and yellow colors of independent Ukraine. Border troops were trying to learn Ukrainian and adapting their Soviet uniforms to include Ukrainian emblems and symbols. While Yeltsin announced his intention to create a

Russian national guard, the Ukrainian parliament went further, claiming dominion over all non-nuclear Soviet military forces in Ukraine and beginning to raise a Ukrainian army between 120,000 and 420,000 strong. . . . In October [1991], a sampling of public opinion found solid support for splitting up the Red Army, with 47 percent welcoming such a development as democratic, 19 percent worrying that it undermined the defensive capability of the country, and 14 percent concerned that it might lead to civil war. (The remaining 20 percent weren't sure how to answer.) In the last months of 1991, Mikhail Gorbachev formally controlled the black briefcase with one of the keys to the Soviet nuclear system, but with the military now siding with the leaders of Russia, Belarus, and Ukraine it seemed likely that Boris Yeltsin and Leonid Kravchuk would soon have their hands on the keys.

Much has been written about Gorbachev's fabled reforms, but it was the failed August coup that spelled the end of Communism and empire. Historians are likely to reject the notion that the failed coup was somehow a victory for glasnost and perestroika. Vladimir Bukovsky has suggested that, far from being its victim, Gorbachev may well have been engaged in preparing the coup. Even if he did not participate in it, he could well have planned to introduce a state of emergency at an appropriate moment. And while Gorbachev may have been held against his will in his Crimean *dacha*, the real targets of the putsch were the growing democratic movement and the centrifugal independence forces in the republics.

Of all the theories about why the coup didn't succeed, the least plausible is the one most readily offered—that its plotters were incompetent bunglers. The coup failed because of a profound split at the heart of the military-industrial complex. One instrument for that split was the USSR Scientific-Industrial Union, a little-known association headed by a former aide to Yuri Andropov—Arkady Volsky. Volsky's organization sharpened the division between the progressive, reform-oriented captains of Soviet industry and their more backward counterparts, and helped link up the industrial molochs of Stalinist economics, including much of the military-industrial complex, with reformist entrepreneurs, cooperative movement activists, and leaseholders. While Volsky himself may have tried to hedge his bets during the coup, many of his colleagues were forthright in their support of Boris Yeltsin. "Our nomenklatura in the military-industrial complex split. If they hadn't split, the putsch might have succeeded," says Vladimir Bokser, a leader of the Democratic Russia movement and the deputy chairman of the Moscow Assembly, a quasi-governmental forum for the leading democratic groups.

Other crucial factors contributed, including the courage of the tens of thousands who took to the streets of Moscow, St. Petersburg, and Kiev. A private detective agency provided security to the defenders of the Russian parliament. Managers of nearby hotels fed the heroic resisters. Farther away, strike committees and emerging free trade unions led resistance among coal miners in Russia and Ukraine, and pro-Yeltsin industrial workers in the Urals.

Another contributing factor was the emerging legitimacy of Russian statehood and the Russian president. Yeltsin's support was especially strong within the military's officer corps. He had won the overwhelming backing of the armed forces in June's presidential elections, despite explicit orders from the center to back former Soviet prime minister Nikolai Ryzhkov. During the coup, many soldiers and officers simply refused to move against their president. Opposition could also be found in the KGB: in Donetsk, in southeastern Ukraine, the local KGB leadership told a miner's strike committee that it would not move against workers if they staged a general strike. It was the official Communist-controlled unions that denounced the free trade unionists and urged workers not to disrupt the "rhythm of work."

The events of August 19–21 [, 1991] destroyed the cohesion of the three pillars of the Soviet state—the Communist party, the KGB, and the military. With the party now banned, its offices shut down, and its bank accounts frozen, the news media in Russia and Ukraine are daily revealing sensational details of illegal and wasteful Communist financial doings. The KGB, which formerly had a force of 488,000 workers, has been broken up along republic lines. The military, which too is fragmenting, is in no mood to intervene to preserve the old order.

The coup created a political vacuum that enabled, indeed encouraged, Boris Yeltsin and other republic leaders to press for independence. Russia's autumn offensive was the product of growing discontent with the central state. As Sergei Stankevich, a top Yeltsin adviser, told me in early October: "Gorbachev and the central authorities are playing a destructive role. Central government structures are creating confusion. Their *main role* is to sow confusion. Managers and administrators are uncertain about which regulations, laws, and decrees to obey. The existence of this dualism of center and republic is paralyzing reform. These questions will soon have to be resolved. On October 28, [1991,] Yeltsin moved decisively to resolve them." Concluding that it would be folly to wait for other republics to fall into line, he announced that Russia would create its own currency, launch its own price reforms, and proceed with a fast-paced privatization. As Vladimir Bokser noted: "Yeltsin's allies decided to opt for the formula of a smaller Russia, but one that can begin to undertake real reforms." The main figure in this turnaround was 35-year-old economist Yegor Gaidar, now Russia's deputy prime minister.

Yeltsin's embrace of Russian democratic nationalism first surfaced in March 1990, when he and other members of his Democratic Russia electoral bloc advanced the idea of Russia's state sovereignty in response to polling data that showed a fundamental shift in Russian public opinion. Among a majority of Russians, weary of the burdens of empire, a new, inward-looking Russian patriotism was taking root. Demographics showed, too, that some two million Russians had left the non-Russian republics in the 1980s to return to the motherland.

The process was slow and full of setbacks. When in May 1990 two parliamentarians—Christian Democrat Vladimir Aksyuchits and Social Democrat Oleg Rumyantsev—unfurled small Russian tricolor flags at a session of the Russian Congress of People's Deputies, they were jeered by a majority of their colleagues. But Yeltsin and the democrats pressed on. They created a national anthem for their republic, provided for a free Russian press and television, extended the offer of Russian citizenship to countrymen living in other republics (going so far as to promise them a "law of return"), and began to define the economic and political prerogatives of sovereignty. They developed a Russian constitution and ensured the democratic election of a Russian president. After the coup, the once-scorned Russian flag was omnipresent.

Accelerating Russia's move to statehood was a similar movement in the republic's historic and cultural sibling, Ukraine, a Texas-sized country of 52 million. There, the move toward independence [was] irreversible and the nation-building euphoria pronounced. The results of Ukraine's independence referendum—90.3 percent in favor, with a turnout of 84 percent—confirm the impact of nationalist ideas. Not a single region failed to support statehood for Ukraine. In western Ukraine (with a 98-percent "yes" vote), democratic nationalists rule with confidence and authority. They have added a patriotic and democratic content to the educational curriculum, reformed the local police, peopling it with newly trained officers; restored and reopened thousands of churches; and wrested control of trade unions from Communist apparatchiks. Indeed, at the time of the coup the Communist party was already a spent force in the western regions of Lviv, Ternopil, and Ivano-Frankivsk. In central Ukraine (95 percent pro-independence), democrats now run the city councils of the capital Kiev and the industrial city of Dniprodzerzhinsk. Although Ukrainians in Kiev are as likely to speak Russian as their native tongue, they are no less determined than their brethren in Lviv to be rid of Moscow's domination.

Patriotic sentiment has also made significant headway in the countryside and in former Cossack strongholds like Zaporozhye, where for two years the democratic Rukh movement has conducted massive Woodstock-style festivals of Cossack culture. As many as half a million participants have thronged to these cultural and historical celebrations that feature song, dance, pageantry, and speechifying. By resurrecting the region's tradition of Cossack self-rule dating back to the seventeenth century, Rukh succeeded in rekindling local pride and support for Ukrainian statehood. On December 1, [1991,] 81 percent of this area's vote was pro-independence. (Youth culture, too, has become fiercely patriotic. Punk bands and rap groups have adopted Ukrainian—the language of the oppressed—for their music, drawing a following of hundreds of thousands of teens. [In early 1991,], radicalized youths forced the resignation of Ukraine's retrograde prime minister. It's become trendy to be Ukrainian.)

Even in the Russian redoubt of Odessa, 85 percent voted for independence. In the southeastern coal-mining Don Basin, where one out of every two workers is Russian and 90 percent of the population is Russophone, support for statehood was 77 percent. When I first met the battle-hardened miners who led the region's strike movement in late 1989, they were suspicious of all politicians—democrats and Communists alike—and regarded the Rukh as extremist. By the summer of 1991, they had embraced Ukrainian sovereignty. In part, their move was born of necessity: Yeltsin's decision to take control of Russia's coal industry meant that Ukrainian miners now had to deal with Kiev. But given a recent report by the Deutsche Bank that rated Ukraine as the republic with the best economic prospects, the workers have good reason for optimism. (Yegor Gaidar believes that if inter-republic trade is based on world prices, both Russia and Ukraine will come out winners, with Central Asia and the Baltics losing out.)

Ukraine's independence movement and its presidential election campaign allowed anti-Communist nationalists to make their case to the people. In the Donetsk and Luhansk regions, anti-Communism is flourishing under the slogan *Kommunyaky na hilyaky* ("Commies to the gallows"). And few have better anti-Communist credentials than Vyacheslav Chornovil, the charismatic, cerebral 53-year-old journalist-turned-political-prisoner who in 1990 was elected governor of Lviv province. A rapid-fire orator, the democratic nationalist Chornovil allayed Russian fears of Ukrainian independence by proposing a federalized Ukraine, in which educational and cultural policy devolves to the regional level. In late October [1991], the leaders of a widely supported strike movement in the Donbas issued a public statement endorsing the integrity of Ukraine, denouncing attempts to redraw the republic's borders, and backing Chornovil. In a series of whistle-stops, he won converts to the independence cause, walking in on meetings of thousands of skeptical coal miners or hundreds of skeptical Jewish and Russian intellectuals and leaving them amid raucous applause. In the end, however, Chornovil lost out to ex-party ideologue Leonid Kravchuk by 61–23 percent, in part because the wily parliamentary leader dominated television and radio.

More significantly, Kravchuk won because he skillfully distanced himself from his servile past and emerged as a leader genuinely committed to Ukrainian statehood. After the failed August coup, Kravchuk banned the Communist party and allowed its property to be seized by local governments. When I met him in Kiev in mid-October [1991], he was forthright in his defense of Ukrainian independence. "We cannot merely pronounce independence. We must create concrete mechanisms, take concrete steps toward statehood," he declared. "In the area of international relations, we have to claim our place in Europe and take full part in the United Nations." He left little doubt about Ukraine's participation in any union of republics: "We do not want today to take part in political unions which have as their aim a central government structure. . . . We have no use for . . . a union that allows someone else to govern on our territory."

Together, Russia and Ukraine account for approximately 70 percent of the former USSR's population and 80 percent of its territory. For centuries their fates have been intertwined. Ukrainians long served in key administrative posts in the czarist empire and do so in today's unraveling USSR (reform economist Grigory Yavlinsky and top Yeltsin aide Sergei Stankevich are both Ukrainian-born), while Russians streamed into Ukraine's cities to live a more comfortable life. The poet Ivan Drach, who is chairman of the Rukh, worries about the fate of Ukraine's dominant neighbor, "Will Russian democracy triumph over Russian chauvinism?" he asks.

Two factors give reason for hope: Boris Yeltsin and the powerful Democratic Russia coalition movement. Yeltsin's democratic inclinations have been the subject of intense speculation, but his recent behavior has demonstrated a commitment to democratic change, economic reform, and a rejection of Russian imperialism. Immediately after the collapse of the coup, the Russian president shut himself off from outside contact. Fearing manipulation by interlopers and fair-weather allies, he insulated himself with a bunch of cronies he's known for decades, apparatchiks from his years as Communist overlord of Sverdlovsk. While this set off alarm bells within the democratic community, Democratic Russia leader Galina Starovoytova is optimist that "Yeltsin has again opened the door to the democrats." In recent weeks he has held a series of consultative meetings with the Democratic Russia leaders, who are satisfied with the positions that have emerged from these deliberations, including Yeltsin's economic reform program. Moreover, the new generation of young democrats and technical experts in Yeltsin's government helped pave the way to the creation of the Commonwealth of Independent States.

Democratic Russia has emerged as the best guarantor of an independent Russia's democratic transformation. Such movement leaders as Starovoytova, Father Gleb Yakunin, Lev Ponomaryov, Bella Denisenko, and Yuri Afanasyev have spoken out clearly on behalf of independence for all the republics. A mass-based organization coalition similar to Poland's Solidarity or the Czech Civic Forum, Democratic Russia has nearly half a million members and is particularly strong outside Moscow and St. Petersburg.

The Ukrainian move to independence has been largely free of chauvinism; it is fueled mainly by practical economic interests, an awareness that prosperous Ukraine has an excellent chance of improving its lot if left alone. The Rukh coalition has sought to engage Russians, Jews, and Poles, blocking the emergence of mass-based "inter-fronts" or other Russian chauvinist structures.

When we met in Moscow in October [1991], Sergei Stankevich, one of the three state counsels to President Yeltsin, was already confronting the possibility of Ukrainian independence. "Losing Ukraine would be like losing an arm, painful but bearable," he told me in Moscow. Such a formulation is a sign of progress. After all, it was Lenin who said three-quarters of a century ago: "To lose Ukraine would be to lose one's head."

On December 1, [1991,] Ukrainian voters launched the final assault on Gorbachev's empire. Russia, which already had agreed to abide by the results of the plebiscite, extended diplomatic recognition to the new state. Other governments followed, including Hungary, Czechoslovakia, Poland, Canada, Lithuania, Bulgaria, Finland, and Switzerland. The road to Ukrainian statehood, of course, was not smooth; nor is its newfound freedom a sure thing. The greatest danger still lies in the attitude of the Soviet military, which remains loyal to Yeltsin and the new Commonwealth. Still, the move toward Ukrainian independence has raised great anxieties within military circles. Soviet Defense Minister Marshal Yevgeny Shaposhnikov, who resisted the coup plotters, at first sharply criticized the Ukrainian legislature's effort to take control of troops and matériel on Ukrainian soil. In early November [1991], however, Marshal Shaposhnikov told the *Moscow News:*

I understand only too well [Ukraine's] desire to be independent. But let's follow a civilized road. . . . It wouldn't pay to withdraw the Army from Ukraine. Most probably, it doesn't want to leave—many officers would likely choose to stay. . . . The most important thing . . . is to immediately start developing a concept of collective security. There is a need to conclude an agreement on the defense alliance of sovereign states. We must prepare and adopt a status on stationing Union troops on the territory of independent republics in the transition period. [It could last about five years.] . . . My prognosis is as follows: the Supreme Soviet of Ukraine will achieve its objective, to create its own armed forces. May God grant them success.

Shaposhnikov made it clear that he would not countenance the army's entanglement in ethnic conflicts or political matters: "No political objective is worth one drop of human blood." His thinking was apparently widespread. For example, some sort of agreement was reached between the Soviet military and the Ukrainian leadership, as could be inferred from reports that soldiers were encouraged to vote for Kravchuk in the December election and from the fact that 80 percent of them supported independence.

Speaking before the Russian parliament on December 12, [1991,] Yeltsin reported that the new Commonwealth of Independent States formed in Minsk just four days earlier was now supported by military leaders. He also revealed that the Commonwealth's military arrangement will involve a "defense alliance within a single command of strategic forces." Ukraine can thus develop its own national armed forces, which will cooperate with Russia's in a NATO-like command. The same day, Kravchuk reported that Soviet military leaders on Ukrainian soil had agreed to abide by a decree making them subject to his control.

This rapprochement would not have been possible without the active involvement of Yeltsin, whose visionary leap toward a loose commonwealth of states holds the promise of a stable evolution toward democracy, and augurs well for resolving the thorny question of what to do with the former Red Army. For the moment, the real basis for military loyalty will be wages, housing, and food. Red Army officers posted in Ukraine realize that they can continue living in comfortable postings in Kiev and Lviv under Ukrainian control or risk expulsion and relocation to such harsh terrain as Russia's long border with China or to Kazakhstan and Uzbekistan. Already, some of them are switching allegiance. And the Ukrainian parliament's call for Ukrainian officers now outside the republic to complete their service at home is being heard.

The most significant aspect of the new Commonwealth of Independent States is that it does not create a new government structure above that of the constituent nation states. Rather, it combines aspects of the European Community and NATO, with a unified military command and a single nuclear force. While it is difficult to predict what the future holds, a likely scenario can be put forward. The community created by Russia, Belarus, and Ukraine is likely to be joined by all but the Baltic states and quirky Georgia. In the long term, however, the Commonwealth may well see the departure of the Central Asian republics and Azerbaijan, which could eventually be drawn into a Pan-Turkic community (the more optimistic prospect) or a fundamentalist Islamic confederation (the darker possibility).

As for Ukraine, many of its political activists already regard the new Commonwealth as a transitional structure. Ukraine is likely to press for a place in the new Europe along with Hungary, Poland, and Czechoslovakia. Georgia is likely to pursue an isolationist course [. . . .] Moldova, which has indicated it wants to join the Commonwealth, in the end will succumb to pressure for re-unification with Romania. Armenia, under pressure from its Turkic neighbors, will cling to a strong alliance with Russia.

Of course, this scenario does not take into account a reaction-ary restoration. With an unraveling economy, the worst grain harvest in recent memory, and price rises, inflation, and unem-ployment likely to heighten social tensions, the possibility of an irredentist Russian fascism cannot be ignored. In the 1991 Rus-sian presidential election, Vladimir Zhirinovsky, a Ukrainian-born chauvinist, received six million votes on a platform that called for abolishing the republics and restoring a great Russian imperial state. Zhirinovsky received financial support from both the KGB and the Communist party. Another imperialist voice is that of Nikolai Travkin, who heads the self-styled Democratic party of Russia.

The Zhirinovsky phenomenon, Travkin's calls to restore the union, and the August coup itself help explain why democratic forces in the republics, which once were ready to support a loose confederation, prefer complete independence today. As My-khaylo Horyn, vice chairman of Rukh, observes: "We do not want to be part of a union that at any time can fall into tyranny. We want to be masters of our own democratic destiny."

While the future of the ex-USSR was being shaped, the U.S. remained a bystander. On the very day 26 million Ukrainian citizens opted for independence, U.S. Ambassador to Gorbachev Robert Strauss was shown on Soviet television handing over $600 million in food credits to Ivan Silayev, the Soviet prime minister without portfolio, if you will. The legacy of this approach is that, as of December 25, [1991,] we had a policy for a country that didn't exist and a close relationship with a leader who had no power. It also meant we had only two U.S. consular staff on the ground in Ukraine, covering a country of 52 million, and no one permanently based in Kazakhstan, Belarus, or the other emerg-ing nation states.

The Bush Administration [. . .] relegated the U.S. to a mar-ginal role in advancing democratic change, which more and more is being shaped by the leaders of Russia and Ukraine. It also means that the U.S. is ill-prepared to play a constructive role in helping resolve major issues that loom on the horizon, even if the new Commonwealth arrangement holds. Among them:

• a possible conflict over ethnically Russian Crimea, which may eventually want to secede from Ukraine;

• fundamental economic reform and economic recovery, which will require a significant U.S. and Western presence in most republics;

• protection of ethnic minority rights in the republics;

• continued efforts by local, regional, and republic-level apparatchiks to cling to power by resorting to nationalist demogogy.

If it is to contribute to the democratic resolution of these matters, the U.S. must recognize that even with the welcome creation of a loose Commonwealth, central authority no longer exists and can only be restored through violence and repression. The age of Gorbachev has come to an end. A new future beckons, so we'd better get used to dealing with Russia and Ukraine—the two largest countries in Europe.

DEATH OF A HERESY[3]

What died in the Soviet Union on August 21, 1991, was, in the strict sense of the term, a heresy. For Communism was never just economic foolishness married (in its Leninist form) to draconian methods of social control: Communism was a false doctrine, a congeries of false teachings about human nature, human community, human history, and human destiny. Therein lay its power: its power to attract, and its power to coerce.

Heresy often consists in the exaggeration of one part of a complex truth, and Communism was no exception to that rule. Indeed, Communism was particularly seductive in the West precisely because the taproots of Western civilization reach back into the stories and images of Jewish and Christian eschatology and apocalyptic. But Communism was evil not just because of its view of history, but because it taught falsely about man. And from that falsehood came both the idiocies of a command economy and, far worse, the Gulag.

What was the Communist heresy? Simply put, it was the cruelest form of a more widespread evil that has beset the West since the prologue to the French Revolution: the tyranny of the political, which began with Rousseau and was itself a radically secu-

[3]Article by George Weigel, author and president of the Ethics and Public Policy Center in Washington, D.C., from *National Review* 44:42–48 Ja 20 '92. Copyright © 1992 by National Review, Inc. Reprinted with permission.

larized version of the Jewish and Christian hope for a messianic age. In the case of Rousseau and his epigones, though, the messiah was "ultramundane": it was $99^{44}/_{100}\%$ transcendence-free. And the project was to remake flawed humanity—to usher in the messianic age of justice and righteousness—through the medium of politics. Communism, the ultimate expression of this heretical project, was Jewish and Christian eschatology forced into history, without God or God's messiah. Little wonder that those who got in the way were ruthlessly eliminated or, in one of Lenin's favorite verbs, "exterminated."

Focusing on Communism as a heresy also helps us grasp the central truth of the Revolution of 1989 and the New Russian Revolution of 1991: that these were first and foremost revolutions of the spirit, in which people said "No" on the basis of a higher and more compelling "Yes."

Throughout the Western world, pundits, academics, and reporters have been scrambling for over two years now to fix an explanatory label on these stunning events. "Delayed modernization" seems to be the bromide of choice at the moment: the Communist countries just couldn't compete economically and technologically, don't you know? But this soft economism is simply a less odious version of the ultramundane heresy. To accept it is to buy into one of the corollaries of Rousseau's false doctrine of the human, *viz..,* that the only real world is the world of the political. This is, of course, a most satisfying fantasy to indulge if you happen to be a member of the political class. And one shouldn't underestimate the degree to which vanity has played a role in the Western elite's grasping at this explanatory straw. But "politics" (as the term is usually understood today) just doesn't explain the revolutions of 1989 and 1991.

For the great truth about these upheavals—the explanation that is commensurate with the nature of the evil that they overthrew—is that they were essentially *pre-political* revolutions. They were revolutions that began "before" politics, with the reconstruction of civil society. As the Polish authorities put it with unintentional accuracy during the martial-law period of 1981–83, Communism was in a "state of war" against society: politics was demanding to fill the space previously occupied by society and culture. The antidote to that tyranny of the political could not be more politics. It had to come from a revolution of the spirit, from a recovery of independent culture and a reconstruction of civil society. Not for nothing did one of the most powerful resistance groups in Poland style itself the "Committee for Social Self-Defense."

Put another way, Communism's tyranny of the political inevitably resulted in the atomization of society. Resistance required that the tissues of society be rebuilt. That meant rediscovering the virtue of social solidarity, of human fellow-feeling and a sense of mutual moral obligation. Solidarity, the virtue, preceded Solidarity, the trade union/political opposition.

A similar process has been under way in the late Soviet Union, noticed by a few Western analysts. While the media and some Western academics indulged in Gorbophilia, others looked at the rising democratic opposition *to Gorbachev* and at the reconstituted elements of civil society from which that opposition grew.

For several years now, S. Frederick Starr of Oberlin College has urged Western analysts to take more seriously the rapid growth of independent social and cultural organizations across the former USSR. Here, Starr argued, was the existential rejection of the tyranny of the political; here was the civic and civil opposition on whose foundations a political opposition with greater tensile strength might be built. Similarly, James H. Billington, the distinguished historian of Russian culture now serving as Librarian of Congress (and the man who certainly should be the U.S. ambassador in Moscow right now), has been writing and speaking for years about the religious renaissance under way in Great Russia and throughout the former Soviet empire.

Had Billington, Starr, and others like them been taken as seriously as they deserved, and had the lessons of that prior revolution of the spirit been absorbed, the West might not have been quite so surprised by the non-violent resistance that checked the Gang That Couldn't Shoot Straight in Moscow [in August 1991] and, in so doing, put the final nail in the coffin of Communism.

In the collapse of the Yalta imperial system and the ultramundane eschatological fantasy it embodied, the persistence, even the resurgence, of moral conscience has been crucial. Vaclav Havel, in his brilliant 1978 essay "The Power of the Powerless," put his finger on both the core, and the point of maximum vulnerability, of the Communist enterprise. It was acquiescence: not enough people were willing to say "No"; too many people were willing to make those small, ritual gestures of consent by which the system reinforced its image as an unchangeable monolith. (Remember Havel's image of the greengrocer who, despite misgivings, nevertheless displays a sign reading "Workers of the World, Unite!" amidst the carrots and onions in his shop window.) That is what changed, over the past decade or so. And that change was the basis of the Revolution of 1989 and the New Russian Revolution.

But whence that new courage? Here, too, there were ironies in the fire. For, in yet another existential refutation of both Marxist theory and Western secularism, the courage to resist was largely religious in origin. Even in its more secular forms (as among several key Solidarity intellectuals), the courage to say "No" came from a "Yes" that transcended and relativized the tyranny of the political.

The first, great symbolic reference point for the revolution of the spirit that made possible the political revolution against Communism was the pilgrimage of John Paul II to his native Poland in June 1979: the moment when millions of Poles, looking at each other at those historic outdoor Masses, came to understand that "we" were a lot more powerful than "they." The end of the line may have come last August when, as James Billington noted, Father Aleksandr Borisov, an Orthodox priest and member of the Moscow City Council, distributed some two thousand Bibles to the soldiers in the tanks outside Boris Yeltsin's Russian parliament (only one soldier refused) and another two thousand to those on the barricades protecting Yeltsin's White House. Borisov then helped convince Patriarch Aleksei to intervene, and the patriarch issued a prayer that, as Billington put it, "anathematized fratricide."

And that, as we might say in another context, was the ballgame.

That most of the policy apparatus of Western governments, and much of the fraternity of Western pundits, has simply missed this revolution of the spirit is an indication of just how deeply what Jacques Ellul called "the illusion of politics" has infected the West. To decry the tyranny of the political is not, of course, to say that politics is unimportant: but it is to put politics in its place. Which means to remember that politics, in the great tradition of the West (the tradition deliberately rejected by Rousseau, Marx, and Lenin) is not in the first instance about the getting and keeping of power. Rather, "politics" is the ongoing and public deliberation about the good man and the good society. Politics is, ineluctably, normative. Politics is, inescapably, a function of culture. And the heart of culture is cult, religion.

The pre-political revolutions of 1989 and 1991 may give birth to the era of the post-political, and sooner rather than later. Rousseau's delusion of the politically driven eschaton will survive, but its devotees will be increasingly marginal. New heresies, similarly eschatological in orientation, will emerge (some already have: look at the New Age section in your local bookstore). But their passion will not be for politics-the-contest-for-power.

The remarkable events of the past [few years] have revealed that the ultramundane heresy of Marxism-Leninism is finished as a world-historical force, and that the primary struggle in the West will be at the level of culture. The new *Kulturkampf* in the developed democracies will touch, at points, on the world of politics; like the poor, the John Frohnmayers of this world will, alas, always be with us. But it is altogether possible, and perhaps even likely, that the men and women of the twenty-first century will look far less to the order of politics as the focus of their energies, and far more to the order of culture. We may even see the revival of a true Judaeo-Christian humanism, in place of the sundry false humanisms that have beset us these past two centuries.

That would, in fact, be a wholly fitting wrap-up to the Revolution of 1989 and the New Russian Revolution. For it was the humanism whose true roots lie in Jewish and Christian concepts of the human person, human society, human history, and human destiny that finally toppled the modern Moloch, the false and anti-human "humanism" of Marxism-Leninism. Today's springtime of nations was born from a springtime of the human spirit. We would do well to think about that, and remember it.

II. POLITICAL FALLOUT

EDITOR'S INTRODUCTION

Two years after the revolution in Eastern Europe, Richard C. Longworth assesses the impact of communism's fall on its people. He discovers that old fears of power and the police state have been replaced by economic fears—communism may have been hard, but at least it was predictable. Writing in *The Bulletin of the Atomic Scientists,* Longworth describes the vitality of people throughout the former Eastern Bloc and their perceptions of the West formed by secretly reading classic American novels during communist rule. In concluding, the author foresees the evolution of demi-democracies in Eastern Europe, giving birth to societies that are economically prosperous but politically "unpleasant."

Using Moscow as a barometer for the rest of Russia and the former Soviet Union, Leonid Zagalsky describes a land and a people beset by economic strife and ethnic warring. His article in *The Bulletin of the Atomic Scientists* paints the picture of a city and country in worse economic shape than it was in the days of former Soviet President Leonid Brezhnev. Intellectuals have either emigrated or become entrepreneurs. Western, and particularly American, cultural ideals have permeated the society through television. Lost in the transformation is an innate humor, which has been replaced by anger and greed.

George J. Church writing in *Time* presents an overview of the outbreak of nationalist and ethnic separatist movements throughout the former Soviet republics and Eastern Europe. While some political scientists have labelled this turmoil a necessary prelude to the new world order, governments shudder in the wake of violence and the inability of Western leaders and international organizations to control the unrest.

The last two articles in this section take up the question of when nationalities should be recognized as states. Writing in *The Nation,* Eric Hobsbawm argues that the notion that every nation should form a state is unworkable, as seen throughout history. Yelena Bonner, the widow of Andrei Sakharov, counters in *New Perspectives Quarterly* that to deny statehood to a nation is undemocratic, and she maintains that self-determination is the essence of human rights.

EASTERN EUROPE: THE PARTY'S OVER[1]

If there is bliss in this cynical world, it was on view in Eastern Europe in the revolutionary autumn of 1989—the Germans chipping their souvenirs from the breached and suddenly irrelevant Wall; the hushed power of the Prague crowd filling Wenceslas Square in the smoggy dusk; even the vengeful glee of Romanians around their television sets, cheering the execution of their mad dictator. Those of us who were there shared the euphoria but knew it couldn't last.

It hasn't. A tour of Eastern Europe two years later is a strange experience that raises a variety of thoughts and musings, happy and otherwise.

The best news is that the fear is gone—or rather, the fear of the police or of "the Power," as many East Europeans called those who ruled their lives. It is impossible to overcelebrate the lifting of this fear, the lightening of what, Laurens van der Post, in *A Journey into All the Russias,* called "a weight upon the soul." Now, when East Europeans tell what it was like, what they say can break your heart.

"I never wanted to think about how it was then," a Romanian businessman says. "I never wanted to really think. Because sometime I might have too much to drink and it would all come out. Better not to think at all."

A Hungarian woman told about her aunt "who kept a painting of Christ on the wall of her apartment. Every time someone rang the doorbell, she took it down and hid it under the bed. Later, she took it out and put it back again. This went on every day for 40 years. No one ever caught her. Nothing ever happened."

But there is now fear about the economic future. Life under communism was hard but, economically speaking, predictable.

---

[1]Article by Richard C. Longworth, a senior writer and former chief European correspondent for the *Chicago Tribune,* from *The Bulletin of the Atomic Scientists* 48:22–29 Ja/F '92. Copyright © 1992 by the Educational Foundation for Nuclear Science. Reprinted with permission.

Even more, there is fear of the political future among men and women who know too well that, with rare exceptions and for brief times, their homelands have never existed without dictators or foreign suzerainty.

In most of Eastern Europe, the bloom is already off the democratic rose. Weariness with free politics is setting in. One reason, of course, is that two years of democracy haven't put much bread on the table. Another is the popular disgust with parliaments that debate issues and non-issues endlessly, instead of issuing instant orders as the last regime did.

Westerners know that democracy is messy, time-consuming, and not always dignified. Easterners are just learning this. One can only pray that their political systems start delivering the goods before their tolerance runs out.

Along with this goes the suspicion that all politicians are ex-communists, on the take, or both. Certainly, many people running Eastern Europe now are the same guys who ran it before, for the simple reason that you have to have some people who know how things work.

Full-scale purges aren't possible, if only because nearly everyone was tainted during the communist years—even the greengrocer, in Vaclav Havel's famous example, who did no more than put a poster in his shop window, urging the workers of the world to unite. Havel pointed out that it was in such mindless, casual compliance that communist power was solidified. So who was pure? Once purges begin, who knows where they'll end? Better not to start.

I think of Endre, a Hungarian friend, born an aristocrat and purged from the Hungarian foreign ministry in 1948 for his parentage, then purged again from journalism after 1956 for his political views. By the time I knew him, he had a low-level journalistic job. His daily rounds, he said, brought him into contact with the very people, diplomats and editors, who were responsible for ruining his life.

"My God, Endre," I said. "What do you do when you see them?"

"Do?" he said. "What can I do? I smile." He paused. "God," he said, "I'm getting tired of smiling."

So he smiled, and drank, and made little accommodations with the Power—a few harmless reports to the police about the foreigners he met, including me—and so he managed until his death a few years ago. But what else could he have done? Emigrate? Many did. But if, like Endre, you loved your country and your wife spoke only Hungarian and you wanted your sons to grow up Hungarian, what could you do? Protest? You could, but read some prison memoirs—Havel's *Letters to Olga* is a good example—and ask yourself if you could have taken it. More likely, you would have smiled and put up the poster and reported to the police, and one day, when the communists vanished and your file was opened, it wouldn't look so good. (The files, of course, won't tell the good things you did, or describe your warmth or humor, or the courage it took just to get through the day.) And if the purges started, you'd be purged.

For Endre, it would have been the third purge, by the good guys or the bad guys. How many purges can a person, or a country, take? In Czechoslovakia, the Nazis purged the Jews. After the war, the winners purged the Nazis. Then the communists purged the anti-communists. Next, the Moscow communists purged the local communists. In 1968, the reformers purged the hardliners. After 1968, the process was reversed. Now they're talking about another purge. In the end, who'll be left?

Better not to start. But this means that some pretty unsavory characters still hold power, and this knowledge is an acid eating at the foundations of the new democracy.

The young of Eastern Europe are a delight. I'm not talking about the mindless skinheads of the ex-East Germany who bash immigrants and give the Nazi salute. I'm talking about the Czech students who led the revolution, the Bulgarian kids on poll-watching teams, the Hungarian youngsters who have formed one of their country's most popular political parties. Where in the world did they come from?

Whole generations of young East Europeans were born under communism, schooled by communist rules, indoctrinated in the glories of communism. Yet they have emerged from the communist cocoon as full-fledged democrats. But democracy isn't simple or easy. Where did they learn it?

They tell different stories. Some simply saw the difference between propaganda and reality. Some countries, like Bulgaria, encouraged Western tourism and the tourists brought news of a different world. Many kids, perhaps most, were quietly re-educated by parents or, more often, by grandparents determined to undo the damage being done by society.

Radio Free Europe and Voice of America were potent

sources. Listening was illegal of course, but everyone listened anyway. At the end, Radio Free Europe had a network of correspondents throughout Eastern Europe who sent their reports to Munich by an elaborate underground telegraph. One VOA [Voice of America] correspondent is virtually a hero now in his native Czechoslovakia. Now out in the open, VOA blares from cafes throughout Bulgaria for customers who adore it, even if most can't understand it. The educational power of Western radio, over the years, was enormous.

Books were crucial. The communists censored what their young people read—but botched it. Courses in communism assigned pre-communist philosophers to serve as horrible examples side by side with the gospel according to Marx and Lenin. The kids, naturally, ignored the "good guys" and soaked up Locke, Mill, and other "bad guys."

To an amazing degree, today's young say they gleaned ideas from slightly dated American novels that authorities allowed to be translated and published, figuring they were safe. But to kids raised under communism, *The Grapes of Wrath, To Kill A Mockingbird,* and Jack Kerouac's *On the Road* were incendiary.

And the most explosive book of all was *A Catcher in the Rye,* possibly the most subversive book ever written. Many East European regimes innocently assigned J. D. Salinger's bombshell to students, never imagining the fuses they were lighting. They must have been nuts.

Communism's most enduring legacy in Eastern Europe may be a landscape of hideous architecture. Apart from some reconstructions—the Old Town in Warsaw, the Vigado in Budapest—and a handful of decent Western-built hotels, it's hard to find a postwar building from the Baltic to the Balkans that is not an insult to the eye.

Virtually every city is a graveyard of stained, crumbling, concrete buildings, as uniform as tombstones, marching for mile on mile of identical streets. They are six or 12 stories tall, festooned with laundry, surrounded by unmowed grass, their entrances unpainted, their apartments cramped, their halls urine-scented, unloved by the tens of millions of persons who pass their lives inside them. The same tens of millions work in office buildings as bad or worse.

The West has its eyesores, of course, from the housing projects of American slums to the bleak estates that encircle Paris.

But nowhere is the ugliness so uniform. In many provincial towns, these lumps are all there is. Even in graceful cities like Budapest, Prague, and Sofia, they surround city centers like sentries, keeping the grace from spreading.

In a more rational society, the residents could have built something better. Now, they no doubt will. But the blocks remain home to the vast majority of East Europeans and can be replaced only gradually. In a few years, the former communist bloc will clean up its pollution, stock its stores, fix its telephones, perhaps even restore trust to its public life. But these hulking blemishes will be the norm of East European housing for decades to come.

Life in these cells provided a corrosive framework for a routine that seemed designed to sap the subjects of communism of all will, all mind. Eastern Europe has produced no Solzhenitsyn, but a number of writers have tried to describe the cumulative effects of this daily degradation. One of the best is the Romanian, Norman Manea, who has written of the "terrible derailments of history, of society, of the psyche" that afflicted his poor country, first under fascism and then under communism—"a national history consisting of a series of catastrophes."

"A whole nation subjugated, hungry, humiliated, and forced to celebrate the crime ceaselessly," he wrote. "Life as a series of postponements, a tumorlike growth of mistrust and fear, an all-encompassing schizophrenia. A step-by-step reduction of private life, and finally its abolition, as time itself becomes subject to ever-increasing taxation and eventually total expropriation by the state: the hours sacrificed to standing in lines, to ritual political meetings and to rallies, on top of the hours at work, and the hours of helpless exposure to the inferno of public transportation on the way to and from work, meetings and shopping: and when you were finally home in your birdcage, you found yourself lost, mute, staring into an emptiness that could be defined as infinite despair.

"You would gradually stop seeing your friends because the buses ran very infrequently and were overcrowded, and it had become impossible to get from one end of the city to the other, and because you . . . were sick of repeating the same lament for the billionth time, and because you didn't want to face the other's defeat—marked each time by new wrinkles—and recognize it as your own."

Unfortunately, as Manea wrote, communism has so discredited all "isms," even the most noble—it has so leached the political soil of all faith—that no belief or creed can take root in the lands where it once ruled. "The deformation of high principle to the point of caricature can discredit faith in principles as such," he says. In Romania, where the dictatorship was the most thorough, all that is left is an atomized society, robbed of trust or truth, with no national myth to bind it, no habit of distinguishing between fact and rumor, no habit of talking honestly with each other. It's no accident that the main opposition organization in Bucharest is called "The Group for Social Dialogue."

Anyone who worked or traveled in Eastern Europe during the communist years was constantly struck, and humbled, by the extraordinary richness of private lives, and by the kindness and generosity of the people.

Public life was bleak and savage. Political orthodoxy strangled talents. Petty bureaucrats dealt out humiliation. Work was unrewarding. Careers degraded lives, not enhanced them. On the street, people elbowed each other in a daily fight for survival. The Soviet system, with its hatred for anything individual or whimsical, drove its subjects in on themselves.

So East Europeans retreated into private lives and friendships of great warmth that provided havens against this jungle. Many dived deep into narrow and arcane realms of scholarship, like porcelain or plainsong, simply because these subjects were beyond politics and they would be left alone. With each other and with strangers, they routinely brought out their last sausage and bottle, even if they didn't have the money to buy more for tomorrow.

This was certainly the most attractive part of life under communism, and it may not outlive communism's death. Suddenly public life has become worth living. Already, public manners are improving. But now that they can pour their energies into rewarding jobs and careers, will East Europeans feel the need—or will they have time—to nurture their private lives? Will they become as busy and as heedless of friendship as we are in the West? Something rare may be lost.

Certainly, the old generosity is going. "We aren't willing to spend our last zloty on our friends any more," a Polish woman told me. "Remember, before, when there were such shortages, there was nothing else to spend our money on. Now there is."

What do we want these countries to become? That's easy: we want them to be prosperous, stable, clean, moral, model democracies. Just like Sweden or Holland.

Forget it. Eastern Europe has suffered too much history—
invasions by Russians and Ottomans, rule by kaisers and emper-
ors, centuries of acting as barriers behind which Western Europe
built its remarkable civilization. By and large, these countries
have no democratic tradition, and they were riven by class hatred
and deformed by a benighted peasantry, reactionary priests,
deep-rooted anti-Semitism, and a taste for corruption. Add to
this 50 years of domination by Nazis and communists, and you
have a part of the world that has been raped by history while the
Western world, if it noticed at all, did nothing.

The people of Eastern Europe have met these tragedies with
courage, grace, and generosity. But the dark side of Eastern Europe is very dark, and it is too much to expect that it will be
overcome.

There are no Swedens here. Rather, with much luck, East
European countries may turn out like Italy or Austria—with
which they share a lot of history—reasonably well-run demi-
democracies, generally prosperous, with unpleasant but not lethal
politics, cheerfully corrupt, tolerant of frailties, free, and friends
to the world.

Everything considered, that's not bad.

SOCIAL REALISM BITES THE DUST[2]

All totalitarian societies are unhappy in the same way. All
democratic societies are unhappy in different ways. (Apologies to
Leo Tolstoy.)

I spent a month in Moscow in November and December 1991,
during the last days of the Soviet Union. I had last been there in
December 1990, but it seemed that an eternity had passed. The
Moscow where I lived for 35 years had nothing to do with the
complete mess I found at the end of 1991. Each day there reminded me of the last days of Pompeii.

A close friend whom I've known for many years has always
been an incurable optimist. He laughed sadly when I asked him

[2]Article by Leonid Zagalsky, a journalism associate at Global Outlook, Palo Alto,
California, and a Western correspondent for *Ogonyok*, from *The Bulletin of the Atomic
Scientists* 48:16–23 March '92. Copyright © 1992 by the Educational Foundation for
Nuclear Science. Reprinted with permission.

what he was going to do the next day. "You know," he said, "it is hard to predict what I will do in the next couple of hours, and you can be sure that these hours will not bring anything positive to my life. In the morning my salary seemed decent enough to feed my family, my three kids. In the afternoon they may change my wages. . . . Who knows what will happen in the evening?"

My friend's words reminded me of a book I read long ago. The major characters were three friends working in a body shop. Every morning they got a paycheck and immediately ran to the bank to cash it, because inflation was so high that they might not have enough money to buy dinner by evening.

Hard Times

What should we call the former Soviet Union? Some people with a sense of humor have created a new euphemism: "economic space." They say that the country should be cleaned with detergent and then sold at auction to foreigners for hard currency.

Yes, it is a space, but certainly not economic. Domestic trade and manufacturing are in ruins. The factory in Georgia can't produce tools because it needs metal from Azerbaijan. The Azerbaijani tobacco factory can't make cigarettes because filters come from Armenia.

But some factories and enterprises are doing pretty well. They are selling their products for hard currency and are able to supply their employees with all necessities. There was little in state stores when I was there, but people were not dying from hunger. Paradoxes abound, and no one can predict what will happen tomorrow.

Ethnic conflicts are breaking out all over the place. Each piece of the country is trying to establish independence and to kick other nationalities out. Moldovans are killing Russians and Jews, Ossetians and Chechens are killing each other, and Georgians are trying to take over both. Armenia and Azerbaijan are in a real war. Newspaper articles about these conflicts resemble reports from battlefields. Journalists are describing events in military terms.

When I visited, the cold winds of winter, destruction, and pain were starting to blow across this endless "economic space," which occupies one-sixth of the earth's land mass, bringing frustration and freezing out the last bits of hope. Some old people in a retirement home in Khabarovsk in Siberia froze to death because there was not enough heat and electricity in the region. The incident evoked strong public indignation, but nothing could be done because there was no way to get enough energy to support such an out-of-the-way city.

Moscow Crumbles

The city of Moscow has always been the mirror of the whole country. The gray sky was hanging very close to the ground—it seemed like there was no room in between. It was getting dark at 2:30 p.m. and there was not enough light in the streets. Most roads were in bad shape; driving a car meant risking falling into a hole. My friend explained that there were many old water and heating pipes in Moscow and that there were always accidents with bursting pipes. I remember learning in school that the Soviet Union produced more metal pipes than any other country. One should hardly count that as an achievement. The rest of the developed world has shifted to plastic or ceramic pipes, which are much cheaper and don't rust.

Buildings are literally falling apart. The city is losing its face.

The traffic police in Moscow are completely corrupt. They don't even ask for bribes. They just stop you on the road and stick their hands into your car window. "It is cold," they say. If they stop you during the daytime and you haven't broken any rules, you can get rid of them with 25–50 rubles. At night they double or triple the price. A drunk driver or lawbreaker will be released for a thousand in cash.

Sergei Belolobov, the KGB officer who was guarding the gate to the Kremlin, told me that his mother had stood in the sugar line for four hours. He was married and had one child. "We will survive this winter because we have lots of things grown at our dacha," Sergei said. He also said lots of unpleasant things about the government he was guarding.

The Food Museum

Prices were incredible, even before the lid was officially lifted from them in January. When I visited, the average monthly salary was enough to buy 10 pounds of meat or half a bottle of cheap whiskey in so-called commercial stores. The goods in these stores were priced 10 times higher than goods in state stores, where there was almost nothing. One of the biggest state stores in Moscow offered only sausages and sour cream—after a long wait. What used to be a clean, sophisticated store, the showcase of the "socialist way of trade" in Brezhnev's times, was dirty, smelly, and nearly empty. Lights were dim, and people in winter coats could hardly see whether there was anything to spend their money on.

But there was one lively, if surrealistic, spot in the store, filled with people: Spanish-made slot machines had been installed and people were gambling. The machines with their bright, colorful lights reminded me of a rattle given to a hungry kid instead of food.

The second floor of the building was given over to an Irish supermarket, which traded for hard currency. It was filled with goods: meat, cheese, milk, butter, oil, ice cream, chocolate, fresh vegetables. The store on the second floor was an unattainable dream for all the people hanging around on the first floor. It could easily have been renamed The Food Museum, a place for parents to bring their kids and say, "Look! This is sausage. It smells like . . ." But they would never find a metaphor to describe the smell of sausage.

Sitting in Line

Some people carry big plastic bags stuffed with money. They pay with piles of it, not even bothering to take the bank wrappings off. But millions of others, especially old people, still use their wallets. They wait near stores in the futile hope of buying something. One enterprising co-op started producing small folding stools, like fishermen use, and it has sold an incredible number of them. A new phrase has appeared: *sitting* in line rather than standing in line.

You eat food and it disappears, leaving only memories. The Germans, who paid with food for unification, have occasioned a sad joke that reflects the circle Soviet-German relations have traced over the last 50 years. During World War II, fascists used to take everything from the peasants in the occupied territories. Today, the joke goes, a German comes to the Russian peasant's house shouting, "Eggs, chicken, and bread!" "We have nothing left," the peasant answers sadly. "Don't worry," says the German. "I've brought everything."

It is naïve to think that Western aid will help the country make the tough transition to democracy. One can only hope that charity will not end up on the black market, as it did in Armenia after the earthquake. Some poor people will get some of the food packs, but there is also a high risk that foreign charity will end up enriching government big cheeses.

Beggars are everywhere. They are desperate for money, and one has to give it to them because they are mostly disabled, which means they can't work. Their pensions are next to nothing and without help they will die of hunger.

Brain Drain

Intellectuals are ready to go to Mars to get out of the country. They discuss emigration opportunities and complain that they don't have enough knowledge of foreign languages. Many who know any language have already emigrated or at least signed contracts to work abroad.

There was a certain unity among the intelligentsia during the period of stagnation. They all hated stupid leaders. They expressed some democratic ideas. They suffered together from the impossibility of overcoming the idiocy of the "epoch of well-developed socialism." Kitchen talk around the vodka bottle was their favorite occupation for years.

Now that is over. The ideas they suffered for suddenly appear ordinary and well-known. What is more, the ideas are all over the mass media, and one can express them freely without fear of the KGB. Many intellectuals feel they have been plundered. Their sacred ideas have been adopted by everyone, with no difficulty. Strangely, instead of feeling good they feel frustrated.

Some intellectuals have joined the big gold rush, forming co-ops, private publishing houses, theaters, and studios. They have started to make big money—and are being condemned by their former friends, the other part of the intelligentsia who still consider making money shameful.

Ninja Turtles

Moscow's children are signs of the times. They reveal detailed knowledge of Teenage Mutant Ninja Turtles and the whole series of "Rocky" movies. They can tell you in detail the difference between an Acura Integra and a Mercedes 190. By the way, video copies of *Terminator II* were available in Moscow before the video was out in the United States. No one cares about copyrights in the former Soviet Union—and Russia will not soon join the world copyright convention. American movies are all over the place, even on central television, and owners of private theaters are making big money on Sylvester Stallone's and Arnold Schwarzenegger's movies.

The best gift for kids is chewing gum or a T-shirt with any brand name on it. Adults appreciate American cigarettes, toothpaste, soap, or almost anything else.

A year ago parents would never have allowed children to listen to "adult talk." They were scared of the KGB and tried to hide their real opinions about the system from children. Now they tell their kids: "Listen to what I'm saying. You must know what an awful country you were born in." All kids now know that Gorbachev was stupid because he didn't move quickly toward a free-market economy and that the KGB is the horror and shame of the epoch. But even most adults don't know what "free market" means, and children often can't explain what KGB stands for.

Sleaze Factor

The old culture of social realism has been destroyed. All the stars of the recent past, all the Heroes of Socialist Labor in art, Lenin Prize winners in music, and State Prize winners in architecture are insignificant in this new environment. The values of communism have been scattered on the ground near the Tretyakov Gallery, the museum of fine arts. People call this place the Garden of Former Chiefs. All the dismantled statues of Lenin, Stalin, Dzerzhinsky, and so on have been put in this garden, protected by a fence.

They need protection from the furious crowd. From this garden, Stalin, the greatest tyrant of all times, who in his more than 25 years of power created the culture of totalitarianism in this country, looks out at you suspiciously. But there was egg on his bronze face when I visited. Half of Lenin's head was lying on the ground, and Dzerzhinsky, the first KGB chief, had the word "shame" painted on his back. They don't terrify anyone any more.

The new culture has not yet appeared, but something is beginning to emerge from the intellectual soup of the day. More than 3,300 new newspapers and magazines have appeared since 1990. At the same time, existing major publications have lost circulation—people call them grandfathers of perestroika and don't buy them any more. The new publications vary greatly in quality and type. There is the oddly named *Global News from Odessa*. A magazine named *Broker* is aimed at a profession that didn't exist two years ago. The truly disgusting *People's Business* published a cover story, "AIDS Is Not Dangerous for White People." Another headline proclaimed, "Iraq Has Won!" The newspaper's trident emblem looks like a swastika.

One new newspaper called *Buy-Sell* publishes only ads. Along with "will buy new car" or "will sell a new dacha," one finds offers like "will trade two cans of black caviar for VCR," and "will trade new vacuum cleaner for new down vest."

But the idea of trade is still new to people. A few years ago one could end up in prison for selling something in the street for one's own price. This was classified as "speculation" in the criminal code and considered as serious as rape or murder. The speculation article still exists in the code, but it is no longer enforced. My friend, a director and producer from New York, filmed a story about the owner of a co-op who was taken to prison for speculation, spent nine months there, and then was released. While she was filming, the man was waiting for trial. He was optimistic. He said, "They are changing the laws every day. There might not be the necessary law in the code when they finally take me to the courtroom."

Four Moscow casinos could hardly be considered cultural centers, but they at least provide entertainment. Gambling houses also reflect the contradictions of perestroika. Gambling is still forbidden by the criminal code, but one can play blackjack or roulette in the Moscow casinos and not go to prison. I visited one called Casino Royale in an old but recently renovated building near the racetrack. Gambling was only allowed in hard currency, but I saw no foreigners. God knows where the gamblers got their dollars. I saw one gangster lose about $10,000 in a couple of minutes.

If someone had told me just a couple of years ago that books would be available in bookstores, I would have laughed. Now people are selling books all over the place. Topics vary from science fiction to Tibetan medicine. But fewer readers are buying them. Books are an example of the forbidden-fruit phenomenon: you want them only when you can't get them. Books are now also very expensive, and intellectuals often have to choose between reading and eating.

Most of the movies in theaters are foreign. Many Soviet directors have settled in Hollywood in the illusory hope of shooting their new films there. Art was never popular among Soviets, and this has not changed.

Amazing things have happened to TV. It is becoming freer in political analysis but not more interesting. Many shows are poor copies of American shows like *Wheel of Fortune* and *The Dating Game*. There are beauty competitions and thrillers about mobsters and cops. My impression was that TV people understand freedom of the press to mean sexual freedom. Nearly naked girls are all over the screen. They are dancing, singing, making love with muscular males—the kind of thing you would see in X-rated films in the United States. They are also the main characters in commercials—a new feature on TV. The advertisements for different firms and enterprises look like they employ the same director and models. It will take time for ads to gain sophistication.

"Somehow"

I was invited to a party celebrating the launching of a new magazine, *Dar* (Gift). The editor said at the press conference that he was grateful to the sponsors who had given 200,000 rubles for the event, because it allowed the new enterprise to rent one of the most fashionable places in Moscow for the party—the Column Hall. Before perestroika this hall had been a place for the Soviet people to say goodbye to the latest dead leader. I remember Brezhnev's dead body and a long line of people passing by his coffin. That was nearly 10 years ago. Now, scantily clad girls were modeling the latest fashions while a new magazine was being huckstered.

But copies of the magazine were not available at the presentation. This was consistent with the Soviet way of doing things. Great! We've got money from a sponsor—let's spend it. It doesn't matter that there is nothing to promote. Everything will be all right, somehow.

This "somehow" is still alive. Somehow we'll transfer to a free market, somehow we'll build this house, somehow we'll publish this magazine.

New Breed

I almost didn't recognize my brother when he met me at the airport. He was concentrated, energetic, and tough. "Here is the car, here is money, if you need something, give me a call," he said and handed me his business card, car keys, and a plastic bag stuffed with money.

He embodied the greatest change in the country. This useless, unhappy communications engineer had become a businessman. "Moscow Commodity Exchange" was written on his business card. He presented me with a pile of white T-shirts with his company's emblem on the sleeve, great presents for my American friends.

The exchange, a very new structure for a nonmarket economy, appeared a year ago. My brother says, with some exaggeration, that he works 24 hours a day and doesn't have holidays. "This work is like a drug. The more you do, the more you are responsible for. It is very interesting and new to be responsible for yourself and your enterprise."

I met a couple of my brother's friends at a fancy restaurant where they could hardly have dreamed of eating a few years ago. The dinner was extremely expensive. My brother's friends were all alike. They had been nobodies, but now they were rich. They had the same energy and ideas. They supported Yeltsin and wanted Gorbachev to resign as soon as possible. (This was in November [1911], before the bloodless Commonwealth coup.) They had all learned about new things like brokerage, stocks, and marketing. They were throwing the terminology around easily, although it seemed to outsiders that they were speaking bird language.

My brother and his friends are the new plants growing in this tremendous "economic space." If the space expands, the harvest will be huge. Now the space is completely chaotic, and no one can predict what will happen there next. But the world will certainly be watching.

I interviewed many big wheels during my trip back to Moscow, but I decided not to quote them. I was not sure whether their pronouncements would matter by the time this essay was published. Who would care in a few months what Gorbachev said at a meeting with World War II veterans? Who would be interested in the important thoughts of a retired or arrested politician?

Nor did I bring back any new jokes from Moscow, like I used to do. There are no more jokes; people are too angry. I only hope we have not had the last laugh.

SPLINTER, SPLINTER LITTLE STATE[3]

The convoluted plot twists and bravura posturing might seem reminiscent of a comic opera. Certainly the so-called Dniester Republic (pop. 600,000) is among the miniest of ministates, proclaimed by ethnic Russians and Ukrainians seceding from a secession. Its citizens refused to stay in the new nation of Moldova (pop. 4.4 million), a former Soviet republic that broke away from Moscow [in August 1991,] because the majority ethnic Romanians were making noises about uniting with their brethren across the border.

But in little more than a week the story [. . .] turned into a blood-soaked tragedy with ominous international implications. As many as 500 people [were] killed in savage fighting between Moldova's Romanians and Slavs, and tens of thousands of refugees [. . .] fled across the border into Ukraine. Worse, Russian-controlled units of the former Soviet army [were] caught up in the battle. Russian President Boris Yeltsin has warned that Moscow may intervene to protect its soldiers and ethnics. That could set a precedent for further interventions on behalf of 25 million Russians living in the Baltic states, the Central Asian republics and other parts of the old Soviet Union, as some of Yeltsin's nationalist opponents are already demanding. At week's end an international conference in Istanbul arranged a ceasefire, but there is serious doubt it will hold.

What is happening in Moldova is of global concern for another reason too. It is a not at all untypical example of one of the two main trends vying to shape the post-cold war world. One is the move toward uniting once jealous sovereignties in economic groupings that also have political ties, like the 12-nation European Community. The contrasting trend is toward splitting up existing states into smaller ethnic nations, some of which then go on to divide amoeba-like into ever smaller pieces. Moldova conceivably might split in three: the Gagauz, a 150,000-member clan of Turkish Muslims, have proclaimed autonomy and appealed to Turkey for protection.

[3]Article by George J. Church, a writer for *Time,* reported by James Carney, William Mader, and J.F.O. McAllister, from *Time* 140:36-39 Jl 6 '92. Copyright © 1992 by Time Inc. Reprinted with permission.

Of the two trends, the one toward what is usually called self-determination might now be the stronger. All over the world, ethnic movements are demanding and frequently getting their own turf, sometimes though not always complete with flag, army, currency and United Nations seat. The secessionist groups range in size from the 50 million citizens of Ukraine to 30,000 Ainu, descendants of the aboriginal inhabitants of northern Japan. They demand "exclusive possession" of two or three small islands in the southern Kuriles—also claimed by Moscow and Tokyo—where they can cluster and preserve their culture.

Not even long-established multiethnic states seem to be immune from breakup. For 74 years Czechoslovakia achieved a mostly peaceful accommodation between Slovaks and Czechs. As recently as 1989 they were solidly united in the "velvet revolution" against communist rule. But now, driven by discontent with their economic lag, the Slovaks have won Czech agreement to effect a "velvet divorce," splitting up peacefully by Sept. 30 [, 1992] into two countries. Both sides are having second thoughts and talking about forming some sort of confederation. But ethnic separatism may be a genie difficult to cram back into the bottle. Says Slovak leader Vladimir Meciar: "We probably will not be able to prevent a breakup."

The thought that self-determination might be the wave of the future makes leaders of the established powers shudder. To them, it threatens instability on a horrendous scale. Secessions often have touched off savage neighbor-vs.-neighbor wars, like those in Moldova; in Georgia, where South Ossetians have been fighting to break away and join ethnic brethren across the border in Russia; and of course in Yugoslavia and in the enclave of Nagorno-Karabakh, caught in a violent tug-of-war between Armenia and Azerbaijan. Even peaceful secessions could spawn a slew of mininations, unable to support themselves economically and dependent on aid from richer nations for survival. At [an] international conference French President Françoise Mitterand worried out loud "whether in the future every tribal group will dispose of its own laws to the exclusion of any common law?" and immediately answered himself, "You can sense how impossible that would be."

Less impossible than irresistible, comes the reply from some political scientists. They view the turmoil as the necessary pain attending the birth of a genuinely new world order no longer dominated by large nation-states but composed mainly of regional associations of smaller countries. It is possible too to see the move toward self-determination as a net gain for liberty. In any case, the day seems to be past when rebellious people can be forced to remain in a state they want no part of. Since resistance to a breakup is usually futile, say many experts, the task for international bodies such as the U.N. is to guide the upheavals into peaceful channels.

That, however, is a mammoth job that would begin very late if it started today. The idea that every group with a common ancestry, language, history and culture should have its own state and write its own laws goes back more than a century. The principle of self-determination got a big boost from Woodrow Wilson at the end of World War I, and in 1945 was written into the Charter of the U.N.

In the Third World the dissolution of Western empires gave birth to many new states whose borders had been drawn for the convenience of colonial administrators and enclosed peoples who had never got along with each other. Jockeying among varied ethnic-religious groups for pieces of the old imperial turf has been igniting secessionist wars ever since. Possibly the deadliest one the insurrection of Hindu Tamil groups against the Buddhist Sinhalese in Sri Lanka. The Washington-based Carnegie Endowment for International Peace counts, among many others, six separate conflicts in India and three each in Burma and Indonesia in which guerrilla groups are seeking independence.

The biggest impulse to the recent explosion, however, has been the end of the cold war. "The reason why the ethnic rivalries and aspirations surfaced so suddenly in the Soviet Union and Eastern Europe is that till recently communism kept them in a time warp," says Oxford history professor Robert O'Neill. Tensions burst forth with explosive fury as soon as the lid of dictatorship was lifted.

By now the movement has begun feeding on itself. In the former Soviet Union, for example, the success of Latvians, Ukrainians, Armenians, Georgians and Tajik, among others, in breaking free from Moscow has encouraged separatist movements inside Russia, Tatars, Chechen, Ingush and Yakut are demanding either greater autonomy within the Russian Federation or full independence. In many areas, though, ethnic groups are so thoroughly mixed that it is impossible to draw neat border lines between their respective turfs. Any attempt to do so only creates new minority problems: a Serb minority in Croatia, for example, instead of a Croat minority in a Serb-dominated Yugoslavia. That leads at best to severe tensions, at worst to savage wars between peoples who once lived in peace.

Yugoslavia, says a U.S. State Department official, is *the* horrible example of "self-determination gone mad." He and others accuse Serbia of adopting a poisonous nationalism that demands ethnic purity at home, enforced by deporting "foreigners" if necessary, and conquest of any lands—portions of Croatia and Bosnia-Herzegovina, for example—to which one's brethren have migrated. Once that spirit takes hold, says the official, "anything becomes justifiable in the name of your kind: expulsion, devastation, murder."

Yugoslavia also provides an example of how badly the international community has been fumbling in managing self-determination. The U.S. and the European Community tried to keep the so-called nation together long after that had become impossible. Then they split over whether to recognize the independence of Slovenia and Croatia. The U.N. sent peacekeeping forces far too late and, by making clear that it would not allow its soldiers to become involved in any fighting, effectively signaled Serbian leader Slobodan Milosevic that nobody would seriously try to stop his efforts to create a Greater Serbia.

But then how should the international community cope with a trend that is both irresistible and extremely dangerous? Thoughtful diplomats and academic analysts offer four general guidelines:

1) Do whatever is possible through preachment, aid and sanctions to encourage the spread of democracy. The most destructive ethnic explosions usually have occurred under repressive regimes. [. . .]

2) Grant a large measure of self-government to dissident ethnic groups. Democracy alone may not satisfy ethnics who suspect that their representatives in a national legislature will be constantly outvoted on such matters as where and how tax money should be spent. [. . .]

3) Develop a set of principles to govern when new states should be given diplomatic recognition, and what they must do to qualify for admission into international bodies. Robert Badinter, president of the French Constitutional Council and head of the E.C. Arbitration Commission on Yugoslavia, suggests that new states must establish democratic institutions, accept international

covenants on human rights, pledge to respect existing frontiers and guarantee respectful treatment of their own ethnic and/or religious minorities.

4) Work out rules for determining when international intervention is necessary to prevent ethnic bloodshed, and develop mechanisms to carry it out. The old idea was that outsiders had no business interfering with anything a government might do within its borders to its own people. That principle has been shattered [. . .] by two events: the dispatch of a U.N. force to northern Iraq to protect Kurds from massacre by Saddam Hussein's forces (the Kurds have since set up what amounts to an autonomous zone there); and the arrival, however tardy, of the U.N. peacekeeping force in Croatia while the Croats were still fighting to break free from Belgrade.

But since the U.N. neither can nor should butt into every secessionist dispute around the world, some standard is needed to judge when intervention is justified. One often heard suggestion is that intervention is defensible whenever a civil war threatens to send floods of refugees across international frontiers. Established powers also need to work out in advance how to organize and finance an intervention force, rather than repeatedly reinventing the wheel. NATO foreign ministers, meeting in Norway [in June 1992], approved for the first time the formation of a force that could be used outside the territory of the alliance states, and U.N. Secretary-General Boutros Boutros-Ghali has called for the creation of a standing U.N. force.

None of this can happen too soon. Demands for ethnic self-determination could [. . .] cause fearsome violence in many more parts of the world. China gives the outside world the impression of being a monolith, yet it contains 55 ethnic minorities numbering perhaps 80 million people, many of whom are bitterly discontented. New violence already has broken out in Tibet, according to reports reaching London. In Europe there are feelings of repression and aspirations toward autonomy, if not independence, among Hungarians in Romania, Turks in Bulgaria and Poles in Lithuania, among others. In Afghanistan civil war could yet pit southern Pashtun against northern Uzbek and Tajik in a conflict that could spill over into neighboring Pakistan and the formerly Soviet republics of Uzbekistan and Tajikistan.

All this adds up to a crazy quilt of ethnic ambition. The task ahead is to ensure that the quilt is not forced into service as a shroud.

THE PERILS OF THE NEW NATIONALISM[4]

At a time when the Marshall Islands have just been admitted to the United Nations, nearly twenty of whose members have a population of less than 250,000, the argument that a territory is too small to constitute a state can no longer be convincingly maintained. Of course such states—even much larger ones—are not independent in any meaningful sense. Politically and militarily they are helpless without outside protection, as Kuwait and Croatia show. Economically they are even more dependent. Few separatist movements hope to go it alone. They want to exchange dependence on a single state economy for dependence on the European Community or some other larger unit that limits its members' economic sovereignty just as much.

Still, if a territory wishes to run up its flag outside the U.N. building in New York and acquire all the other fringe benefits of statehood—a national anthem, a national airline and a few embassies in attractive or politically important capitals—the chances today seem better than ever.

But why should anyone wish to set up such a state, mostly by breaking up existing political units in Eurasia and Africa? (There is so far no significant tendency to do so in the Americas, except in Canada.) The usual reason given by would-be state-builders is that the people of the territory concerned have constituted a "nation" from the beginning of time, a special ethnic group, usually with its own language, which cannot live under the rule of strangers. The right of self-determination, they argue, implies states that coincide with nations.

Almost everything about this argument is historically wrong, but as Ernest Renan noted more than a century ago, "Forgetting history, and even historical error, are an essential factor in the formation of a nation." However, we are concerned not with history or with rationality but with politics. Here one thing has to be stated very clearly. The nationalist belief, first expressed in the nineteenth century by Giuseppe Mazzini, that every nation should form a state, and that there should be only one state

[4]Article by Eric Hobsbawm, professor emeritus at London University and teacher at the New School for Social Research, from *The Nation* 255:537+ S 4 '92. Copyright © 1992 by The Nation Company, Inc. Reprinted with permission.

for each nation, is and always was quite unworkable in ethnic-linguistic terms.

There are, with the exception of some island ministates, probably not more than a dozen ethnically and linguistically homogeneous states among the 170 or so of the world's political entities, and probably none that include anything like the totality of the "nation" they claim to embody. The territorial distribution of the human race is older than the idea of ethnic-linguistic nation-states and therefore does not correspond to it. Development in the modern world economy, because it generates vast population movements, constantly undermines ethnic-linguistic homogeneity. Multiethnicity and plurilinguality are quite unavoidable, except temporarily by mass exclusion, forcible assimilation, mass expulsion or genocide—in short, by coercion. There is only a dark future for a world of nation-states such as the new government of Georgia, which wants to deny citizenship rights to any inhabitant who cannot prove that his or her ancestors were Georgian speakers and lived in the territory before 1801.

There are today four rather different reasons such sentiments, and their political expression in separatism, are widely supported. The first is that the collapse of the Communist system, which imposed political stability over a large part of Europe, has reopened the wounds of World War I, or, more precisely, of the misconceived and unrealistic peace settlements after it. The explosive nationalist issues in Central and Eastern Europe today are not ancient ethnic conflicts but those created during the formation of the successor states to the collapsing multi-ethnic Habsburg, Ottoman and Czarist Russian empires. Baltic and Caucasian separatism, and conflicts between Serbs and Croats, and Czechs and Slovaks, were not serious problems in 1917, or could not have existed before the establishment of Yugoslavia and Czechoslovakia. What has made those problems acute is not the strength of national feeling, which was no greater than in countries like Britain and Spain, but the disintegration of central power, for this forced even Soviet or Yugoslav republics that did not dream of separation, like Kazakhstan and Macedonia, to assert independence as a means of self-preservation.

The breakdown of Communist systems has given separatist agitations elsewhere enormous encouragement, but it has no direct bearing on them. Such as they are, the prospects of independence for, say, Scotland, Quebec, Euskadi (the Basque country) or Corsica remain the same as before. They do not depend on what happens in the East.

The second reason is more general, though probably more important in the West than in the East. The massive population movements of the past forty years—within and between countries and continents—have made xenophobia into a major political phenomenon, as the earlier mass migrations of 1880–1920 did to a smaller extent. Xenophobia encourages ethnic nationalism, since the essence of both is hostility to other groups (the "not-we"). United States nationalism is by origin entirely nonlinguistic. It is only because of mass Hispanic immigration that today demands are made, for the first time, that English should be the *official* language of the United States. However, mutual ethnic hatred does not necessarily produce separatism, as the United States also proves.

The third reason is that the politics of group identity are easier to understand than any others, especially for peoples who, after several decades of dictatorship, lack both political education and experience. In Central Europe, argues Miroslav Hroch, a leading Czech historian, language is once again replacing complicated concepts like constitutions and civil rights. Nationalism is among the simple, intuitively comprehensible beliefs that substitute for less understandable political programs. It is not the only one.

The fourth reason is perhaps the most fundamental. To quote the Czech historian: "Where an old regime disintegrates, where old social relations have become unstable, amid the rise of general insecurity, belonging to a common language and culture may become the only certainty in society, the only value beyond ambiguity and doubt." In the former Communist countries this insecurity and disorientation may derive from the collapse of the predictable planned economy and the social security that went with it. In the West there are other forms of disorientation and insecurity that have built up during the past decades, when the world and human life changed more rapidly and profoundly than ever before in human history.

Is it an accident that Quebec separatism as a serious political factor emerged at the end of a decade when a traditional, Catholic, pious and clerical community that had preserved the values of seventeenth-century French peasants suddenly gave way to a society in which people no longer went to church and the birthrate fell almost vertically? After two generations, when continents of peasants have become continents of city dwellers, when the relations between the generations, and increasingly between the sexes, have been transformed and past wisdom seems irrelevant to present problems, the world is full of people who long for something that still looks like an old, and unchallengeable, certainty. It is not surprising that at such times they turn to group identity, of which national identity is one form, or that the demand for a political unit exclusively for the members of the group, in the form of ethniclinguistic nation-states, once again comes to the fore.

However, if we can understand the forces that lead to a revival of the politics of national consciousness, and even sympathize with the feelings that inspire it, let us have no illusions. Adding another few dozen to the member-states of the U.N. will not give any of them any more control over their affairs than they had before they became independent. It will not solve or diminish the problems of cultural or any other autonomy in the world, any more than it did in 1919.

Establishing nation-states on the post-World War I model is not necessarily a recipe for disaster. Among the potential new nation-states there may well be one or two future Netherlands and Switzerlands, bastions of tolerance, democracy and civilization. But who, looking at Serbia and Croatia, at Slovakia and Lithuania, at Georgia, Quebec and the rest, would today expect many of the newly separated nation-states to go that way? And who would expect a Europe of such new states to be a zone of peace?

FOR EVERY NATIONALITY, A STATE[5]

With a flourish befitting an Isaac Asimov novel, three days in August [1991] transported us into an entirely different country. And the West must relate to this new system-in-the-making on an entirely different basis than it did before August 21.

Having staked everything on Mikhail Gorbachev, who had proclaimed *perestroika* but impeded actual changes that would inevitably limit his power, the West tirelessly strived for the preservation of the Soviet Union. Although it ecstatically greeted the

[5]Article by Yelena Bonner, a human rights activist in the former Soviet Union and widow of Andrei Sakharov, from *New Perspectives Quarterly* 8:15–17 Fall '91. Copyright © 1991 by the Center for the Study of Democratic Institutions. Reprinted with permission.

liberation of Eastern Europe, the West steadfastly denied the right of freedom for the Soviet peoples.

By focusing on the issue of leadership at the center and paying no heed to the national aspirations of the republics, the West proved to be profoundly undemocratic. Before the coup, Western interest in Soviet affairs revolved around the conflict of two personalities, Gorbachev and Boris Yeltsin. But the issue was actually something entirely different: whether a given people—the people of Lithuania, Estonia, the Ukraine, Byelorussia, Armenia or any other nation, republic, or autonomous region, including Russia itself—has the right to choose its own statehood and destiny.

On March 12, 1990, Lithuania declared its independence. Why did it take a year and nine months to recognize its legitimacy, as well as that of Latvia and Estonia? For that matter, what could possibly explain why the West refused to recognize the right to independence of Slovenia and Croatia from the very start? Is it easier to normalize international relations after a blood-bath?

The most popular responses to these questions sound rather naïve today: "We were trying to help Gorbachev and *perestroika*. We were hoping to preserve the USSR." And why was that? To facilitate the West's dealings with the country? And what about the people who live in it?

Are Western democrats truly indifferent to how people fare under totalitarianism? Is this why they so easily forgive anything at all, even a nightmare like tanks crushing students in Tiananmen Square?

The West must not only rethink the approach it has taken over the past six years, it must also rethink the very concept of human-be based on the meager charity of the Helsinki Accords, obtained in exchange for legitimization of the postwar partition of Europe, but rather on the Universal Declaration of Human Rights, the principal charter of humanity under the flag of the UN. Most of us have for decades defended the rights of the individual person as listed in its thirty articles. And yet we bypassed the preamble, which says: "It is necessary for human rights to be protected by the power of the law, in order for a person not to have to use the last resort of rebellion against tyranny and oppression."

These words pertain to nations, not individuals. They speak of the right of Iraqi Kurds, Lithuanians, Croatians, or Armenian peasants from Nagorno-Karabakh to struggle against tyranny.

They require of the international community, if not an outright armed intervention as called for on behalf of Kurds and Shiites in Iraq, then at the very least immediate international diplomatic support in the cases of Eastern European countries, republics of Yugoslavia and all republics of the former Soviet Union that have proclaimed their independence.

Diplomatic recognition and positive attitudes toward such declarations of independence serve as safeguards of one of the most fundamental rights—that of self-determination. Such recognition can often prevent otherwise imminent bloodshed. No geopolitical or so-called *Realpolitik* considerations can take precedence over the protection of human rights and the right of a given people's self-determination.

For nearly half a century, we have honored the principle of inviolability of borders, while forgetting just what the principle applies to. It is accepted that national borders are not to be breached from without, as in Afghanistan or Kuwait. But this concept has not been applied to Lithuania or Slovenia, for example, when their people or lawful parliaments decided to create or restore their sovereign statehood. Isn't that, too, an inviolable right?

Until such a time when international law clearly defines and codifies the principles of inviolability of borders *and* national self-determination, we will be unable to defend human rights—the rights of peoples and individuals—in their full scope.

This is the most crucial and urgent issue in my country today.

Although the republics all face complex problems, this is particularly true of Russia. Because of its historical role and actual influence, Russia will be the first to grapple with the issue of the future political structure of the former Union.

Russia's choice between a democratic and totalitarian future will greatly influence the course adopted by the other republics. In order to become a democratic state, it will have to deliver on the promise of self-determination for its own multinational constituencies and serve as an example to the rest of the republics. It will have to escape the menace of converting from a Soviet regime, where religion is separate from the state, to a Russian Orthodox ideological state. It will have to forever bid *adieu* to the Messianic role of Russia that was so nurtured over the centuries.

Is the parliament capable of all that? Is Yeltsin, for that matter?

Can Gorbachev review the lessons of *perestroika* and live with the realization that democratic development of the people of the former USSR means he would be leader of a center with very limited functions delegated by the republics?

All these conditions are a must. Otherwise, the victory over the coup will prove to be a hollow one for the people. Russia will once more become a totalitarian government, having merely changed one ideology for another.

III. TO MARKET, TO MARKET

EDITOR'S INTRODUCTION

The economic revolution begun in 1989 has been accompanied by an atmosphere of false gloom in Eastern Europe, according to Mark Kramer, writing in *Foreign Policy*. While living standards have dropped and unemployment risen, economic figures do not measure qualitative improvements in people's lives or unreported income. Furthermore, Kramer argues that faulty figures disguise the level of unemployment that existed during the communist era. The author details the impact of historical events on Eastern Europe's new economies and examines the relative success of reforms. He concludes that the most unfortunate and dangerous consequences for these frail economies would be caused by a continued lack of interest by the West. Kramer therefore outlines specific recommendations for the Western nations in addressing Eastern Europe, including the dimination of trade barriers, access to foreign private investment, and a greater emphasis on privatization.

In *USA Today*, Karen LaFollette examines the establishment of free enterprise in the former Soviet republics. She maintains that the Commonwealth of Independent States will disintegrate. Loans from government and private banks to the new republics will damage rather than help their economies. Instead, LaFollette advocates the shoring up of the collapsing economies from within by establishing private property and market economies as the basis for creating successful new societies.

More positive about the potential success of Russian capitalism, Jude Wanniski in an article reprinted from *Foreign Affairs*, considers whether a newly designed Russian system might become the envy of the world in the next century. Free from the excesses of current Western economies, Russia could build a new form of capitalism. The author proposes that Russian leaders refrain from devaluing their currency, and instead draw upon the country's vast natural assets, and privatize. Finally, the author suggests the new Russian system should strive for simplicity in creating economic and tax laws and regulations.

The concluding piece in this section is by Kenneth L. Adelman and Norman R. Augustine, who examine the challenges posed by the conversion of the massive military-industrial complex that was the centerpiece of both sides of the Cold War economy. The authors provide a unique point of view as businesspeople who were a part of that economy and who, in their article for *Foreign Affairs,* examine possible transitions of the world to a peacetime economy from a historical, political, philosophical, and economic perspective. Adelman and Augustine conclude that the trip will not be an easy one and offer suggestions to improve the likelihood of a successful change both in the United States and across the Atlantic.

EASTERN EUROPE GOES TO MARKET[1]

The collapse of communist rule in Eastern Europe in the autumn of 1989 brought with it widespread euphoria about the prospects for democratic change and economic prosperity. By the start of 1992, however, the optimism of 1989 had been supplanted by a sense of gloom. This deepening pessimism stemmed in part from the resurgence of old political rivalries and nationalist conflicts, including the bloody civil war in Yugoslavia and the turbulent dissolution of the Soviet Union. As Western Europe moved toward greater political and economic integration, Eastern Europe faced disintegration and internecine warfare.

Even if these ethnic and political fissures had remained submerged, the growing public awareness in Eastern Europe of the region's economic plight would have been enough to sustain a mood of pessimism. The task of replacing dysfunctional state-controlled economies with viable free-market systems would have been formidable under the best of circumstances. In Eastern Europe, the task has been further complicated by a series of external economic shocks and by the lack of clear guidance from past experience. Although previous transitions from authoritarianism

[1]Article by Mark Kramer, a research fellow at Brown University's Center for Foreign Policy Development and a fellow of Harvard University's Russian Research Center, from *Foreign Policy* 86:134–157 Spring '92. Copyright © 1992 by the Carnegie Endowment for International Peace. Reprinted with Permission.

to democracy in Latin America, the Iberian countries, and Greece are instructive, the economic and political challenges facing Eastern Europe have no ready parallel in modern history. The East European countries find themselves embarking on a painful and prolonged economic transformation without any guarantee that their sacrifices will pay off in the end—but with the risk of growing social and political unrest.

Official statistics in all the East European countries paint a grim picture of the first two years of postcommunist transitions, revealing substantial declines in both production and living standards. Advocates of a cautious approach to reform widely cite these statistics, claiming that the cure of "shock therapy" is killing the patient. In reality, the gloomy statistics tell only part of the story and, in some respects, are highly misleading. The decline in production in each country came exclusively in the inefficient state sector, where most of what was lost would have had no place in a viable free-market economy. Moreover, the production statistics often understate the growth and vibrancy of the private sector, especially the rise of small-scale entrepreneurs. In Poland, for example, some 1.4 million private businesses opened between December 1989 and December 1991, and their impact by the economy is not always given due weight by statisticians.

Official data showing a precipitous drop in living standards and a sharp rise in unemployment are misleading as well. These figures do not adequately reflect qualitative improvements in people's lives, such as the disappearance of lines and the improved quality of consumer goods and services. Nor do the figures take into account money people earn in the private sector but fail to report in order to avoid paying taxes. The statistics also exaggerate unemployment, counting as unemployed those who actually work in the "second," or unofficial, economy. The unemployment figures also include people who in previous years had been paid wages for work they never performed. The disguised unemployment of the communist era has now simply been acknowledged.

In short, from an economic standpoint, the initial results of the postcommunist transitions are less discouraging than the official statistics indicate. From a political standpoint, however, the situation is altogether different. In the political arena, the actual (or projected) achievements of the economic reforms matter less than the public perception of those achievements. On this score, there seems little basis for optimism. The electoral results in Poland in October 1991, the sporadic demonstrations against price increases in Hungary, the labor unrest and widening ethnic divisions in Czechoslovakia, and the violent rampages by miners in Romania all bear witness to growing popular discontent with the hardships and austerity that economic reform requires. The basic question for the East European countries over the next few years is whether the proponents of economic shock therapy will survive the political fallout of their reforms and, if not, what the consequences of a gradual approach or even outright failure might be.

Why have the postcommunist economic transitions in Eastern Europe encountered such difficulty, and what might be done to improve the situation? Four basic problems have complicated the economic transformation of these countries: disruption of foreign trade, the ambiguity of property rights, worker resistance, and uncertainty about the appropriate sequencing of reforms. The first category refers to the external climate for reform, whereas the second, third, and fourth categories concern internal matters. These four problems are not the only ones that the postcommunist states have confronted, but they are the most important and they bear, at least indirectly, on all other obstacles to the creation of free-market systems.

Trade Shocks

From the late 1940s until 1989, the Soviet Union was by far the largest trading partner of all the countries in the region. The East European states depended heavily on Soviet supplies of energy and raw materials, and many East European firms relied on the USSR as their main customer for finished goods. By contrast, the USSR, as a largely autarkic state, depended relatively little on its imports from Eastern Europe and could easily shift its exports of energy and raw materials to the West.

Soon after the upheavals of 1989, Soviet-East European trade began to crumble. In 1990 the Soviet Union reduced its deliveries of oil and natural gas to Eastern Europe and sought to export more to the West for hard currency. Starting in January 1991, the USSR and East European countries replaced the transferable ruble with the U.S. dollar as the basis for all transactions. This change, carried out at Soviet insistence, forced the East European and Soviet governments to use world-market prices for the goods they traded (including Soviet oil), thus ending the artificial pricing system that had long existed within the Council for Mutual

Economic Assistance (COMECON). Fittingly enough, COME-CON, which had been moribund since late 1989, was formally disbanded in June 1991. The shift to hard-currency financing not only forced the East European states to pay more for Soviet energy supplies and raw materials; it also deprived them of vital markets. Because Soviet officials and enterprise managers for the most part had to use scarce hard currency reserves to pay for East European goods, they chose instead to buy what they needed from Western suppliers, whose products were of much better quality and only slightly more expensive.

The resulting decline in orders from the USSR for East European products dealt a sharp blow to East European firms as yet unable to compete in Western markets. In the first quarter of 1991, Czechoslovak and Hungarian exports to the Soviet Union fell by 80 per cent, and for the year as a whole they declined by nearly the same amount, despite a partial return to barter trade in the second half of 1991. The drop in Polish exports to the USSR was almost as steep, around 60 per cent. The reductions particularly hurt pharmaceutical, transportation, cosmetics, and food processing industries, leaving them with warehouses of unsold goods that were unmarketable in the West.

The growing chaos in the Soviet economy further disrupted Soviet-East European trade. By mid-1991, most of the USSR's foreign trading responsibilities had devolved to enterprises and republic governments, but many of the enterprises did not have enough hard currency to pay for imports from both Western and Eastern Europe. Consequently, they fell far behind in their payments to East European suppliers, and the republic governments declined to cover the debts for them. The growing unreliability of Soviet enterprises prompted East European firms to withhold further supplies to the USSR in the absence of bank guarantees, which proved difficult to obtain. This credit cutoff prevented additional financial losses for Eastern Europe, but it did nothing to bolster export opportunities or recover outstanding Soviet debts.

The erosion of trade with the USSR in the first half of 1991 was the most serious of the external shocks to the East European economies, but other developments also contributed to the turmoil. Trade with the German Democratic Republic (GDR), especially important for Czechoslovakia and Poland, came to an end with the reunification of East and West Germany in October 1990. Until then, the GDR had provided markets for East European agricultural and industrial goods and had been a major supplier of scarce industrial components and high-technology products. Following German reunification, Czechoslovakia and Poland temporarily lost access to these markets and supplies. Further, the German-based companies frequently outmaneuvered their East European competitors in the quest for Soviet and Western markets. Thus, the demise of the GDR cut into East European trade from two angles.

In addition to the disruption of trade caused by German reunification, trade among all the East European countries dropped sharply for several months after the shift to hard-currency accounting within COMECON. The same considerations that induced Soviet managers to cut back on imports from Eastern Europe led the East European countries themselves to forgo purchases from one another. To help ease the problem, Czechoslovakia, Hungary, and Poland tentatively agreed in December 1991 to phase out customs duties, quantitative restrictions, and other trade barriers among themselves. The agreement, however, could not redeem the damage that had already been done, nor could it immediately revive trade among the three.

East European trade also suffered as a result of the United Nations-sponsored embargo against Iraq. Iraq had been a major trading partner for Eastern Europe and several countries in the region lost hundreds of millions of dollars in uncollected debts and unfulfilled contracts. The brief surge in oil prices during the Persian Gulf crisis further weakened Eastern Europe. Although the losses did not cause permanent harm, they were an onerous burden during a critical early stage of the economic transitions.

If the East European states weather the short-term dislocation from these external shocks, the outlook over the medium to longer terms will be much brighter. The reorientation of East European trade away from the former Soviet Union, though painful in the short term, will work to the long-term advantage of Eastern Europe. Having been forced to reduce their reliance on Soviet energy and markets, the East European economies will emerge more capable of trading with the West. In 1990 and 1991, trade between Eastern Europe and members of the European Community (EC) expanded significantly, as a number of East European firms adjusted surprisingly well to competition on the world market. Moreover, the increase would have been larger without the barriers that the EC still has in place against such products as textiles, steel, and agricultural goods. The growth of trade with

the EC, though not as substantial as the East European governments had desired and not enough to offset the losses in trade
with former COMECON partners, provided some hope that
Czechoslovakia, Hungary, and Poland might be ready to join the
EC within the next decade.

Private Property

The fundamental pillar of any capitalist system is the private
ownership of property. If communism achieved anything in Eastern Europe, it was the abolition of private property rights as state
bureaucracies assumed control of all land and production facilities. Thus, one of the most urgent tasks confronting the postcommunist governments has been the legalization of private ownership and the transfer of state property to private hands. Although
small-scale privatization has been underway for some time
throughout Eastern Europe and programs for large-scale privatization have been adopted in Czechoslovakia, Hungary, Poland,
and even Romania, a number of thorny problems regarding fair-
ness, speed, and efficiency have arisen.

The controversy surrounding restitution or compensation for
citizens whose property was expropriated by the communist regimes complicates the whole question of privatization. The value
of affected property in Czechoslovakia, Hungary, and Poland has
been estimated at more than $22 billion. Because the notion of
shifting ownership to private hands is predicted on the assumption that the state owns the property to be transferred, ambiguity
about the state's claim poses obvious difficulties for privatization.
Potential buyers of state assets will be reluctant to purchase anything that might later be subject to restitution claims. Moreover,
the lengthy process needed to verify potential claims could delay
privatization indefinitely, thereby thwarting hopes of swift ownership transfer.

The restitution issue roused heated debate both inside and
outside the East European governments and became a factor in
local and national elections. In Hungary, one of the contending
parties, the Independent Small-holders, made the demand for
restitution of farmland its main electoral plank. Ultimately, the
East European governments tried to reach compromises that
would be deemed fair by the public, yet would minimally affect
plans for privatization. In Poland, a compromise bill limited restitution in kind to property seized in violation of the laws existing

at the time of seizure. Vouchers that could be used to purchase shares in privatized firms would be granted to all other successful claimants. Hungary provided for compensation in the form of property bonds that could be used in land auctions or exchanged for shares in privatized companies. Only Czechoslovakia permitted restitution in kind on a wider scale, and even there dispossessed owners had to fulfill strict conditions and file claims within a limited time. Thus, although lingering pressure for expanded restitution remained an obstacle to privatization, the acute uncertainty that arose in 1990 and early 1991 had largely subsided by the end of 1991.

Other formidable obstacles to privatization remained, however. During the first two years of their economic transitions, Czechoslovakia, Hungary, and Poland took widely differing approaches to privatization. Hungary adopted the most cautious approach, eschewing plans involving either a mass giveaway of state-owned companies through vouchers or the broad transfer of ownership to workers and managers. Instead, Hungarian officials sought to privatize on a case-by-case basis using traditional sales methods. That approach had the virtue of simplicity, but the results it produced in 1990 and 1991 were not especially encouraging: The sale of just one of the most successful Hungarian companies took many months longer than expected. By mid-1991, some Hungarian officials, including Finance Minister Mihály Kupa, openly complained that privatization would take several decades or even centuries if the government relied exclusively on selling off companies one at a time.

Case-by-case privatization faced the same difficulties in Czechoslovakia and Poland. Unlike Hungary, however, Czechoslovakia and Poland responded by devising mass giveaway schemes that they hoped would expedite the privatization process. The Polish plan called for the establishment of 12 investment management funds, headed by Western financial consultants, that would control 60 percent of the shares of Poland's several hundred largest companies. The state treasury and the company's employees would divide the remaining 40 per cent of shares in each company. The investment funds were to start trading shares in the companies immediately after the initial allocation in 1992. At the same time, an equal number of shares from each investment fund were to be distributed free of charge to all 28 million Polish adults, who would be entitled to trade shares in the funds starting in mid-1993.

The Czechoslovak government came up with a more elaborate approach, which called for 3,000 large state-owned companies to be sold off by means of "coupon privatization." All companies selected for the program had to submit a privatization plan by November 1991 and, except for a few firms of particular national importance, were entitled to sell shares to any interested buyers, including foreigners. The large majority of companies, which were unable to sell enough of their shares by standard methods, were then channeled into the "coupon privatization" scheme. Under that scheme, shares in enterprises were to be auctioned off in two waves to holders of investment vouchers, which were available to all adult citizens of Czechoslovakia for a nominal price of 1,035 crowns (roughly $35). Initial estimates suggested that some 3–4 million people—approximately one-third of the adult population—would purchase vouchers; the actual number of buyers in 1991 amounted to only about 450,000. A last-minute rush of purchases in January 1992, however, brought the total up to the initial projections.

Neither the Polish nor the Czechoslovak plan has turned out to be entirely feasible and both are potentially susceptible to abuse. The Czechoslovak proposal has been criticized for failing to introduce the new capital and management expertise that is needed to revive ailing industries and stem the growing obsolescence of the industrial base. If most of the newly privatized companies quickly go bankrupt, the experience could permanently set back the cause of mass privatization in Czechoslovakia and elsewhere. Quite apart from that problem, the Czechoslovak approach is prone to the dangers of insider trading and fraud. Because most Czechoslovak citizens lack the information required to make sound investment decisions, the most valuable shares may end up going to voucher holders with access to inside information. This drawback could be mitigated somewhat if workers and managers used their vouchers to buy shares in their own firms, but the potential for abuse cannot be eliminated altogether. Finally, the plan has been attacked by both Czech and Slovak politicians for endangering the interests of their respective republics by enabling foreign investment funds to make quick profits from undervalued companies. So bitter did their complaints become by the fall of 1991 that they delayed the implementation of the entire program, much to the dismay of the federal government.

Although the Polish plan avoids most of the Czechoslovak

proposal's shortcomings, it is dependent on the government's ability to recruit a sufficient number of Western fund managers who can adjust to doing business in Poland, itself a daunting task. Further, the long-term financial underpinnings of the program, including compensation to fund managers and operation of the stock market, have never been fully clarified. Nor has there been any concrete vision of the investment funds' role over the longer term: whether they will be preserved, liquidated, or broken up. The concept of distributing investment shares to every Polish adult has also come under attack from legislators who believe the approach is too slow and financially unpredictable. Because of these problems, the scope of the plan was scaled back substantially in October 1991, when 171 of the proposed 400 enterprises were dropped from the first round of the distribution scheme, including some of the largest Polish companies. Later on, other companies were excluded because of antitrust concerns, raising further doubts about the plan.

The slow pace of case-by-case privatization in Hungary, and the problems connected with the Czechoslovak and Polish versions of mass privatization prompted some East European officials to reconsider the idea of condoning spontaneous privatization—the transfer of ownership to workers and managers—at least for small- and medium-size firms. Initially, the East European governments were reluctant to promote spontaneous privatization because of a widespread and accurate perception that it had been exploited by ex-Communist party officials to retain influence in society through the ownership of fraudulently acquired property. To preclude a recurrence of such abuses, East European advocates of spontaneous privatization, such as Hungary's Kupa, proposed new legal safeguards ensuring that workers as well as managers would benefit from the process. Although supporters of spontaneous privatization had gained considerable ground by the start of 1992 in Hungary and Poland, the debate regarding privatization may not be fully settled for years to come.

Even in the unlikely event that all the shortcomings in the privatization schemes could be worked out, private property rights would remain ambiguous. Over the last few years, the East European countries have created new forms of property that cannot be neatly classified as either state-owned or private. Early reforms to decentralize economic decision making without actually privatizing firms led to the emergence of enterprises governed by workers' councils or by a combination of workers and managers who had not been given formal title to the property. In both cases, the state still nominally owned the companies, but those who actually ran them were accountable only to themselves and behaved accordingly. Eventually, these nebulous companies may be transformed into commercial enterprises governed by boards of directors, which can then be either retained by the state or privatized. Until clarification occurs across the board, enterprises existing in the limbo between state and private ownership will severely impede East European economic performance.

Worker Resistance

Until 1989, blue-collar workers in all East European countries lived under broadly similar political and labor conditions. For the most part, they were allowed only ritual participation in national politics, and were strictly limited in their participation in the workplace and at the local level. In return for their political and labor quiescence, most workers received certain economic benefits from the state, including job security, stable and subsidized prices, and a lax work regime with low performance standards. Recent advances toward a free-market orientation introduced blue-collar workers to heightened performance pressures, job insecurity, and income disparities. At the same time, workers began, openly and legally, to articulate demands, organize independent unions, and exert political influence. The convergence of these two developments—economic hardships coupled with much greater political freedom—spurred workers in Eastern Europe to join in opposing some of the harshest austerity measures.

The degree of worker resistance to shock therapy programs has varied from country to country, but in every case some of the strongest opposition has come from workers whose job security and living standards have been threatened. In Czechoslovakia, for example, the threat of widespread labor unrest in early 1991 forced the federal government to back away from its plan to quadruple the prices of electricity, gasoline, and heating. Similarly, protests by workers in Slovakia, who feared losing their jobs, helped induce the government to refrain from closing down inefficient factories in the Slovak Republic. After initially promising to halt all arms transfers to the Third World, Czechoslovak officials gave in to worker pressure and permitted Slovak factories to continue producing tanks, air-defense missiles, training aircraft, and related equipment for export to Iran, Syria, and other countries. Although Czechoslovakia suspended all weapons sales to the Middle East in October 1991 to facilitate the Arab-Israeli peace negotiations, growing pressure from Slovak industrial workers later compelled the federal government to allow the sales to go forward and to seek potential arms customers elsewhere.

Even after the Czechoslovak government took steps to preserve jobs in the military industries, however, labor unrest in Slovakia persisted. Three hundred and eighty thousand metalworkers staged a one-hour warning strike in Bratislava in November 1991 to protest higher prices and the decline in living standards. Similar protests occurred in other industries in Slovakia. The federal government also found itself under attack from workers on collective farms in both Slovakia and the Czech lands, who feared unemployment if plans for the privatization of agriculture went ahead. This unexpected resistance crippled efforts to decollectivize agriculture in 1990 and 1991. By the start of 1992, worker unrest in Czechoslovakia had proven to be a key impediment to all types of economic reform, especially the federal government's plans for large-scale privatization.

In Poland, too, the first threats to the shock therapy program that then prime minister Tadeusz Mazowiecki's noncommunist-led government implemented in January 1990 came from miners, shipbuilders, and other workers who were concerned about unemployment. Mazowiecki's program enjoyed unusually strong popular support for several months and produced dramatic results, but by the late summer of 1990, public approval had ebbed and labor protests had begun. These growing signs of discontent induced the government to slow down its plans for privatization and afforded Lech Wałęsa an opportunity to seek the Polish presidency. The presidential elections of late 1990 ended in a decisive rebuff for Mazowiecki and an equally decisive victory for Wałęsa, confirming the extent of popular dissatisfaction with the austerity program.

Once Wałęsa had taken office, however, unrest among workers continued to grow, as the basic framework of the shock therapy policies remained in place and the main architect of those policies, Finance Minister Leszek Balcerowicz, retained his post. Workers demanded that large factories be kept open and that wage restraints be eliminated or at least eased. On the former point, the government had made significant concessions by the fall of 1991. The inconclusive results and low turnout in the parliamentary elections of October 1991, the substantial protest-vote that went to the former Communist party, the two months of wrangling before a less reform-minded government emerged under Jan Olszewski, and the proliferation of strikes across Poland all suggested that resistance among workers to shock therapy would hinder attempts to proceed further with radical reforms in Poland.

In Hungary as well, labor unrest caused extensive disruption and generated pressure on the government to relax its austerity program. In October 1990, a cab drivers' strike brought Budapest to a virtual standstill for several days, dramatically illustrating the growing public discontent. A few months later, the threat of mass protests by workers at the huge Ikarus bus-manufacturing plant influenced the decision of Hungarian leaders to seek outside investment to keep the ailing factory in business. During the summer of 1991, the Hungarian government abandoned its plans to cut agricultural subsidies after farm workers organized large rallies nationwide to protest grain surpluses and call for higher grain prices.

Workers in other East European countries protested austerity measures as well. In September 1991 thousands of coal miners from the Jiu Valley in western Romania stormed into Bucharest seeking higher wages, lower prices, and the government's resignation. Ensuing clashes with the police and security forces left three people dead and dozens injured. In Bulgaria, labor protests did not erupt into mass violence in 1990 or 1991, but strikes and work stoppages helped bring down the communist-dominated government in November 1990 and impeded the economic reforms of the new, noncommunist government. For example, a strike by 27,000 Bulgarian coal miners in August 1991 led to significant wage increases, contravening the government's anti-inflationary policies. Subsequent waves of strikes, including one by more than 4,000 workers at the Arsenal weapons factory in December 1991, brought additional pressure to bear on the government.

Workers in Eastern Europe have good reason to be leery of drastic economic reform. The experience of eastern Germany demonstrated that the sacrifices required during the transition from a state-controlled economy to a free-market system fall disproportionately on blue-collar workers. Unemployment in eastern Germany soared to 30 per cent in 1991, and the rate would have been even higher if underemployment and part-time work were taken into account. Without the advantages that reunification brought to eastern Germany, the sacrifices that will be required in the other East European countries may make the situation in the former GDR seem pleasant by comparison.

The extent to which worker resistance becomes a crippling obstacle to reform will depend, in part, on the precautionary measures to cushion shock therapy. The Hungarian government has sought to soften the impact of rising unemployment, which reached 6.1 per cent in September 1991, by providing generous unemployment benefits of up to three times the minimum wage for as long as two years. Similarly, Romanian officials have tried to head off labor unrest by preserving housing subsidies and a few other price supports. Although these policies have obvious drawbacks, they are indicative of the trade-offs that may be required to ensure worker support for—or at least acquiescence to—radical economic measures. Although precautions of this sort will insulate the East European governments to some degree, the success of economic reform in Eastern Europe will ultimately depend on the readiness of workers to put up with austerity—perhaps severe austerity—over the short to medium term in return for much greater political freedom and the hope of eventual prosperity.

Sequencing Reforms

The ideal shock therapy program would pursue the full range of reforms—macroeconomic stabilization, price liberalization, currency convertibility, trade and banking reform, labor deregulation, broad privatization, and appropriate legal and social measures—simultaneously. For both political and economic reasons, however, a truly comprehensive package has been impossible except in the very special case of eastern Germany. The other East European governments have found it necessary to choose among certain steps rather than pursue all avenues at once. Unfortunately, some measures have little or no effect unless combined with other measures, and it is often difficult to evaluate a sequence of reforms before implementation. Further, if the austerity required during the early stages of a shock therapy program generates enough popular opposition and discord among elites, it will complicate the subsequent enactment of any deferred reforms.

This problem has been evident in Poland, the first East European country to undertake shock therapy. Enacted in January 1990, the Polish program removed controls on prices, countered inflation through wage restraints, restricted the money supply, reduced trade barriers, and devalued the złoty to make the currency convertible. Although the program envisioned large-scale privatization, it deferred that goal pending the success of the initial reforms. From a political standpoint, the delay in implementing privatization may have been necessary; and economically, freeing prices would help in deciding which companies were worth trying to sell to private buyers. However, the decline in Polish living standards during the first two years of shock therapy has made the public wary of future reforms, including plans for privatization.

Looking back in late 1991, Polish minister of privatization Janusz Lewandowski publicly regretted the sequence of reforms that his government had chosen. In an interview with the Moscow weekly *Novoe Vremya*, he said:

So risky a measure as the freeing of prices should have been carried out *simultaneously* with the greatest possible introduction of private enterprise and large-scale privatization. We made that mistake here. At first we freed prices and strengthened the złoty, and only a year later got down to privatization. Instead, we should have done the two simultaneously, or better yet, privatization should have come ahead of the decontrol of price formation. Then the hyperinflation could have been overcome earlier and without such a shock.

Lewandowski's comments illustrate the difficulty of formulating an economically viable sequence of reforms that will also be politically acceptable. The approach that the Polish government took in 1990 and 1991 has made it inordinately difficult for any future government to close down inefficient factories. Efforts to privatize firms that might be efficient if they were to reduce their labor force have been similarly hindered. For example, during the October 1991 electoral campaign, Prime Minister Jan Bielecki's government found it necessary to promise to bail out the giant Ursus tractor plant and a number of ailing military factories. The uncertainty that has followed the October 1991 elections will further complicate efforts at privatization in Poland.

Polish officials face obstacles that are typical of those bedeviling all the East European countries. In 1990 and most of 1991, officials in Czechoslovakia, Hungary, and Poland concentrated primarily on dealing with the easiest problems first—macroeconomic stabilization and the control of inflation. They were less inclined to call for measures that would bring about large-scale unemployment. The experience of the former GDR, where industrial output fell by 50 per cent and unemployment rose to 30 per cent in the first year after reunification, reinforced the cautious inclinations of governments elsewhere in Eastern Europe. Although the painfully compressed transition in eastern Germany created the basis for a near-term recovery, the other East European countries could not endure a similar course because they lack the protection that the former GDR received. Since these governments have to proceed more gradually, the way they handle three sets of reforms will be critical to the success of their shock therapy designs:

Currency Convertibility. Currency convertibility and trade liberalization can be invaluable in the earliest stages of a reform program. If prices in Poland had been freed without a convertible currency and a lowering of trade barriers, the high degree of monopoly in Polish industry might have thwarted the development of a meaningful pricing system. By allowing foreign competition, the Polish program ensured that prices, once freed, would become true market prices. However, foreign competition could swiftly render domestic industries obsolete, denying them the opportunity to become internationally competitive. Even if allowing the unprofitable majority of companies to go bankrupt makes economic sense, the experience in eastern Germany demonstrates that the unemployment resulting from widespread de-industrialization carries severe political costs. A string of violent protests against rising unemployment and other hardships could undermine the East European governments' ability to sustain their shock therapy programs.

Financial Restructuring. Without an elaborate system of commercial banks and stock markets, the allocation of capital to East European industries, whether privatized or stateowned, is likely to remain skewed. Establishing a viable financial system, especially private banks, should therefore be one of the highest priorities for the East European governments. Nevertheless, the Polish experience suggests that the task is much harder than one might expect. Because almost all the loans held by banks are to firms that have not yet been privatized, there are problems in determining whether existing banks can be run efficiently. In addition, the banking scandal that came to light in Poland in mid-1991 is but one illustration of the serious risks of abuse and corruption that plague the newly formed systems. That experience prompted the chief inspector for Poland's National Bank to warn that "the establishment of a safe banking system" would be "extremely costly" and could take more than a decade.

Privatization. The longer the task of privatization is delayed, the harder it becomes to implement. The East European states thus have an incentive to proceed rapidly in privatizing companies. The Polish experience reveals some of the dangers in putting off privatization. Nevertheless, the obstacles to privatization evident throughout Eastern Europe provide little reason to doubt economist Josef Brada's prediction in a 1991 essay that

for a rather indefinite future [the East European] countries will have economies where large industrial units partly or wholly owned by the state will co-exist with or indeed, predominate over, large privatized firms in the hands of residents or foreigners and small industrial units that will arise as the result of the efforts of indigenous entrepreneurs.

But if this prediction is indeed borne out (that is, if large-scale privatization does take a very long time to accomplish), the whole future of postcommunist economic reforms will be endangered. The Hungarian economist János Kornai has argued that the impossibility of privatizing in a "big bang" will mean that "for a long time, inevitably, a large part of [every East European] economy, in particular the gradually shrinking, but still rather large state-owned sector, will run inefficiently," dragging down the private sector with it.

There is no universally applicable way that these three types of reforms (or others) should be implemented. Because Hungary has not experienced the acute crisis that Poland did in late 1989, officials in Budapest have been able to proceed more gradually in all three areas. Hungarian proponents of shock therapy argue, however, that the gradualist approach may be safer in the short term, but it will prove more costly over the long term once drastic measures are required. Czechoslovakia, for its part, has come closer to adopting Polish-style shock therapy reforms, thanks largely to the tenacity of the finance minister, Václav Klaus. But the Czechoslovak reforms have not been as sweeping as those in Poland, nor have they fared any better with the issue of privatization.

Questions of sequencing also have begun to arise in Bulgaria and Romania, both of which were initially slow to undertake economic reforms. Since mid-1991, the two countries, particularly Bulgaria, have shown signs of eventually moving toward some version of shock therapy, which could prove even more complicated than analogous programs elsewhere. For example, neither Bulgaria nor Romania has much of an industrial base; hence, they may be far less willing than Poland was to proceed immediately with currency convertibility and trade liberalization, for fear that their capital stock will be undermined by a flood of imports. (In the Polish case, this problem was forestalled by the huge devaluation of the złoty.) In any event, whatever the precise sequence of reforms that individual East European countries arrange, there is bound to be a good deal of trial and error, with many adjustments along the way.

The West will play a crucial role in the economic transformation of Eastern Europe, but the exact nature of this role will depend on the actions of the East European states themselves. Ultimately, successful reform will have to come from within. If the East European countries cannot endure the painful steps required to bring about genuine prosperity, no amount of Western assistance will help. In fact, Western aid—financial or otherwise— would be counterproductive if used by the recipients as an excuse to avoid or defer meaningful reforms.

So far, however, the Bulgarian, Czechoslovak, Hungarian, and Polish governments have embraced the very measures long urged by Western officials and economists. Unlike the former Soviet republics, the East European states have moved far more boldly down the path of reform than most observers had expected. Yet, ironically, almost all the recent debate about Western financial and technical aid has focused on what can be done for the former Soviet Union. Billions of dollars in loans, grants, and humanitarian aid have flowed to the Soviet government and the republics, overshadowing the amounts that have been used more efficiently by the East European countries. Memories of the dramatic events of 1989 have faded, and there emerges the possibility that Eastern Europe will once again become a forgotten region for the West.

This loss of interest in Eastern Europe is unfortunate and dangerous. Facilitating successful reform in Eastern Europe is vital not only because economic collapse could spur floods of refugees and violent civil disorder, but also because a failed transition in Eastern Europe would discredit the move from socialism to capitalism. This would play into the hands of anti-reformist elements in the former Soviet republics and would set back the cause of free markets and democracy all across Europe.

To be sure, severe budgetary constraints in the West will limit the direct contribution the United States and its allies can make to the economic development of Eastern Europe. The German government's experience in meeting the costs of reunification illustrates the problems that will arise in other cases as reforms progress. Even with these constraints, however, relatively modest increases in technical and economic assistance, if properly targeted, could prove decisive.

No step would be more welcome for the East European countries than the elimination of EC and U.S. trade barriers, particularly for agricultural products, textiles, and steel. The East European states can successfully compete with Western producers in these three industries, but they have been barred from entering prospective markets. Projections by the Overseas Development Council suggest that East European exports of textiles and apparel to the West could increase nearly fourfold if trade barriers were removed. Exports of steel and agricultural products could also rise far beyond current levels. Although there will be strong political resistance in Western Europe to the easing or elimination of trade barriers, the United States should emphasize the incongruity of the EC's urging the enactment of free-market reforms in Eastern Europe while adopting policies that greatly impede those reforms. The United States should also be willing to dismantle all or most of its own remaining barriers to East European trade without demanding immediate reciprocity from the East European countries, as was done with Czechoslovakia in October 1991.

Access to foreign private investment will also be vital for the East European countries during their economic transitions, but relatively little investment has flowed into the region so far. Only about $2.5 billion actually arrived between late 1989 and mid-1991, and that money was distributed very unevenly, with roughly 60 per cent of the total invested in Hungary. Accelerating privatization in all the East European countries will require much larger sums, perhaps $20 billion or more. Of course, the amount of private investment in Eastern Europe will depend in the long term on the prospects for profit. Those prospects, in turn, will grow only if political stability is ensured and economic conditions begin to improve, criteria that may not be fully met for at least several years, if at all.

In the meantime, however, Western governments and nongovernmental organizations can foster a propitious climate for foreign investment. The "association" agreements that several East European countries recently concluded with the EC will help boost investor confidence, but that status would be far more valuable if combined with the elimination of trade barriers. The increased use of export credit guarantees from Western governments and international financial organizations should also help create a better investment climate without requiring additional direct expenditures. The climate for investment can be further improved through the development of a suitable business infrastructure in each country. Western governments can provide technical support and expertise on keeping accurate statistics, running financial and banking systems, and monitoring and maintaining adequate environmental standards. In this regard, programs like the "twinning" of Polish banks with Western counterparts, sponsored by the World Bank and the International Finance Corporation, will be invaluable. So too will the programs that have recently been set up to train East European company managers and entrepreneurs at Western business schools.

Another key step for Western governments will be to give greater emphasis to privatization than to conversion. Starting in the early 1950s, the Soviet Union required most of the East European countries to maintain large defense industries. Now, with communism abandoned and the Warsaw Pact defunct, all the East European states have been seeking to reduce, or at least stabilize, their military spending and convert a significant portion of their military factories to civilian production. Plans for conversion have won support in the West and should certainly be encouraged, especially when conversion is cost-effective. Successes include the huge Slovakian manufacturing complex *Zavody Tažkého Strojárstva* (ZTS), which received help from German investors in converting some of its assembly lines from the production of tanks to tractors, bulldozers, earth movers, steam rollers, and dump trucks. If the whole of ZTS can be sold off to private investors, it could well become one of the largest European producers of civilian heavy vehicles. In Hungary, a former military factory known as the Gamma Works, which produced equipment for defense against chemical and nuclear attacks, has successfully reoriented its facilities to produce nuclear medical diagnostic instruments, automation systems, and other nonmilitary goods.

Despite these successes, officials in both East and West should be aware that plans for conversion do not always make much sense. In many cases, factories that produced military equipment cannot shift over to civilian production at an acceptable cost; or if they do shift over, they have no hope of making a profit. It would make more sense for the East European governments to shut down those factories. The urgent need is to privatize factories, not merely convert them. Otherwise, conversion may become a way of preserving subsidies to inherently unprofitable firms. Private owners of factories have every incentive to convert to civilian production if it would make economic sense to do so; if it did not make sense, they would not have bought the factories in the first place. The best way for the West to encourage conversion in Eastern Europe—aside from providing modest technical advice—is to encourage privatization and let the market decide which factories will be viable in producing civilian goods.

Debt relief is another urgent priority. Except in Romania, and to some extent Czechoslovakia, large foreign debts accumulated by the old East European communist regimes have impeded economic reforms. It is unwise and unfair to compel the fledgling democratic governments to shoulder the burden of their predecessors' mistakes. The agreement by the Paris Club (the group of 17 major Western governmental creditors) in March 1991 to write off half of Poland's government-held debt provided a deserved reward to a country that had undertaken drastic internal reforms. Other states in the region can benefit from similar measures as they embark on their own shock therapy programs. Just as important will be the relaxation of commercial debts, something that the Paris Club agreement required of the Polish government. No doubt, negotiations between the East European states and their commercial creditors will proceed more slowly than the government-to-government talks, but a forthcoming approach by governmental lenders should expedite far-reaching reductions in Eastern Europe's commercial debts.

Finally, even if Western officials do their best to encourage private investment and reduce trade barriers, increased governmental assistance to the East European countries will be essential. Substantial amounts of aid have already been channeled through the EC, the European Bank, the International Monetary Fund, and the World Bank, but the total falls far short of the amounts the East European states will need to sustain themselves through the transition. East European leaders have acknowledged that unemployment in their countries could double, triple, or even quadruple in 1992 and 1993, bringing with it the risk of "disorder" and "strike after strike." Economic crises could rapidly overwhelm the social "safety-net" programs that Czechoslovakia, Hungary, and Poland have set up. Increased Western aid will be needed simply to ease the growing hardships ahead.

Whatever the political rationale for increased Western aid,

such aid will not be of long-term benefit unless it is put to productive use. Western governments should provide a large-scale aid, $5 billion to $10 billion a year, specifically targeted for infrastructure development and environmental cleanup. Roughly one-third of this money would come from the United States and would be distributed both bilaterally and via the major international lending institutions. The East European countries lack modern transportation and communications networks, and sorely need to address the disastrous environmental degradation that occurred during the communist era. Funding from the West for these objectives would improve long-term prospects for economic growth in Eastern Europe, and would also absorb tens of thousands of workers who would otherwise be unemployed.

These policy guidelines alone will not be enough to stimulate economic recovery in Eastern Europe, but at least they will enable the West to play as constructive a role as possible. As Polish prime minister Bielecki emphasized recently, failure is not inevitable just because "a miracle cannot happen," and the economic transitions may take more than a decade. The road ahead in Eastern Europe is long, but the postcommunist states are undertaking radical solutions to the daunting problems they confront, and that is no small accomplishment.

ESTABLISHING FREE ENTERPRISE IN FORMER SOVIET REPUBLICS[2]

The world seems awash in mismanaged, unpayable government debts. The London-based *Financial Times* reported in January, 1992, that the foreign debt of the former Soviet Union, incurred mainly to finance Western imports, totals [$65 billion]. The World Bank faces arrears on [$2.7 billion] in principal loan balances outstanding to Third World countries, and the International Monetary Fund (IMF) faces arrears on principal loan balances outstanding of [$1.7 billion]. The Bush Administration is

[2]Article by Karen LaFollette, a research associate at the Institute for Political Economy in Washington, D.C.—this article is based on a Cato Institute Foreign Policy Brief, from *USA Today* (Magazine) 120:64–66 May '92. Copyright © 1992 by the Society for the Advancement of Education. Reprinted with permission.

proceeding with efforts to forgive debts owed the U.S. government by Poland, sub-Saharan African countries, and Latin American nations. Many of these are to the U.S. Export-Import Bank. As of Sept. 30, 1991, the Ex-Im Bank wrote down [$2.6 billion] in loans, almost 30% of its outstanding loan balance. A number of those same countries have received, or are seeking, forgiveness of the debts they incurred to private banks.

Government-to-government loans, as well as private bank loans to governments, are managed by bureaucrats whose own money is not at stake and who necessarily make investment decisions according to political criteria. Thus, valuable resources are used for a variety of unproductive ends. For all the rhetoric about the need for further economic progress, the unprecedented levels of public and private loans to developing country governments throughout the 1970s and 1980s promoted or led to graft, expansionist bureaucracies that frustrate private sector activity, and debts that can not be repaid. Ignoring that lesson, the Bush Administration and other Western nations continued promoting debt-financed development, through government-to-government loans, for the countries of the former Soviet Union.

The failed August, 1991, coup and its aftermath brought new urgency to the issue of aiding the disintegrating Soviet economy and shoring up the collapsing union. Many analysts advocated the G-7 nations' rapid approval of Soviet central government membership in the IMF and World Bank, organizations with which it had initiated official contact in September, 1990.

In October, 1991, the G-7 approved special associate status in the IMF and a technical assistance agreement with the World Bank for the Soviet central government. This enabled it to receive economic advice and technical assistance and paved the way to full membership, which would have entitled it to receive loans from the international institutions.

The collapse of the Soviet central government in December, 1991, left the aid institutions scrambling to expand offices rapidly in the 15 republics and broaden dialogues they already had initiated with each of the republics. In February, 1992, the G-7 and the Russian government were pushing for rapid full membership in the IMF, the World Bank, and various aid institutions for Russia and the other independent states. Acceptance of an IMF economic adjustment program is a prerequisite for full membership.

Meanwhile, the Commonwealth of Independent States, a

loose political confederation based on tentative agreements, is beset with conflict and headed for disintegration, while the new leaders of the Central Eurasian countries have yet to consolidate their power. They may never do so. The staying power of leaders who implement unpopular economic policies, such as Boris Yeltsin, is uncertain. Moreover, Yeltsin's example of standing up to the communist old guard during the coup has inspired nationalist leaders of peoples forcibly annexed to the republics to make their own bid for independence. The successful showdown of the breakaway Chechen-Ingush Autonomous Republic against Russian authorities portends the fragmentation of the former Soviet republics into feuding fiefdoms. Into this morass, the IMF and World Bank are poised to begin development programs that only will prolong government retrenchment and hook the nations of Central Eurasia on the same types of subsidized loans that have financed big government throughout the developing world.

The Failure of Development Planning

The 20th century has witnessed two dramatic socialist failures—the fall of communism and the largest government-to-government transfers in the history of mankind. Communism, with its central planning of the economy, utterly failed to provide an acceptable living standard for the population. Instead, it caused the moral, political, social, and economic collapse of all societies that implemented it. Meanwhile, Western development institutions spoon fed more than one trillion dollars in foreign aid to Third World governments, tying their largess (in the form of grants and loans) to development planning. That approach substituted foreign aid for domestic and foreign equity so that the investment process could be controlled by the recipient government's development scheme drawn up by Western planners. Countries which utilized that approach are experiencing a level of crisis akin to that of the former Soviet Union.

Development planning was inspired in no small part by Western observers' hopeful interpretation of Soviet central planning. Hatred of the market led many experts to reject the capitalist development of their own societies and view the U.S.S.R. and Eastern Europe as a better model for development in the Third World. Highly exaggerated Soviet statistics were accepted by economists such as John Kenneth Galbraith and Ragnar Nurkse as evidence that rapid growth could be achieved by comprehen-

sive economic planning. Nobel laureate Gunnar Myrdal viewed
the Soviet model "as fundamentally a system for the development
of underdeveloped countries. This particular point cannot be
stressed too much." Nurkse even expressed the opinion that "it
may be that the iron curtain is necessary for the maintenance of a
high rate of saving and investment in the Soviet Union."

Such statements sound absurd today. Yet, from the 1950s
through the 1980s, the most influential experts recommend planning for the Third World, while those who saw the folly of the
approach were shunned.

In the 1950s and 1960s, Third World leaders were quick to
adopt socialist development planning, as they correctly perceived
an unprecedented opportunity to use foreign monies to further
entrench and expand their already extensive control over their
economies, at the expense of society. For example, multilateral
development bank loans can finance the growth of the state power company, while elites rake off national tax revenues for their
own use.

Nobel laureate James Buchanan has observed that competition for government largesse and protected profits emerges as a
significant social phenomenon when institutions move away from
ordered markets toward the near chaos of direct political allocation. In the Third World, from the 1950s onward, the organization of cartels and interest groups to compete for government
protection and favors became all-important because, with one
stroke, the state could declare a monopoly or promulgate damag-
ing regulations, thereby enriching or bankrupting private firms.
Moreover, as bureaucrats could not possess the billions of pieces
of information upon which individual entrepreneurs base their
investment decisions, bribery of them emerged as the most efficient way to allocate government resources.

Government employees in developing countries came to believe that state property belonged to them. Give that such people
manage property in their own interest, it is not surprising that
bureaucrats have become a new aristocracy, complete with Swiss
bank accounts and palatial mansions, similar to the communist
nomenklatura (Establishment] described by Milovan Djilas in *The
New Class*. Graft and corruption proliferated as Third World
elites skimmed off billions in purported commissions for themselves and squirreled them away in Western banks.

Because government investments were not guided by any
sense of market profitability, they did not generate the wealth to

pay back the foreign loans. The [$429 billion] Latin American debt and Third World landscapes littered with bloated and inefficient state companies stand as monuments to this failed approach.

Now, Western experts are pushing debt-financed development on the former Soviet Union. Western governments are rushing to revive collapsed planned economies throughout Central Eurasia with billions of dollars in direct aid, export credits, and loan guarantees. In January, 1992, approximately $80,000,000,000 in total assistance had been pledged to the former Soviet Union since September, 1990, more than half of it from Germany. As of February, the U.S. had committed or disbursed $3,900,000,000 in food aid and grain export credit guarantees, and its cargo planes carried out an international airlift of food and medical supplies to 23 locations in the former Soviet territories. This included the ferrying of about $78,000,000 worth of American emergency aid, most of it surplus U.S. military rations and medical supplies left over from the Persian Gulf conflict. Japan committed a package of [$3 billion] in financial assistance for government food and medical supply loans and export credit insurance, and Saudi Arabia pledged [$1.5 billion] in assistance.

To build successful societies, Russia and the other independent states need to establish private property and a market economy. As has been demonstrated in the Third World, foreign aid does not help to reorient economies. In the case of the former Soviet Union, it will foster the growth of government and run counter to efforts of democratic leaders to cut the bureaucracy. In November, 1991, at the same time that Yeltsin cut off or drastically reduced funding to 80 government ministries and departments, leaving 40,000 bureaucrats looking for work, international aid officials were studying how to revitalize state enterprises and eventually channel loans for infrastructure development through them.

The Soviet economy failed because, as Paul Craig Roberts and I explained in our 1990 book (*Meltdown: Inside the Soviet Economy*), Mikhail Gorbachev's six years of *perestroika* and *glasnost* did not eliminate the linchpin of communist economic organization—production to meet gross output quotas. Piecemeal economic reforms only served to destroy the decrepit state supply distribution system while blocking the establishment of a market economy, resulting in chaos. In November, 1991, Moscow Mayor Gavril Popov wrote in the *Washington Times* that Russia is undergoing "a critical transitional moment, when the old system has died, but the new one has not yet been born." Today, Russia is plagued with severe shortages of basic necessities such as milk, butter, and bread, and high inflation makes consumer goods available in the free market unaffordable to the average worker.

The Need for Privatization

Private property is the basis of the market economy and, as Paul Craig Roberts has pointed out in *Wall Street Journal* and *Business Week* articles, getting widespread property rights into the hands of the people is critical to jump-starting a free enterprise system in the former Soviet territories. The establishment of private property is critical because bureaucrats are not entrepreneurs and allocate resources according to political criteria, leading to waste and inefficiency. They must cede control to owners, who will allocate them according to the best available return. Only in such a system can freely floating prices serve the dual function of limiting the demand for goods and stimulating greater supply.

A battle over property is raging in Central Eurasia, not about privatization *per se*, but who will enjoy the benefits of private property. Russian citizens complain that *nomenklatura* managers in control of parts of state firms and agricultural collectives commonly cease operations, only to reopen as "private" cooperatives. In October, 1991, journalist S. Razin complained to *Komsomolskaya Pravda* that "at present the Democrats are making life difficult for one another in the corridors of power and the former nomenklatura is cheerfully carrying out privatization. Where previously there were departments, now corporations are shining brightly— for example, 'Transstroy,' the petroleum and gas industry and others."

Privatization at least is proceeding, albeit in a decidedly unjust manner. New businesses are sprouting daily, but the Central Eurasian peoples are becoming increasingly disaffected as they witness the old-guard *apparatchiks* throughout the territories taking full advantage of their control over state resources to charge ahead with *de facto* privatization in their own behalf.

On Jan. 2, 1992, Yeltsin announced the freeing of prices in Russia with the aim of rapidly creating a market economy. He intended to begin priority privatization of small and medium enterprises and collective farms, while laying the foundation for a sound financial system through tough monetary and financial credit policy and tax reform to strengthen the ruble. Larger industrial enterprises were to be reorganized and left in state hands for the time being.

As of February, Yeltsin had not been able to do much more than free prices, while simultaneously establishing disincentives to production in the form of high taxes—a combination that may end up costing the Russian leader his job. Former *nomenklatura* members are resisting government privatization and demonopolization plans. Meanwhile, the Russian government's imposition of a 28% value-added tax, a policy in keeping with the usual IMF advice, further burdens an emerging private sector already faced with high costs due to unclear property rights and heavy regulation. The response of a monopolistic economy to these policies is hoarding, falling production, and soaring prices, as producers enjoy high demand for their consumer goods without the competition that would bring down prices. Falling production leads to a drop in tax revenues, and, at the rate the Russian government is printing rubles to cover the budget deficit, hyperinflation will result soon.

A pall of discontent in Russia is stimulating anti-Yeltsin demonstrations. With the average person earning 400 to 800 rubles in late January, 1992, and a basket of the minimum consumer goods to ensure survival costing 1,944 rubles, Russia is on the verge of a social explosion. Unsavory elements are increasingly vocal. On Feb. 9, [1992,] about 15,000 demonstrators proclaimed messages of chauvinism, communist nostalgia, and anti-Semitism.

Democratic reformers are convinced that rapid privatization to get widespread property ownership among the population is crucial. In January, Yeltsin vowed to overcome "difficult conditions—economic crisis, collapse of the union" and "the resistance of mafia structures striving to retain dominance in distribution" in order to speed up privatization and smash monopolies.

Others are joining in his focus on privatization. The *Financial Times* recently reported that, under the leadership of president Nursultan Nazarbayev, Kazakhstan has begun privatizing services, housing, and industry. In Armenia, Prime Minister Grant Bagratian claimed that 70% of cultivated land in the republic had been sold since spring, 1991.

Amidst the turmoil in the former Soviet territories, citizens gradually are obtaining property rights and markets are beginning to form, without large-scale Western development assistance. Yet, the statist IMF is promoting the message that external assistance is crucial to the transformation of the former Soviet

Union into a market-based system and should include financial and technical assistance as well as improved access to Western markets. The IMF is exhorting the implementation of a "comprehensive program of macroeconomic stabilization and systemic reforms," not unlike the austerity programs it has foisted upon the Third World. Typically, such programs entail fiscal restraint (while keeping in place deficit-ridden state enterprises), currency devaluations, and tax increases to cut domestic demand. Implementation of such a plan further would pave the way to full-scale project assistance.

Far from helping to build viable economies, such programs have sparked social unrest in the Third World. Economic recovery in countries such as Mexico and Argentina only began once they ignored the IMF's advice and cut taxes and eliminated regulations.

The World Bank also is providing technical assistance to the former Soviet territories in preparation for a full-scale aid program. In November, 1991, Mikhail Gorbachev and World Bank president Lewis Preston signed a technical assistance treaty giving the Soviet central government access to a $30,000,000 trust fund to hire and pay for experts to help in establishing a market economy in the former union. The World Bank is focusing upon four areas of reform: the macroeconomic system, including revamping the financial system, privatization, and Western investments; changes in specific sectors of the economy, such as transport, agriculture, power engineering, and communications; organization of a social welfare system; and the instruction and training of cadres.

While it is unclear whether leaders such as Boris Yeltsin even will have the authority to implement their economic programs fully, they should maintain their stated focus on incentives to production. Reformers should steer clear of the demand management austerity programs advocated by the IMF/World Bank, which would strangle a nascent market economy. Czechoslovakia Finance Minister Vaclav Klaus recently said at a United States Information Agency conference in Washington that his country was not interested in the market socialism dreams of international experts. According to him, "the third way is the fastest way toward the Third World." If such plans are adopted in the post-Soviet republics, the peoples are likely to face the same disincentives and economic regimentation that have destroyed the prospects of so-called developing countries.

Amid the swarms of international aid officials and conflicting advice circulating through Russia and other Central Eurasian countries these days, native officials should not lose sight of the fact that the peoples themselves ultimately are responsible for creating functioning market economies out of the debris of central planning. Perhaps the hurtling pace of change in the former Soviet Union will have the saving grace that it will safeguard the peoples from dependency on foreign aid, since international bureaucrats can not get a firm foothold in government structures that constantly are changing. The loans and advice of the IMF and World Bank have impoverished and indebted the Third World. The Bush Administration and other Western governments should not push bureaucratically managed, debt-financed development on Central Eurasia.

THE FUTURE OF RUSSIAN CAPITALISM[3]

For years Western observers had assumed that as the transition from socialism to capitalism proceeded in the Soviet Union there would appear a gradual shift away from strict state control of production toward some form of market socialism. Some property and productive assets would move from collective to individual ownership, but not all that much. Market forces of supply and demand would take over some of the responsibilities of allocating resources, but the state would retain a dominant role in protecting the population from the excesses of capitalism. Russia would more or less fit itself into the Swedish model. The dynamic of capitalism would be safely subordinated to the imperatives of a welfare state. How could it be otherwise? After seven decades of collectivism, the people of Russia and the former Soviet republics must surely have lost all memory of commercial competitiveness.

In fact quite the opposite conclusion might be drawn. During the 70 years of the communist experiment the competitive impulse of Soviet man has not been extinguished at all, but rather

[3]Article by Jude Wanniski, president of Polyconomics, Inc., an economic consulting firm in Morristown, New Jersey, from *Foreign Affairs* 71:17–25 Spring '92. Copyright © 1992 by the Council on Foreign Relations, Inc. Reprinted with permission.

has been channeled into the awkward mazes and blind alleys that ultimately led to abandonment of the Marxist-Leninist idea. Now freed of these constraints, it is easy to imagine these competitive impulses racing ahead of our Western form of corporate capitalism, which has grown flabby and slow. It is possible to imagine a future of Russian capitalism that asserts itself early in the 21st century as the envy of the world.

In this difficult time of Russia's conversion from one system of political economy to another, it might seem sheer fantasy to present such a notion. The objective, as an alternative to the Swedish model, is worth considering, however. The Russian people are now engaged in nothing less than designing the basic architecture of a brand new country. Why not consider all possibilities? Why not design the Russian system of capitalism to be the best?

Before exploring the future of Russian capitalism, we should be clear about the past. Karl Marx was extremely close to the truth when he completed his examination of capitalism in the midst of the nineteenth century: capitalism could not succeed because capitalists would sow the seeds of their own destruction. That is, if capitalism requires relentless competition, yet capitalists are doing everything they can do to destroy competition, we have a system that is inherently unsustainable—as with animals who devour their young.

Here is the problem: if successful capitalists can control the apparatus of government in order to prevent a new growth of capitalists, the system will inevitably destruct. If a system can be devised that prevents successful capitalists from controlling the apparatus of government for their narrow interests, though, there is at least a chance of renewal and a prospect of success.

The system Marx did not contemplate took another half century to reveal itself. It came in the form of a secret political ballot, the key to democratic choice, the key to unlocking the wisdom of the masses. If the people collectively know which course of action is the wisest, as I believe they do, they must be provided a safe channel to express that opinion.

In creating a system of Russian capitalism there is no more important ingredient than this—a democratic mechanism that protects the collective wisdom of the electorate. Mikhail Gorbachev called it glasnost. In that he was correct: the democratic structure of the political economy is far more important than the

economic structure. The economic structure must change continually to keep pace with changing times in a competitive world
economy; an optimum democratic structure provides the foundation for such change, enabling the people to exert their wisdom
guiding the direction and contour of economic change.

Even then it is not enough to have democratic mechanisms
alone to thwart the most determined corruptors of capitalism.
Capitalists are forever trying to use their power in government to
protect their businesses against foreign competition, through
higher tariffs or nontariff regulatory barriers. The Wall Street
Crash of 1929 and the Great Depression of the 1930s were the
direct result of such trade protectionism in the United States.
The American public at the time did not vote for such policies.
Indeed it voted for politicians who were seemingly opposed to
trade protection.

The worst policy errors occur not because of voting decisions
of ordinary people, but because politicians break their promises
to the people between elections. For this reason, in the design of a
democratic political mechanism for Russia, the most advanced
democratic processes should be adopted, including national initiatives and referendums that can be triggered at any time between national elections in order to keep politicians from straying
from the commonweal.

At the moment no such mechanism exists, but there is immediate need for economic relief. From a distance, standing outside
the unfolding history of events now under way in the republics,
one arrives at certain elemental considerations.

Think of the current status of Russia and the other republics
as bankruptcy proceedings, the bankruptcy of the old U.S.S.R.
The corporation that we had called the Soviet Union can no longer pay its bills. And, as in any bankruptcy proceeding, the creditors are crowding in to get paid, trying to elbow their way to the
front of the line. There are two classes of creditors here, foreign
and domestic. Thus far, the foreign creditors have been more
successful, persuading first the Gorbachev government, then the
Yeltsin government, to put them at the head of the queue. The
government has put domestic creditors—the people of the old
Soviet Union—at the end of the line.

Indeed the government has come close to advising the people
that it intends to cheat them out of their ruble claims against it,
their lifetime savings and pensions. This has been the advice of
Western creditors, who suggest that the ruble savings of the ordi-

nary people of the republics is a barrier to progress. They see it as a "ruble overhang" that could suddenly come out of savings for spending purposes, igniting inflation. Of course this is nonsense. The ruble savings of the people are the foundation of the new Russian capitalism and should be preserved and protected. We must include here the value of pensions, which should be restored to their level of purchasing power that existed prior to the recent inflation.

Because of the nature of the failed experiment with communism, the wealth of the nation is held collectively; a strategy must be developed that will, as equitably as possible, turn collective wealth over to private hands. The new managers of the state will, of course, try to preserve as much wealth in state hands as they can. Foreign investors will also try to crowd into privileged positions when state assets are offered for sale. It is the strength of the democracy alone that can offset these forces and place the assets where they belong, at least to begin with, in the hands of the ordinary citizens. The political leadership must be determined to place at least half the nation's collective wealth into individual hands, insisting that foreign individuals or corporations be permitted to buy assets only from the citizens in the open market. Because great wealth and natural resources are involved, it will take impressive political resolve to prevent the people from being cheated of their due through bribery and corruption. Russian capitalism must have this moral foundation.

Much is made by some Western analysts of the absence of the legal pillars of capitalism: courts to enforce contracts, a clear legal code, a transparent system for making regulatory decisions that affect business. This argument has great merit, because in Western democracies the state stands over the marketplace as referee, discouraging individuals from cheating one another, just as the police discourage individuals from robbing each other in the street.

Even more fundamental to the success of Russian capitalism is that the state abstain from cheating the people by demeaning the value of the currency through inflationary policies. In that regard Western democracies are not as pure as they might like to represent. If one individual owes another $100 and decides to pay only $50, the creditor has recourse to the courts to exact payment. But if the state decides to reduce the purchasing power of its currency, debtors (including the state, which is always the biggest debtor) gain from devaluation of the currency, while creditors lose. Devaluation thus redistributes wealth arbitrarily among citizens.

In Russia, where private debt does not exist for all practical purposes, the devaluation of the ruble represents nothing more than a transfer of wealth from individuals to the state. Excepting automobiles, household appliances, furniture and hoards of consumer goods, all private wealth in the republics of the former U.S.S.R. takes the form of currency or bank deposits held by individual citizens. These are debts owed by the state to the people. If the state devalues the ruble, it cheats the people out of their savings. What good is contract law or courts if the state can rob the people with impunity?

Western economists, as well as the Russian government, agree that the Russian economy can only recover if the state transfers property to the people. Under the advice of Western creditors the Russian government has gone in precisely the opposite direction. While the government negotiates with the West over $10 billion or $20 billion of emergency credits, it has virtually eliminated 600 billion rubles of private wealth through the devaluation of the currency. This savings wealth accumulated over decades in which the purchasing power of the ruble was roughly equivalent to a dollar: a dollar could buy a loaf of bread, so could a ruble. In that light the people have had the bulk of their personal wealth, 600 billion rubles, repudiated by the state. In sheer size that is an expropriation of private wealth comparable to the forced collectivization of agriculture during the 1930s. Its economic consequences are no less devastating, even though the move was accomplished without violence and deportations.

To estimate the disaster wrought upon Russia by the devaluation of the currency, we must begin with a concept that Marx omitted from his economic model, what Western economists call "transaction costs." Transaction costs are ultimately determined by the degree of risk involved in economic activity. The social cost of a commodity is quite different if a producer can sell it in a moment in an efficient market, or if the same producer must hire a dozen bodyguards to avert robbery on the way to the market. To avert robbery by the state, citizens of Russia must first convert their rubles into some store of value and then find the means to barter these stores of value for products they need. Farmers will not sell wheat or milk for worthless rubles; they would rather feed their produce to pigs, which represent an interim store of value. Thus we see ordinary citizens waiting on queues for many hours to exchange depreciating rubles for consumer goods, individuals spending hours in the market trying to exchange one good for another, and industrial managers spending weeks attempting to obtain goods they need by an elaborate chain of barter.

In a modern industrial economy whose daily activity requires a division of labor of millions of workers producing tens of thousands of different commodities, the social costs of a barter system are catastrophic; the costs of simple transactions eat up most of the economic effort of society. It is no surprise, then, that Russia is now experiencing a spiraling economic collapse, with the great majority of its citizens reduced to the most abject poverty, the diet of most citizens limited to sufficient carbohydrate calories to sustain life itself. No one believes that this situation can continue for long without catastrophic social and political consequences. It is equally obvious that the state must convince the people that it will not rob them—that it will preserve the value of its debt held by the people, for the crisis to be overcome. Once the state honors its obligations to the people, the creation of a legal code for business and related matters can be attended to expeditiously.

But how is this to be done? The state itself is in the grip of a vicious cycle: the collapse of the ruble has forced an ever-growing proportion of transactions into the barter system, wiping out government revenues. The state, in turn, is forced to print money to meet essential expenditures, since its revenues shrink much faster than it can reduce spending. By flooding the market with newly printed money, the state further reduces confidence in the ruble.

If the Russian state were a private firm within a Western industrial country, the problem would never have arisen. Russia is rich: the assets of the state, land, structures, capital equipment and mineral resources amount to trillions of dollars by the most conservative measure. Its debt totals less than one trillion rubles. Even if the ruble were valued at 1 : 1 to the dollar, its assets would exceed its liabilities many times over. A Western firm with such a favorable position would have no difficulty raising ready cash by borrowing against the collateral of its assets or selling some of its assets to investors. The existence of capital markets capable of converting wealth into ready cash, though, depends upon the existence of trust between creditors and debtors, something that Russia has yet to achieve.

By the most optimistic estimate Russia will require several years to privatize the bulk of state properties. It cannot exchange the state debt in the form of currency or deposits for houses, mineral rights or industrial shares quickly enough to stabilize the ruble. It must therefore persuade the people to wait for a number of years, offering capital instruments—bonds—with a corresponding maturity. The value of the ruble should be in accord with the value of Russian labor; at the current black market exchange rate a Russian worker earning the average wage of about 900 rubles a month earns barely $6 a month. Assuming that Russian labor is worth on the international market what workers earn in middle-income developing countries, the proper exchange rate for the ruble should be around two to the dollar. That should be the target for the exchange rate. The government bonds must be indexed to gold or foreign exchange at this high rate.

Russian officials worry that the people may not trust the government sufficiently to have confidence that these bonds will be redeemed at a favorable exchange rate. The building of trust is a formidable task and will require all of the state's resources to accomplish. One avenue toward that end would be to guarantee that part of a gold-indexed bond issue could be sold on international markets to Western investors. A secondary market would then exist for such bonds in hard currency; Russian citizens would, if they chose, be able to sell bonds bought with today's rubles for hard currency in this secondary market. This is an essential element for establishing trust.

It is important to recognize, though, that the state has never attempted to offer the people the chance to hold financial assets that will preserve the value of their savings. It has offered them only low-interest deposits or low-interest, long-term bonds that the public has rejected. If the government clearly explains the nature of the problem to the people and shows how it intends to make good on its obligations to the people, it still has a fighting chance to win their confidence.

Once current rubles are convertible into a financial asset that pays a dollar for every two rubles, rather than every 100 at today's distorted black market rate, a floor will be placed under the ruble's value. It is hard to tell where that floor will be, since it depends on the public's confidence in the new government bonds. Certainly the ruble's value will rise to fewer than ten to the dollar, perhaps to fewer than five. Farmers will again sell wheat and milk for rubles, rather than feed them to pigs, and a flood of hoarded goods will reappear in the stores.

These measures alone will not solve Russia's economic problems. On the contrary: they are the precondition for solving them. Russia will require the new aforementioned legal system, a tax structure that permits producers to operate with the least burdens, regulatory mechanisms that do not impede economic activity and a variety of other reforms. All these improvements are possible once a basic condition of trust is achieved between the state and the public. If the state accepts the premise that its obligations to the people are sacrosanct, Russia's leaders will have little difficulty persuading the public that all these reforms are in the general interest, since the vast majority of individuals will stand to benefit from them.

It was in just this fashion that the United States began its national life more than 200 years ago. The early American experience is endlessly fascinating to today's Russian officials and opinion leaders. There were voices in the first administration of George Washington who urged a policy of debt repudiation. The new country was burdened with great debts to its own people, incurred during the fighting of the War of Independence. It also owed a large amount to creditors in Holland, who had helped finance the war. The first American treasury secretary, Alexander Hamilton, insisted this was not the way to begin as a new nation, by declaring bankruptcy, thereby cheating creditors at home and abroad. A new country should be expected to incur debt for many years before it matures and is able to redeem its obligations. The United States began on this moral principle, establishing a bond of confidence between the state and the people that became the foundation of the great enterprise that soon became the envy of the world. The new Commonwealth of Independent States will find this policy serving it just as effectively. Investment will soon flow from abroad, and from the toil of the people, as they note the integrity of the new government.

The future of Russian capitalism lies in the lessons of America's past. Honesty in its money is but one element. Simplicity in law is another. In the United States more than 700,000 lawyers ply their trade, draining off the energies and talents of a nation in empty legal skirmishing. Battalions of accountants are required to fathom the dispiriting intricacies of the tax laws. Bank regulations have become so incomprehensible that ordinary people increasingly find it impossible to borrow. The government has become dominated by aging capitalists who add layers of complexities to prevent new competition from below. The freedom and flexibility of America's youth has become bound like Gulliver.

If Russia is to leap ahead after 75 years of stagnation it should be resisting all advice that comes from the West that complicates growth. Americans can now only dream of how nice it would be to start anew, with a blank slate on which we could write simple tax and regulatory legislation. Complexity serves the interests of the elite, who know how to pay their way around it. It confounds the interests and opportunities of ordinary people who are hoping to get ahead. If Russia can think of itself as a nation of young capitalists, striving to attain a potential that now seems limitless, the path to its prosperous future will more easily be seen.

Two centuries ago the elite of the Old World looked smugly on the ragtag enterprise of the new United States of America. We can be sure there were many who doubted whether Americans would ever amount to much. These Americans would surely be confounded by the wilderness, the native savages, and the absence of experienced institutions capable of dealing with the intricacies of modern politics and commerce.

We Americans, in turn, may now be tempted to become Old Worldly ourselves, viewing the new Russian enterprise with patronizing amusement and skepticism: it will surely take these Cold War losers a generation or two before they learn the sophisticated nuances of modern business and finance, to the point where they will understand the profound importance of a leveraged buyout. Will it not?

Or perhaps we could consider the Commonwealth as a kind of new frontier, an adventure on the planet that will soon be exploring far more interesting possibilities than leveraged buyouts and convertible debentures. Across the great expanse of 11 time zones, Russia and the republics are like so many liberated colonies, freed of the straitjacket of the communist idea. We should not forget that the idea was simply one that subsumed individual risk-taking and reward to the security of the community, the commune. The experiment in political economy did not work, and the people who were subjected to it are eager for a system that will.

If our own history is any guide, we should expect in this brand new country an eagerness for opportunity and an explosion of risk-taking and entrepreneurial ferment. The people of Russia clearly look to the United States, not Europe or Asia, as the exemplary model. We should be happy they do and counsel them in that spirit, not as old adversaries or potential new competitors, but as converts and potential new allies. It will make a great difference to the shape of the 21st century.

DEFENSE CONVERSION: BULLDOZING THE MANAGEMENT[4]

The record of massive defense conversion is one unblemished by success, with two notable exceptions: the defense-dominated economies and mammoth military facilities of Japan and Germany, which were converted into civilian production after World War II. Then, the two defeated powers were militarily occupied, their defense industries were immediately destroyed and rebuilt with extensive foreign aid; now, decades later, both countries enjoy economic prosperity.

Similar solutions are being proposed today for the former Warsaw Pact nations, using Western bulldozers rather than Allied tanks, since true defense conversion is readily dismissed as impossible or at least impracticable. There are sound grounds for such dismissal. In our travels throughout the onetime communist countries—talking to plant managers, workers, academics and government officials alike—we came to sense the staggering obstacles they confront. The greater these obstacles appeared relative to anything known in the West, where defense conversion has largely failed, the darker their prospects seemed. And where the need is greatest, in the former Soviet Union, the impediments are greatest and the trends most pernicious.

Something needs to be done. On that almost everyone concurs. On exactly what, almost everyone seems to differ. We offer our views from a rather unique perspective among analysts of this topic, since one of us has actually had to operate and alter defense production plants over the years.

Defense conversion in the United States has been bedeviled by two conflicting objectives: how to shift firms out of defense

[4]Article by Kenneth L. Adelman (syndicated columnist and vice president of the Institute of Contemporary Studies) and Norman R. Augustine (chairman and CEO of Martin Marietta), from *Foreign Affairs* 71:26–47 Spring '92. Copyright © 1992 by the Council on Foreign Relations, Inc. Reprinted with permission.

and into civilian pursuits, and how to preserve a mobilization base to meet conceivable future defense needs.

Twenty-six years ago an Arms Control and Disarmament Agency report examined attempts at commercial diversification by U.S. defense firms. It found "a discouraging history of failure." Two years ago ACDA reexamined the same issue and came to the same conclusion: "Successful examples of such conversion are difficult to find. Detailed research has not identified a successful product in our economy today which was developed through a military-to-civilian conversion approach. . . . As of 1990 there are very few concrete examples of actual conversion."

Defense conversion attempts have been made, some laughable and in retrospect almost all dismal. Kaman Aerospace successfully ventured into guitar-making, but its effort affected only about 100 workers. Rohr Industries moved from aerospace into mass transit. Boeing Vertol from helicopters also to mass transit. Grumman into the bus-making business and Martin Marietta into the electronic-pager market; in virtually all these cases, the results were disappointing, at best. Nor have prospects brightened recently. The latest ACDA report on the subject states: "Studies sponsored by some defense contractors have shown that if they were to attempt conversion projects, about 85 percent would be doomed to failure." This assessment comes from firms historically accused of making chronically rosy forecasts.

The reason for this solid record of failure is simple: defense work has little in common with civilian work. These two areas demand different skills and marketing techniques and have different cultures and organizations. Clearly the defense business, even in the United States, has little to do with free enterprise. Defense contractors have a single customer who directs them from above, rather than many customers who show their preferences in the market below.

Defense contractors lack expertise in mass marketing and in making high-volume, low unit-cost items. Their distribution network is, in the commercial sense, nonexistent. Their capitalization is modest. Their product servicing is limited. And their bookkeeping and reporting requirements are staggering. Defense firms know little of consumer tastes, establishing customer credit or pricing to compete in the commercial marketplace. They know nothing of market research. Much of their work is performed under cost-reimbursable contracts—they are paid whatever costs they incur, which encourages taking huge technological risks. In a nutshell, defense contractors have adapted to their unique monopsonistic environment in a Darwinian fashion. To further complicate matters, embedded within this monopsony are occasional monopolies, since only a single firm can sell the "customer" a B-2 bomber or MiG-29 fighter.

When venturing out of their natural habitat, defense firms seek to retain the same organizational structure and company culture and to use the same operating methods. This accounts for a majority of defense conversion failures. Even the few switch-hitting firms—those successfully engaged in both military and commercial work—commonly erect an impenetrable iron curtain between the two sides of the house. And when astute U.S. defense firms acquire a commercial firm, they retain the prior management and culture and give it wide operating freedom. While this approach is best, it precludes any of the synergism that is at least initially used to justify most corporate mergers and acquisitions. Little "value added" is realized, as the defense firm merely becomes a holding company; scant else is thereby accomplished—certainly nothing to help preserve its own employees' endangered jobs.

Most such acquisitions fail anyway. A recent McKinsey & Co. study done for General Dynamics reveals that 80 percent of commercial acquisitions by defense contractors prove financially harmful. This is not reassuring to defense companies, already heavily burdened with debt and selling at a 60 percent discount in the equity market. Many firms now stand practically one mistake away from extinction.

Postwar experiences of individual U.S. defense companies are distinct from those of the country as a whole. The U.S. economy has expanded in various postwar periods, none as dramatic as that immediately after World War II when U.S. defense spending fell by 90 percent. Defense spending plummeted from 41 percent of GNP [gross national product] in 1944 to 6 percent just three years later. But while some 19 million GIs were demobilized, unemployment rates stayed beneath the four percent level.

While a remarkable record, it is a singular experience. For rather than a successful example of massive defense conversion, the post-World War II case was a special instance of defense *reconversion*. Most wartime defense plants were only temporarily such; they reverted to their prewar civilian activities when the war ended. Enormous demand for civilian goods followed V-E Day, as did the farsighted GI Bill that provided educational, retraining and counseling opportunities for millions who had served in uniform. This enhanced their purchasing power and lifted their living standard. Moreover America's massive postwar conversion was successful, in part, because of high rates of wartime savings coupled with President Truman's prudent expansionary economic policy to fuel a quick recovery.

The Korean and Vietnam wars were far less demanding on U.S. industry. Existing defense facilities were expanded rather than new ones created to meet those wartime needs. Worker and capital mobility helped minimize disruptions in those postwar transitions. Most important, all such transformations occurred in a fundamentally sound economy. Herein lies the prime difference between the post-World War II U.S. experience and the present challenges in the newly free Soviet and east European states: their economies were tenuous, at best, long before defense conversion became a top priority. Almost nothing, it now seems, worked—at least not well. And that which did work under the old Soviet system seems to have been confined to the commercially irrelevant defense sector.

In trips across eastern Europe and the former Soviet Union we often found inferior technology, inadequate capital, bankrupt consumers, poor work practices and scant experience with the free-market system they say they now seek. Their defense sectors have just one advantage over those in the United States: they are not seeking to penetrate established and crowded markets already populated with strong and quasi-threatened competitors.

That a centrally controlled economy does not and cannot work is now accepted. The once-raging war of ideas—capitalism versus communism, central control versus free enterprise—has ended with the clear contrast between the economies of west and east Germany, Taiwan and China, Puerto Rico and Cuba, and South and North Korea.

While the destination is clear, the means of getting there are not. Libraries are full of books on the transition from capitalism to communism, but few were written on the transition from communism to capitalism. Such manuals are needed now to guide the first crop of newly elected politicians, who worry whether they will have enough time to manage the transition. They fear the attempt may be overtaken by economic collapse, civil war, authoritarianism or some combination. And people now constantly worry about losing their jobs.

Under communism there was no official unemployment, just massive underemployment. Everyone had a job, though nobody had to work. Conversations with plant managers and workers throughout the area led us to a rough conclusion: one-third to one-half of all employees would no longer be needed if their plant had modern technology and competitively oriented management. Efficiently run firms could not afford to keep them on the payroll.

Nonetheless no government can tolerate such massive unemployment, even during a transition period. Never having acknowledged joblessness before, the former Warsaw Pact nations lack both the social "safety net" structures found in the West and the funds to launch such programs. To be unemployed is a big blow to self-image, even in countries where some unemployment is common. But where everyone has been employed for nearly as long as anyone can remember, as in the onetime communist countries, it constitutes a psychological shock of immeasurable proportion.

Besides it has become a phenomenon of modern life—in free and managed economies alike—that when government causes unemployment, people mobilize to resist, but when private companies cause unemployment, people mobilize to find other jobs. After the Pentagon canceled the A-12 aircraft, for instance, thousands of industrial workers were laid off, with hardly a whimper. Yet when a government laboratory or military base is subject to closure, even if it employs only a handful of people, massive political pressure is mounted and is often successful enough to stop the proposed closure—and this in a free enterprise nation.

Thus the main dilemma of defense conversion: how to manage a first-ever transfer from central to a market-driven economy, starting with bankrupt political and financial structures, ending soon enough to preclude unmanageable social unrest and with as little unemployment as possible along the way. What we have here is a world-class challenge.

From Leonid Brezhnev through Mikhail Gorbachev, Soviet attempts at defense conversion had led to some ludicrous results. The Ministry of Aviation Industry was given responsibility to process fruits and vegetables and to make starch, syrup and pasta. A few years ago the minister himself appeared before the Soviet Council of Ministers to boast of creating the country's first macaroni production line. Under Gorbachev the ministry charged with making nuclear weapons began to manufacture cheese-making equipment. Initially it received orders for 10 units and then, within a few weeks, orders for 2,300 units, causing the plant manager to sigh: "Of course now we are somewhat bewildered." Stories have been rampant of children's sleds adorned with titanium runners, of gasoline refiners producing somewhat dubious champagne.

The problem of defense conversion, however, is no laughing matter. And the conversion situation is unique, just as the Soviet economy was unique. The U.S.S.R. spent perhaps three to five times more of its GNP on defense than the United States, and up to 25 times more than Japan. Around one-fourth of all Soviet industrial production went for its military. For a large number of cities in Russia and Ukraine—two republics that accounted for some 85 to 90 percent of all Soviet defense production—this one sector comprised four-fifths of all industrial enterprise.

Over time the distinction between military and civilian sectors became increasingly blurred. The so-called military sector relied upon civilian plants for its raw materials and finished goods—all produced under military priorities. And the civilian sector relied upon the military sector for much of its goods. In 1971 Brezhnev boasted that 42 percent of the Soviet defense industry's output served civilian purposes. In 1991 the 3,000-plus Soviet defense firms made some 2,000 types of consumer goods, including nearly all televisions and refrigerators and some two-thirds of vacuum cleaners and washing machines.

The expansion of the defense sector into civilian production came in part because defense industries seemed the most successful. While enjoying some triumphs in its core business—from launching Sputnik to making first-rate weapons in enormous quantities—the Soviet defense sector's overall efficiency, even in high-tech military equipment, was far below that of the West.

In its heyday the Soviet industrial-military complex worked as well as it did because it was politically favored and thus generously funded. It received a hefty budget, any needed raw materials and the best and brightest scientists and engineers. It attracted the ablest managers, who received the highest salaries, biggest bonuses and newest dwellings. Its workers lived in the most comfortable apartments of any workers in this once-touted "worker's paradise."

Whenever bottlenecks developed, the defense sector expanded by vertical integration. The Ministry of Aviation Industry, for instance, made aluminum for its airframes and grew rubber plants for its tires. Assisting those engaged in defense and intervening at the first sign of a dip in production by suppliers were the party apparatchik and KGB operatives. They kept things in line, as they did elsewhere in Soviet society.

Gorbachev left this system relatively intact during his first three years as Soviet leader. In March 1988 he began an energetic campaign for defense conversion—although in an all too typically injurious way. His campaign did not move defense plants into the commercial sector, but incongruously moved at least 260 civil plants into the defense sector as defense management took over ongoing operations in other fields.

Gorbachev had embarked on the wrong path. His faltering attempt at defense conversion was a failure of leadership. Expanding the defense sector further into civilian production merely expanded the military's role in an already vastly overmilitarized society. This approach could not help satisfy popular needs, because in such an environment consumer goods would invariably take second priority to defense manufacturing. As one Soviet production official remarked, "We should not delude ourselves here. We must always remember that we are responsible for defense above all."

Hence those least willing or able to make consumer products were given authority to do just that. Gorbachev's conversion plans were devised by the Ministry of Defense and implemented by the military production ministries—neither of which was known for championing reform. Those efforts were like using rabbits to deliver lettuce. Besides, at lower levels many defense managers and technicians resisted such changes. They saw the development and production of consumer goods as less professionally challenging and certainly less rewarding than building spacecraft, precision-guided missiles and supersonic aircraft. They would be less assured of acquiring necessary supplies and having ready markets.

Defense firms generally lack the skills needed for successful civilian work. Their managers face problems at both ends of the business spectrum—in obtaining supplies and finding markets—and in between at running responsive factories. Workers lack the geographical mobility to adapt to a changing labor market. Like their Western counterparts, defense producers in ex-communist states lack knowledge of consumer preferences, marketing, distribution, pricing and commercial accounting. They understand little of market research or turnover cycles, or inventory strategy or promotion. And in the ex-communist nations they understand nothing of capitalization, leverage, depreciation or product warranties. It is not surprising, then, that Soviet consumer goods cost more when produced within the defense industry than by a specialized civilian plant.

Such products were often overdesigned by overly skilled engineers and produced on overcomplicated machinery run by overly sophisticated machinists—all overseen by legions of bureaucrats. Thus washing machines passed through 20 different cycles for each load. And thus Gorbachev's most celebrated conversion was to have the Votkinsk machine plant, which manufactured all the SS-20 missiles before the Intermediate-range Nuclear Forces (INF) Treaty ended that production, begin to manufacture baby carriages and beer containers. Likewise having airplane plants produce saucepans makes scant practical sense. The tale of a Soviet defense factory reconfiguring itself to make titanium wheelbarrows is indeed a technological breakthrough of the first magnitude—but only for someone willing to spend $10,000 on a wheelbarrow that will last 1,000 years.

Gorbachev's five-year effort increased consumer output little, if any. If did increase the grasp and power of the Soviet military, which was not helpful to him or his citizens. Gorbachev's approach somehow managed to lower the already abysmal quality of consumer goods while simultaneously raising their prices. He apparently wanted defense conversion in the worst way—regardless of the consequences—and that is how he implemented it.

The new leaders of Russia and Ukraine have already taken the single most important step toward defense conversion by severely slicing defense production. U.S. intelligence reports estimated that Russian military procurement for the first quarter of 1992 was cut by a whopping 80 percent from the same period last year. That figure may be a big high; other indications are that procurement was down 50 percent. Either figure, though, constitutes a staggering decrease in such a short time. And a discomforting one for that monstrous industrial-military complex.

Since power has devolved to local authorities, plant managers are now scrambling to adjust. In part of Ukraine the situation has on occasion become both comical and ironic. When a generation ago Nikita Khrushchev bragged that the Soviet Union could produce rockets like sausages, he had in mind heavy missile factories like that in Dnepropetrovsk, Ukraine. Once the biggest integrated missile producing plant anywhere, the Iuzhmash factory recently went into sausage-making—literally. "When we built our first 30 sausage machines." its chief engineer said, "they all fell apart." Problems developed elsewhere, as heat chambers for rocket boosters were transformed into high-speed rose-petal dryers to make perfume, booster rockets into farm granaries and trolley buses, and machinery was retooled to churn out umbrellas, tractors and microwave ovens.

More sensible have been changes in the Znamya Truda ("Banner of Labor") Plant 30 in Moscow—once a showplace for the Soviet military aircraft industry as it produced MiG-29 fighters and transport aircraft. Managers there now plan to stop producing MiGs and begin making the I1-114 civilian airliner, currently undergoing fight testing. To help them over the transition hurdle, plant officials attempted to build industrial juice processors, but the results have been nothing short of lemons.

The Klimov Engine Plant in St. Petersburg had long made engines for military and civilian fixed-wing aircraft and helicopters. It now plans to manufacture the engine for a new civilian airliner. To help them through the transition, managers are working to produce shoemaking equipment, but his effort may end as the attempt at juice processors did.

The massive conversion of the defense sector seems dubious at best, although a few such local attempts could conceivably succeed. The new Russian government under Boris Yeltsin has formed some 16 new committees to deal with this problem—an ominous sign in itself, as anyone familiar with the U.S. Congress realizes—and top-level pronouncements have hardly been reassuring.

The good news is that most Russian leaders recognize that Gorbachev was wrong to view defense conversion as paving the way for perestroika. They sense that the reverse is true—moving beyond perestroika to form a functioning market economy must lead the way for successful defense conversion. Hence Yeltsin's adoption of shock therapy for the whole Russian economy.

And hence Mikhail Bazhanov, the head of the Russian State Committee for Defense Industry Conversion, lamenting [in January 1992] that there is no market to help defense conversion. The defense complex must "be taught the market," he said in a televised interview. "Furthermore, one cannot talk about real conversion. I call it convulsion rather than conversion." Bazhanov recognizes the ill-conceived attempts made by most defense factories thus far:

They are looking feverishly for what they should do, if only to earn something, if only to provide social support for their workers. Pans and beds and whatever else you like are therefore indeed being produced, along with hat stands and coat hangers—you name it. Children's beds that often cost more to produce than they're worth.

While on the mark with the problem, Bazhanov is off track on the solution. He still views defense conversion as a centralized effort—one demanding a complete catalogue of every plant's qualifications, technology, output and potential: sort of a centralized decentralization. Bazhanov talked as if his committee (or any committee for that matter) could manage "a conversion program for the enterprise, then for the region" and then "an overall program for the conversion of Russia." For this, he said he needs "approximately 150 billion rubles" for the next five to six years, "and incidentally I am calculating this according to the prices that were in force before now." Such huge sums are required even though "so far not a single kopek has been allocated for conversion. At any rate, I haven't seen any."

Should such funds miraculously come his way, Bazhanov would begin his "certification of production facilities," encourage them to branch out and "offer those enterprises technologies that we have in the committee's data bank. That is the only way."

But centralized planning for defense conversion can work no better than centralized planning for economic development. The plans of Bazhanov, who worked for many years in the Soviet industrial-military complex, have been roundly and rightly criticized by Russian free-market advocates. That is not "the only way." There is a better way, as we will present shortly.

No central east European country was as thoroughly militarized—or is as economically failing, politically splintering, ethnically clashing or bureaucratically stifling—as the U.S.S.R. While these populations often complain about their predicament, they now at least have hope. This, like so many other things, they lacked for a half century.

Being smaller, more monolithic and certainly more manageable, east European states have greater opportunities for outside aid to make a genuine contribution. The ex-Soviet Union is simply so large that plausible levels of foreign aid cannot be expected to make a dent, other than in specialized areas such as medical supplies. And in eastern Europe the living standard has been higher and the work ethic stronger than in the former Soviet republics. Forty-five years of communism is less corrosive than seventy-five years.

One U.S. automaker reports that its plants in western Europe are 25 percent less productive than those in the United States (which in turn are generally less productive than those in Japan), leaving little to the imagination about the productivity in eastern Europe—let alone Russia, Ukraine, Georgia and the other republics. Plants across ex-communist lands are hopelessly outdated— "veritable museums of industrial archaeology," as aptly put by one commentator. A visit to those factories turns one into a Rip Van Winkle in reverse.

East European countries, however, are at least heading in the right direction, toward privatization. Over half the defense plants in Czechoslovakia, Poland and Hungary have now been slated for such conversion or, for many, closure. In east Germany an aggressive program is underway to privatize all manufacturing—an effort destined to succeed given the support of its wealthy cohort, but surely with much greater difficulty and more delay than ever anticipated.

In many cases east European governments have simply flung defense concerns into the commercial marketplace—"the sink-or-swim school" of conversion. Most of these are not real "companies" at all, but factories. For years their managers have been told what to build, their workers when and how to build it. Much to their current disadvantage the defense factories in eastern Europe produced mostly small arms or component parts; in the case of larger systems, their factories and products were simply copied from Soviet designs.

Though east European technology lagged a generation behind the Soviet Union's, at least those countries led in management skills, particularly Hungary. Budapest gained a decade head start in moving toward a free-market system through a tacit agreement with Moscow, which tolerated economic experimentation as long as the political line was toed.

The enormous demands on industrial managers in a free-market eastern Europe pale in comparison with the demands placed upon policymakers overseeing and directing this transformation. Many of their new political leaders were former dissidents; they were intellectuals, poets or unionists, not managers. Some patriots spent many of the communist years confined in jail, and thus lack essential experience. Poland's second postcommunist prime minister admitted that "my experience in politics was close to zero" before he took the key political position.

Now that their countries are strapped for hard cash, they are tempted to continue making military equipment for export. President Yeltsin has explicitly supported arms export in his public statements. This becomes worrisome, since those countries with the most hard cash to buy weapons are precisely those Middle Eastern or Persian Gulf nations that the United States might wish not to be more heavily armed. It is also worrisome since it just postpones the day when massive defense conversion must be tackled.

The classic example of such an exporter is Czechoslovakia. Its inspiring playwright-turned-president, Václav Havel, was one of the most defiant opposition leaders. He nonetheless reversed initial plans to phase out the country's defense production, due to Czechoslovakia's need for hard cash and to preserve jobs. Ethnic tensions also played a major role, since drawing down the defense business would have devastated the poorer republic of Slovakia, which manufactures some 75 percent of the country's arms. In east European states, defense production has been geographically concentrated, with many regions almost wholly dependent upon defense. In one area of Czechoslovakia, for example, the local economy was dominated by a huge underground plant originally built before World War II to manufacture tanks for defense against the Germans. Captured and operated by the Germans throughout most of the war, it eventually fell into the hands of the Soviets. Today it is largely unused, a monument to past wars—and to future environmental cleanups.

The breakup of political links has shattered market relationships. Other former Warsaw Pact nations used to account for half of Czechoslovakia's arms sales—formerly the seventh largest in the world—but these countries no longer want the weapons, nor can they afford them. Consequently many Slovakian defense plants have huge inventories, few customers and a government with an increasingly desperate need for hard currency. Thus the Havel government has approved a $200 million tank sale to Syria and a rocket launcher sale to Iran, both over the West's strong objections. Recent reports tell of Slovak-made weapons heading to factions in Yugoslavia and to Syria.

Such may be the pain of transition. And the transition will be long and hard. After all it took the already developed nations of

Japan and West Germany a quarter century—aided by benevo-
lent foreign occupation and massive infusions of foreign assistance—to convert their economies after World War II. It took
South Korea about the same time after its war in the early 1950s,
again with massive aid (but no occupation).

People are understandably frightened. Polish President Lech
Wałęsa reflected this sentiment when addressing the Council of
Europe last February: "Nowadays our own people are not getting
the feeling they are better off. . . . Democracy is losing its supporters. Some people even say, 'Let's go back to authoritarian
rule'." And in fact, Poland has gone through three prime ministers in the past two and a half years, largely as a result of its jolting
economic reforms.

Capitalism demands individual initiative, an often alien concept for those who lived under communist rule. But promising
signs are emerging, including the thriving black market in Moscow, which prompted David Johnson at Plan-Econ in Washington
to identify the main defense conversion problem as: "They don't
have any experience with how to do it legally."

Defense conversion throughout the ex-communist states leads
to a bundle of woes that accompany the unprecedented leap from
communism to capitalism, from communes to companies. They
raise several questions.

Ownership. Who owns the land, building, or company originally seized by the communist government? Or by the Nazis and
then by the communists? What date does the government choose
to honor restitution? Or should the government not honor
restitution—giving the land or real property back—and instead
merely honor compensation? Who owns the plant? The center,
the local authority or the plant manager?

Privatization. How is one to convert existing facilities from the
government to private hands? Who gains ownership, since few
citizens (besides high-ranking ex-communists with suspicious
sums of money) have the means to buy major facilities? How
much foreign ownership will be allowed? Can an investor be certain that the laws made today will hold five years from now? What
is the sanctity of a contract? How are legal disputes to be resolved?
What standing will foreign firms have? Will domestic firms that
operated these facilities prior to World War II be given preferen-
tial treatment?

Personal Allegations. How much in the millions of raw intelligence reports is to be believed? How can one clear his or her name of allegations? When will this be done? Until it is done, who prominent in these societies can rest assured that they will not shortly be smeared with a leak, no matter how unfounded? In Russia how did a certain individual conduct himself or herself during the attempted coup in August 1991?

Entrepreneurial Talent. Where is one to find or train potential business leaders with a host of skills never needed under communism? How long will it take to create a critical mass of such skills in each country? What happens to the existing cadre of managers?

Conversion of Currency. How do foreign firms repatriate their earnings? At what exchange rates? With what level of taxation? Is this likely to change dramatically?

Environmental Liability. What happens if a newly purchased facility is later found to have a major environment problem? Is the answer the German approach, where officials simply indicate that indemnification will be provided?

Political Stability. With whom within a government does one negotiate? (In Czechoslovakia there are three foreign ministers; in the former U.S.S.R., fifteen.) With what government? For how long? Should commercial agreements be made with the central government, the republics, the cities' mayors or the factory managers?

The dearth of answers to those questions represents the greatest deterrent to foreign investment and provides what may be the last great refuge of the established bureaucrat.

Problems of defense conversion naturally ease as the economy improves. Prosperity, or even relative improvement, is a catalyst to transition. That, in turn, depends on a measure of stability. Money is a coward; few risk great sums in periods of great uncertainty—especially when the world is rich with opportunities from Malaysia to Mexico for risk capital. Reports indicate some 3,400 foreign partnerships have been established with firms in the former Soviet Union, but in reality only a few have left the drawing board.

In a grand sense Britain prospered in the nineteenth century because of four factors: a clear, simple and dependable legal system, which assured both property rights and the sanctity of contracts; real, fully convertible money; relatively low taxes; and an absence of corruption (whose existence prevents any political system from encouraging economic growth). These four elements remain key to prosperity today.

For conversion to work best, capital must flow into private enterprises led by a new class of entrepreneurs sensitive to consumer needs. It will not work when production is assigned to existing defense facilities commanded by the military elite. Nor will it work well if it consists of simply answering the question posed to a Western visitor touring a Ukrainian plant, "How do we sell AK-47s abroad?"

Fortunately the critical step for conversion—privatization—is occurring in eastern Europe, as throughout much of the world. In 1990 some 25 governments worldwide sold state-owned enterprises—incidentally accruing some $30 billion in revenues. Such actions are frequently controversial, sparking demonstrations from India to Argentina when government-owned assets were put up for sale, but such actions are needed.

Privatization must come with greater incentives for workers and managers to engage in civilian projects rather than military programs. The traditional Soviet mania for secrecy must be lifted to open the way for joint ventures with foreign firms. Only justice is blindfolded; no worthy potential business partner will emerge so adorned.

Asking what to do leads to the Rosetta Stone of defense conversion—to wit, defense conversion should not be viewed as "conversion" at all. Rather it is the result of two independent and parallel actions: *shedding* many elements of the defense sector; and *absorbing* those assets into a new entrepreneurial consumer sector. The way to increase the production of sausage-making machines is to expand the sausage factory, letting it hire the employees of the defense firm and rent or buy its factories—not to anoint the rocket makers as sausage makers. The first step is already being done rapidly throughout the world, especially in Russia and Ukraine, where defense shedding is happening much faster than was imaginable, even under Gorbachev.

Ex-military workers can be employed in similar civilian jobs; welding a tank resembles welding a truck. Even design engineers may be salvageable; designing a radar resembles designing a television. Some capital assets can be retained; factory buildings care little whether rifles or refrigerators are made within them. The bad news here is for the managers, most of whom become unsalvageable.

Hence our main message on defense conversion: bulldoze the management, not the factories. And, while they are at it, bulldoze the corporate culture. For every industrial organization, as every individual, has a "personality" or culture that is resistant to change. Buildings can be razed and replaced, machines moved in and out, workers hired and fired—but the culture lives on. It is established over considerable time by deed, not by word, and emanates from the top, only to seep through the layers of managers in an organization. Managers in those countries who stand to lose the most by change must therefore be replaced if the culture is to be fundamentally changed, as it must.

And as it can. Dramatic cultural changes have occurred, as when Japanese firms took over the operation of U.S.-based automotive or electronic manufacturing facilities and achieved remarkable improvements in quality and productivity with the same workers, plants and products—but new management cultures.

Various models exist for transforming a defense industry into commercial pursuits. Many of them have been tried in past cycles of defense downturns in one country or another. None, however, has been fully tested during a shift of the entire economy from a managed to a free-market structure.

First is the "insertion model," similar to what was unsuccessfully tried during the Soviet Union's final years. Here commercial work and market share are assigned by the central government to defense manufacturers. A rocket plant is given responsibility for making refrigerators or perfume. This unworkable approach depends illogically upon a centrally managed economy, which is itself unworkable, and is not an attractive model.

Second is the "conversion model," whereby defense contractors simply seek to use their technology and manufacturing capabilities to shove their way into the commercial sector. They launch major initiatives of new products, such as canoes, buses, coffins or beepers. This approach has been repeatedly tried—notably by U.S. defense manufacturers during the defense downturns of 1944, 1955 and 1969—and has regularly failed.

The third, unlike the first two not a proven failure, is the "evolution model." This version is characterized by a gradual movement into selected commercial markets closely related to the basic skills of existing defense firms—endeavors marked by high-tech, systems engineering, "large" products, low-rate production and arrangements with a few large customers, whether governments or major corporations. This approach offers some promise. Yet it affords only limited opportunity to offset job losses in traditional defense activities since it excludes major market segments and does little for the consumer. Nonetheless this is the best model today for recasting the U.S. defense industry. It could work reasonably well in a controlled defense downturn, as opposed to a defense budget collapse. No model can manage a free-fall.

Fourth is the "substitution model," which we recommend along with accompanying actions for the ex-communist states. This consists of providing government assistance and incentives to small start-up, entrepreneurial enterprises that then selectively hire away the employees of the existing defense firms and, in some cases, even buy or rent parts of existing defense factories. This approach helps assure that the existing management and culture are left behind eventually to wither away, residues of excessive government-imposed bureaucratic oversight attuned to a different era. Under this model technology is transferred the way it has always been transferred—although seldom recognized as such—in the minds and skills of the workers.

This substitution model can be facilitated by the leaders of these ex-communist states allowing joint ventures with foreign firms, on a company-to-company (not government-to-government) basis, to provide manufacturing expertise and capital in exchange for equity ownership. Start-up funds could also be raised from the sale of state-owned land and buildings. But to be effective the old management must be bulldozed aside and replaced with a cadre of fresh leaders, who make up for their lack of experience not only with a vision but also with a stake in that vision.

Decisive action is needed, and needed fast. The "muddle of the road" approach can only lead to economic failure, which invariably leads to political failure.

Leaders of these ex-communist states, now longing for capitalism, must realize that conversions of all kinds are endemic to that system. Joseph Schumpeter identified the essence of capitalism as "creative destruction" since companies, and even entire industries, constantly rise and fall. Manufacturers of buggy whips are down, while those of microchips are up. Employment in defense firms ebbs and flows as foreign threats rise and fall.

Any transition can be eased by enlightened government policy. In such an environment defense conversion largely "happens" rather than being directed or dictated. The U.S. government conversion policy is basically a hands-off policy. The Pentagon has only a minuscule office to help, the Office of Economic Adjustment, which uses its $4 million annual budget to assist some local communities.

Under capitalism the market redistributes whatever human and capital assets are displaced during defense downturns. After the INF treaty was signed in December 1987 American workers in Pershing II missile plants did not then start to make baby carriages in their factories. Rather some moved on to other projects in their companies while others moved on to other companies or other industries.

Defense conversion is a continual and natural part of change in Western economies. Downsizing leads to consolidation. During World War II, some 20 major contractors built fixed-wing aircraft in the United States; today only a half-dozen do. As U.S. defense spending continues to decline from a high of 6.3 percent of GNP in 1986 to below an estimated 4 percent in 1995, the number of defense firms contracting with the Pentagon will continue to decline. Likewise in France and Britain; each had some ten manufacturers of military aircraft in the 1950s. They now have one or two.

Thus do people in free-market societies move on to other activities when a market recedes—not without pain, but with the knowledge that this is how it goes. Or how it should go, if alternatives exist, as with the U.S. economy, which typically generates some one to two million new jobs each year.

Sadly this is not how it goes in most ex-communist countries. Leaders there cannot delay defense conversion until their economies start to hum. They must begin now, and can begin, naturally, by building on their comparative advantages. Work forces in most east European countries are well educated and fairly well motivated. Their number of craftsmen is high and factory labor costs low.

Given appropriate tax and investment incentives in a stable situation, Western firms could use these comparative advantages to build new (or even modify existing) facilities for relatively low-cost production—similar to what has happened in the Pacific Rim and Mexico.

How to accomplish such a transformation? We offer seven steps, none simple, but all clear.

The first task is to help assure political stability. Foreign investors shy away from committing assets if they are uncertain which government will hold power tomorrow—or, worse yet, which government holds power today. Likewise, layers of bureaucracy must be scraped away, for they do little else than impede productivity.

Second, a business-friendly infrastructure must be constructed with clear laws of property ownership, assuring the sanctity of a contract, environmental accountability and an encouraging tax policy. This entails a legal system for dispute resolution and protecting intellectual property, ways for foreign investors to repatriate earnings, insurance for bank deposits, an economic safety net for employees displaced during the transition period, and much more.

Third, privatization should be expedited with a generous stance toward foreign ownership, including special tax incentives to reward job creation. Only then can productive assets be taken from the hands of bureaucrats and passed to the entrepreneurs, while raising capital.

Fourth, conversion must be need-driven, not capacity-driven. To launch the defense conversion effort these new leaders should direct assets into the essentials of a society—medical care, food processing and distribution, housing and energy generation. This, of course, is not the path upon which many Russian or Ukrainian factories are embarked; they prefer instead more glamorous high-tech pursuits. What remains of the old Soviet army, or new republic armies, should use the military's logistics system to help rebuild the infrastructure of highways, railroads, airports and telecommunications as well as for environmental clean-ups. The focus should be on internal markets since that need is greatest and today's capabilities are generally inadequate to match worldwide competition in the export realm.

Surely the sole constructive measure taken by the former East German government occurred in its final gasping days, when it assigned those drafted into the army to spend only three months in basic training and then begin national service in construction work or health care for the duration of their time in uniform. A civilian conservation corps of people displaced from the military and defense projects could help avoid massive unemployment and actually build up the infrastructure.

Fifth, ex-communist countries must develop sources of hard currency by doing what in the nondefense realm they do best. Eastern Europe still produces agricultural goods, and tourism there and in Russia, Ukraine, Georgia and elsewhere can attract Westerners anxious to see once forbidden and foreboding sites. Officials could jump-start tourism as a potentially major source of foreign exchange.

Western firms could also be given equity stakes in developing oil resources in the Russian and other republics, whose resources are said to rival those in the Persian Gulf. This takes new approaches and firm decisions. Chevron's attempts to develop the Tenghiz oil field in Kazakhstan, for instance, has been frustrated for more than four years by bureaucratic infighting among sundry Soviet authorities.

Sixth, civilian manufacturing capacity should be generated, not by converting defense plants to refrigerator factories, as is now done, but by permitting entrepreneurs outside those plants to create new businesses. Something similar to this happens in the black market; it can and should be legalized and encouraged. Then government authorities could offer the new entrepreneurs use of privatized defense plants, besides facilitating the construction of new plants as needed.

Seventh, as an interim measure to help them, Western efforts should be made to inhibit top-notice ex-Soviet scientists and engineers from peddling their expertise elsewhere. Libya, Iraq and other countries are reported to have offered scientists jobs at salaries of several thousand dollars a month—undoubtedly tempting for people now drawing the equivalent of $10 per month. For decades Washington paid American farmers not to farm. Over the next couple of years Washington should pay many Russian and Ukrainian nuclear workers not to work—or at least to work on less threatening projects.

Ideally the U.S. government should identify the top 20 or so nuclear engineers and scientists (those of potential Nobel Prize caliber) and recruit them for work in U.S. labs and universities. The next rung, the thousand or so skilled in this area and possessing the expertise to make nuclear weapons, could be employed to destroy, or at least defuse, existing nuclear weapons throughout the land, to participate on a new U.S.-Russian cooperative Strategic Defense Initiative program, or they could be retrained for other high-tech but low-lethality projects. As for the tens of thousands of scientists at the bottom rung, they must cope with the new situation, much like their fellow citizens.

Overall we propose a policy of substitution rather than direct conversion through the two-step process of shedding defense assets and encouraging the absorption of such labor and capital by newly created companies.

Training in free-market principles is sorely needed if a new corporate culture is to be created. Despite all the talk, knowledge of how to operate within a free market is scarce. After a tour of former Warsaw Pact countries on defense conversion, U.S. Deputy Secretary of Defense Donald Atwood reportedly said, "We found almost universal acceptance of what the problem is—lack of understanding of how free enterprise works."

An infusion of retired Western executives with proven track records could guide the new entrepreneurs. Such activities, dubbed the "paunch corps," are already underway but need to be expanded both in numbers and in time of individual service (to a year or two). Launching a number of "how to" business courses in these countries would likewise help create a new cadre of entrepreneurs with a new corporate agenda. Corporate executive exchanges in both directions could assist as well, as could massive student exchange programs. Western aid to partially guarantee the seed capital for joint start-up businesses would be helpful.

Once on their way the ex-communist countries could model themselves on the step-by-step rise of postwar Japan, which deliberately proceeded from manufacturing baseball gloves to motorcycles to steel to automobiles to consumer electronics and now to aerospace.

International trade is also essential. Lowering, or better yet scrapping, the European Community's protectionist wall against commerce with countries to the east remains the most critical contribution any outside governments can make. It is ironic that a formidable wall harming the peoples of eastern Europe today has been erected and maintained by the west Europeans.

Above all time and determination prove critical. While the newly liberated people of these nations fixate on defense conversion per se, they are actually embarked on a much grander and nobler conversion, into a system of freedom and free markets. Theirs is an effort certainly worthy of pursuit and strong support.

IV. THE NEW WORLD ORDER?

EDITOR'S INTRODUCTION

In the opening selection, political scientist Charles Gati addresses the impact of communist rule on Eastern Europe, postulating that it has created an atmosphere in which the people have placed unrealistic expectations on democracy. Writing in *Foreign Affairs,* he explains that the danger in this is what he calls the Weimar syndrome, in which democracy becomes the villain rather than the liberator, and the people end up embracing authoritarian or semi-authoritarian regimes. The economic developmental backwardness of Eastern Europe, the weakness of the area's professional and entrepreneurial middle classes, and the economic legacy of communism all have exacerbated the difficulties this region is likely to face on the road to democracy. He sees a strong role for America in the region's future, but fears that the United States is turning inward.

The second article, reprinted from *Society,* looks at the reunification of Germany and examines its possible role in Europe. Gregory F. Treverton and Barbara Bicksler describe the political history of the new Germany and the strain reunification has put on the domestic economy. Their article then outlines the new Germany's relationship with Eastern and Western Europe, the former Soviet Union, and the United States. They conclude that Germany will attempt to develop multiple relationships in an attempt to balance the broad spectrum of German interests. As such, they warn the rest of the world not to develop ambitious political expectations from Europe's economic giant.

The five Central Asian republics of the former Soviet Union are relatively unknown in this country. Having long been under Soviet and czarist Russian domination, their officials and citizens are eager for close relations with the United States. James Rupert's article in *Foreign Policy* considers and rejects the possibility that these new countries will form part of a pan-Turkic or pan-Islamic movement as long as they can make progress on the tasks they face before political desperation sets in. The author notes that violence in the region has more often stemmed from economic frustration than from religious militancy. However, because of geography and cultural ties, Rupert believes the Central Asian governments are likely to develop close economic relations with Middle Eastern and Asian countries sharing their borders. In response to this, America should become involved in the area as a means to exert its own economic and political influence.

Because of its long authoritarian history, many observers are skeptical about Russia's and, in particular, Boris Yeltsin's intentions. Writing in *The Nation,* Tatyana Vorzheikina acknowledges the possibility of authoritarian rule reemerging and warns about recent trends that have bolstered the power of the executive branch. The framework for establishing a true democracy is present only if free elections cause the decentralization of power and a strong legislature is allowed to take root.

Dr. Llewellyn D. Howell, writing in *USA Today,* presents five provocative scenarios for the new world order in the year 2017. In what he considers the most likely of these, he sees the Commonwealth of Independent States abandoned in the late 1990s and Russia becoming the preeminent economic and political international power with strong economic ties to Germany and Japan. In this scenario, the Central Asian states form a loose Islamic federation, while the United States degrades into a second rate economic power.

Finally, Joseph S. Nye, Jr., offers advice to the United States in its efforts to establish and keep a power base in the new world order—an order, he argues, that is in a period of evolution from a national to a transnational entity. Nye's article in *Foreign Affairs* encourages the United States to maintain a strong military capable of responding to regional unrest through extra-governmental institutions like the United Nations. He adds that it will be in the national interest of the United States to promote a global balance of power in the near future, and to further the global spread of democratic values and institutions for the long run.

FROM SARAJEVO TO SARAJEVO[1]

From Gdansk on the Baltic to Dubrovnik on the Adriatic, from Prague in the heart of the old continent to Sofia near Eu-

[1]Article by Charles Gati, author and professor of political science at Union College, from *Foreign Affairs* 71:64–78 Fall '92. Copyright © 1992 by the Council on Foreign Relations, Inc. Reprinted with permission.

rope's eastern periphery, freedom has come to east-central Europe: freedom of assembly, freedom of the press and freedom of religion. Throughout the region elected governments are in place.

Unfortunately, if understandably, what attracts more attention is the ugly underside of the transition to democracy: war, political fragmentation and economic despair. Instead of dialogue and debate, there is demagoguery. Instead of consensus, there is contention and confrontation. Instead of new governments adopting a forgive-but-do-not-forget policy toward the communist past in order to deal with the tasks ahead, mysterious sources leak politically inspired, doctored lists of former agents, informers and collaborators. Especially in countries where the communist regimes were relatively mild, as in Poland and in Hungary, there are even signs of nostalgia now for the authoritarian order of recent years.

The main questions remain as they have been since 1989: Will the fragile democracies of east-central Europe take hold and last? Will they become stable enough to join the west European political and economic order? The war tearing Yugoslavia apart now overshadows these questions and exacerbates the problems of transition to democracy. The related but more pressing questions today are the war's international repercussions and implications: Does it portend the beginning of the Balkanization of Europe, east and possibly west? If so, do American and west European interests call for more timely and active Western engagement aimed not only at preventing the proliferation of small wars but moderating the region's growing instability as well?

The horrors of Sarajevo 1992 bear scant resemblance to the events that followed Sarajevo 1914, but the collapse of communism has rekindled ancient political feuds as antagonistic and passionate as ever. They spring from the suddenly freed stresses and strains of the communist era itself, from the memory of destruction and dislocations during and after World War II and from real and perceived injustices imposed by the post-World War I territorial settlements. Countering if not canceling the region's democratic impulse, these passions—the enduring historical legacy of the twentieth century—delimit the pace and define the substance of postcommunist transformation.

Mainly because of the powerful lasting impact of Communist political culture, the road to democracy in east-central Europe is paved not only with bumps but with long detours that could lead to dead ends. Making it so are unrealistically high popular expectations of prosperity and, in general, the widespread identification of democracy with economic well-being. Few people in the area understand, and even fewer accept, the proposition that democracy is but a means to electoral choice; that democracies, unlike communist systems, base their claim to legitimacy more on respect for proper constitutional procedures than on economic performance.

For those raised in a communist political culture the distinction between delivering the goods and upholding the sanctity of the process is often lost if not altogether meaningless. Thus if they blame democracy and not only their current governments for economic pain, the Weimar syndrome may recur, meaning that people will turn from freedom altogether and embrace authoritarian rule, transforming their disillusionment with performance into a rejection of democracy itself. Another possibility—that which is happening in Poland already—is a recurrence of the Italian way, meaning that people will continue to opt for democracy but will produce constantly changing, unstable governments and thus experience protracted political crises. The most likely result, however, is somewhere between the Weimar and Italian models: the proliferation of semi-authoritarian regimes masquerading in democratic disguise (as in Romania today).

Among those who may fish in troubled waters in the years ahead will be former communist party members. In countries where they present themselves as social democrats, as many of them have become, they are now quiescent, even accommodating—but numerous. About a quarter of the region's present adult population belonged to a communist party at some time since 1945. The early recruits may have joined out of idealism; those who followed them were often opportunists in search of power and privilege. Today former party members, believers and opportunists alike, are suspect. Few have lost their jobs but many expect to do so, assuming that in the present political climate their careers will soon come to an end. Only those with marketable skills in the private sector get ahead, earning more money than ever before but missing the status and prestige conferred on members of the old political and economic elite.

Except for Serbia, Croatia, Romania and Slovakia, where communists parading as nationalists are in power, former party members everywhere else hold mid-level positions in the press and in the state bureaucracies, including the potentially critical ministries of defense and internal affairs. These officials and professionals constitute a large section of the region's frustrated, disaffected and often disoriented middle class. They cast a long shadow over the processes of democratic transformation, not because of what they are presently doing but because it is unclear what they could or would do in a moment of systemic crisis born of major domestic confrontation, intra-regional conflicts or outbursts of large-scale violence in the former Soviet Union.

The communist past also reveals itself in the intemperate personal attacks voiced in the region's legislatures and published in the press. Those who make the charges are not veteran anticommunist democrats of long standing, nor—with some exceptions—are leading communist officials the usual targets. Instead the most preposterous accusations and nasty insinuations are being advanced by populist demagogues of questionable background who were not known for their oppositional political views or activities during the communist era. Compensating for their acquiescence in the old order, these McCarthyites of east-central Europe are presently ransacking their current political rivals' past in search of evidence of collaboration with the communists.

Thus Lech Wałęsa, the heart and soul of the Solidarity movement that toppled the Polish communist regime, has been publicly accused of ties to the old secret police and then promptly disavowed even by his fellow rebels at the labor union's last congress. Thus Václav Havel, hero of Czechoslovakia's "velvet revolution," has been the subject of persistent rumors about his past. The prevailing atmosphere of recklessness has left leaders of the pre-1989 democratic opposition disheartened and disgusted; some have withdrawn from the political arena, others have failed to get reelected. As always the revolution is devouring its children.

The lies and insinuations that have surfaced may resemble charges made during heated, hard-fought election campaigns in many Western countries. The difference is that in east-central Europe practically everyone but the very young is politically scarred and thus vulnerable; few have impeccable credentials. Could it not be said that the chief accountant of a much-hated collective farm, who performed his job conscientiously, "supported" communism? Did not the museum director, who accepted a state award for his devoted service from a communist minister of culture, "serve" the system? What about the scholar who reported to the so-called international department of the academy of science on his foreign trips, and thus kept the police informed, in order to assure future professional association with Western colleagues—did he not "aid and abet" the regime and compromise his integrity?

The fact is that, Poland aside, no more than a few hundred people in all of east-central Europe actively confronted tyranny in the years prior to 1989. Those staying on the sideline may have been apathetic, fatalistic, cautious, timid, calculating or fearful, but for the most part they were decent. In a memorable passage, the Polish writer Kazimierz Brandys summed up the chilling dilemma faced by those unfortunate enough to have lived under communism: "Two intellectuals—a scientist and a film director—were once asked to sign a protest," Brandys relates. "One refused: 'I can't. I have a son.' The other one unscrewed the cap of his pen: 'I have to sign, because I have a son'." Havel explained the consequences this way: "We have all become used to the totalitarian system. . . . None of us is just a victim; we are all responsible for it."

As the psychological legacy of communism is thus an environment contaminated with guilt and suspicion, and as the political arena is already overcharged with ambition, the sine qua non of democracy—tolerance—is all but absent. This is why the region's legislatures should adopt a new approach, forgive-but-do-not-forget, which would heal old wounds and thereby ease the problems of transition. For the same reason the populist guardians of probity should overcome the Manichean political mentality that communism has bequeathed—a mentality they profess to spurn but in practice, ironically, exhibit—and start treating their rivals as opponents rather than as enemies.

Obstructing the processes of transition in more tangible ways are the consequences of World War II and especially World War I. Yugoslavia's civil war is the obvious case in point; but the painful, if so far peaceful, separation of Czechs and Slovaks reminds us that the Yugoslav experience is hardly unique. While international borders have not changed, there is growing interest in revising them so that they correspond more closely to ethnic and linguistic characteristics. Romania has already proposed a "treaty of fraternity and integration" with Moldova, now a war-torn sovereign republic with a Romanian-speaking majority, which turned the offer down. Albanians dream of Greater Albania of the World War II era that would include the now-Serbian province of Kosovo with a 90 percent Albanian and only 10 percent Serbian and Montenegrin population. Raising a seemingly subtle if potentially ominous point, the Hungarian prime minister has noted that the territories his country lost to Yugoslavia followed the Paris peace conference of 1919–20 were ceded to a state that no longer exists.

The issues that divide stem from the collapse of four empires—Ottoman, Russian, German and Austro-Hungarian—at the end of World War I, and from subsequent territorial settlements that created the two new nation-states of Yugoslavia and Czechoslovakia, revised the boundaries of several others and restored Poland's sovereignty. The principles that concerned the peacemakers, notably President Wilson, were ethnic justice for the peoples of east-central Europe and, to a lesser extent, the curtailment of German and Russian (Soviet) potential for war. Pressure for ethnic justice and self-determination followed a century of nationalism in Europe, accelerating during World War I especially in the Balkans. That the new nation-states, like the empires they would supplant, also included a number of antagonistic minorities, and that the new states would be too weak to resist either Germany or Russia later on, were seen as serious problems but were left unresolved. The main task for the peacemakers was to deal with the burning issues of the past and present rather than anticipate those that might arise in the future.

Thus they carved out Yugoslavia from the already independent states of Serbia and Montenegro; from the formerly Austro-Hungarian Slovenia, Istria, Dalmatia, Croatia-Slavonia, Vojvodina and Bosnia-Herzegovina; and from the once Ottoman-ruled Macedonia. Fragmented by regional, economic, cultural, linguistic and religious differences that prevailed both among and within these communities, peoples of the new kingdom of Yugoslavia—whose state was no more homogeneous than the empires it replaced—nevertheless welcomed the withdrawal of imperial powers.

As for Czechoslovakia, the other newcomer and a seemingly more viable entity, it was made up of the traditional Czech lands of Bohemia and Moravia that had been under Austrian control; of Slovakia and Ruthenia that had belonged to Hungary for a thousand years; and of a small section of Silesia with a largely Polish-speaking population. From the beginning Czechoslovakia suffered from divisive ethnic strife that would eventually contribute to its dismemberment. The tragic finale to Czech-German discord in the Sudetenland, an ethnically German area in Bohemia and Moravia, was the 1938 Munich accord that assigned the Sudetenland to Germany. The same year, assisted by German and Italian diplomacy, Hungary recovered some of the heavily Hungarian-populated chunks of southern Slovakia and southern Ruthenia. In March 1939, after what was left of Slovakia declared its independence, Czechoslovakia—the pride of the Paris peace-makers—was no more.

Poland, having been repeatedly partitioned by Prussia, Austria and Russia, reemerged as the largest state in east-central Europe in 1918, though some of its frontiers were set only in 1922. With two-thirds of its population Polish and Catholic, the country's ethnic problems with the Ukrainian-Ruthenian, Jewish, German and Belorussian minorities were serious but not quite as troubling as its preoccupation with the security of its borders. Memories of sovereignty lost and gained throughout its thousand-year history, combined with fear of German and Russian revenge, made Poland both apprehensive and vulnerable. Its fears turned into a nightmare in 1939 when, experiencing still another partition (the fourth), the country was swallowed up by the invading armies of Nazi Germany and Soviet Russia.

Unlike Yugoslavia and Czechoslovakia, which were created in Paris, and unlike Poland whose sovereign existence was restored in the aftermath of World War I, Romania benefited from the peace conference by having its prewar territory and population enlarged. More than doubling the area under its control, Greater Romania was pieced together by Hungary giving up Transylvania, Austria relinquished Bukovina, Russia returning Bessarabia (part of which now belongs to Moldova) and Bulgaria ceding southern Dobruja. With about two-thirds of its population composed of ethnic Romanians, the country's integration seemed a more promising prospect, and a somewhat less complex task, than that of ethnically fragmented Yugoslavia. However, persistent Hungarian complaints about Romanian assimilationist pressures against the significant Hungarian minority in Transylvania and strong Romanian rejoinders about Hungarian interference in Romania's internal affairs circumvented the goal of integration from the beginning. In 1940, supported by Germany and Italy, Hungary recovered and then held during the war a large part of Transylvania, which was then returned to Romania in 1945. Traditional mistrust and antagonism between the two countries have yet to subside.

The beneficiaries—Yugoslavia, Czechoslovakia, Poland and

Romania—had little reason to celebrate; their triumph, such as it was, was bittersweet. Throughout the interwar period their security was precarious, their internal peace shaky. While Austria, ready to attach itself to Germany, rather graciously adjusted to the loss of empire, Hungary and to a lesser extent Bulgaria pressed hard for a major revision of the Paris peace treaties.

Hungary justified its irredentism by claiming losses that were indeed excessive, not only in absolute terms but also compared to those of World War I's main culprit, Germany. According to Western rather than Hungarian calculations (as the latter included the loss of Croatia-Slavonia as well), Hungary was left with only one-third of its former territory and two-fifths of its population, becoming a rump state smaller than the territories it ceded to Romania alone. More than half of the 3.5 million ethnic Hungarians who were separated from their homeland lived in areas contiguous to Hungary. By comparison Bulgaria's losses were modest—less than ten percent of its prewar territory—but its lack of access to the Aegean Sea and the burden of heavy reparations produced considerable economic hardship and a stormy political climate. Incensed especially by the controversial transfer of part of Macedonia to Yugoslavia, various irredentist groups and parties succeeded in making that issue dominate political life in interwar Bulgaria.

In the West the multitude of claims, counterclaims, arguments and rebuttals was received with indifference bordering on contempt. Observations that these weak and small states were but inviting targets for German and Russian penetration were rather lightly dismissed; and proposals for a confederation or a federation of east-central European countries to temper intra-regional conflicts gained no Western sponsor. In 1920 the British historian E. H. Carr expressed the unspoken consensus when he cautioned a group of Western ambassadors "not to take the new nations of Europe too seriously" because their affairs "belong to the sphere of farce."

Now, with more than 20,000 people dead in the former Yugoslavia, and with over two million people homeless, the farce that never was must be seen as the tragedy it has always been. Indeed, with the old hatreds and ancient feuds so much in evidence, it seems as if little of significance has changed. The worlds of Sarajevo 1992 and Sarajevo 1914 suffer from the same disease.

One wonders who is unfortunate enough to be next in line on Serbia's list of victims: the Albanians of Kosovo or the Hungarians

of Vojvodina? How much additional territory will satisfy Croatia?
Further north, can Czechs and Slovaks conclude their divorce
without a fight? Unrestrained by Prague, will the fervently nationalist Slovaks ever learn to live in peace with their large Hungarian minority? Sad to say, the harrowing ethnic problems the
past has bequeathed to the region's fragile democracies are as
intractable as they may be destructive in their consequences for
European stability.

Further aggravating the problems of transition are at least
three economic trends and circumstances that history has passed
on to the countries of east-central Europe.

First is the region's relative developmental backwardness, especially of its southeastern parts. These areas have almost always
been on Europe's economic periphery, their condition altered
but a few times under high-minded political leadership. In the
1880s and 1890s, for example, several countries of the Austro-
Hungarian empire experienced a long period—a golden age—of
rapid industrialization, urbanization and modernization that
brought the region's transportation and communications facilities, as well as its literacy rates and institutions of higher education, within striking distance of west European standards.

Because of irredentist fervor and the rise of fascism, combined with the consequences of the Great Depression, that hopeful trend was reversed during the interwar period. The political
and economic environment generated by the region's authoritarian or semi-authoritarian regimes was inhospitable to business
and discriminatory against most foreign investors. Once again
east-central Europe found itself on the periphery—but once
again there was an exception. Thanks to Czechoslovakia's democratic leadership, Bohemia and Moravia were able to defy the
prevailing trend of economic decline. As late as the mid-1930s, in
the shadow of Nazi Germany, they managed to keep pace with
neighboring Austria and Germany.

While being stuck in Europe's economic periphery was thus
almost always a fact of life and a problem, it was never so widely
recognized and so acutely felt as it is today. Tens of millions of
people can now watch Western television and millions travel
abroad, seeing for the first time the contrast between Western
prosperity and Eastern backwardness and wondering about the
discrepancy. Without denying the heavy legacy of over four decades of communist economics, they ask why the region's eco-

nomic decline has accelerated, and the gap between East and West widened, following the collapse of the communist regimes. Could it be that the new regimes they have put in power, the Czech lands excepted, are not supportive enough or private enterprise? While the recent experience of having observed Western achievements at first hand does not change the fact of economic backwardness, it may yet induce pressure for a more liberal political order that would help move the region up and away from the periphery.

The second economic circumstance—the combined consequence of fascism in the interwar years, World War II and the communist era—is the weakness of the region's professional and entrepreneurial middle classes, which used to include large numbers of Jews and ethnic Germans. During the golden era of the late nineteenth and early twentieth centuries these entrepreneurs played an active and indeed critical role in bringing countries like Poland and Hungary closer to west European norms. Jews, for example, were allowed to advance and excel in business, finance, medicine, journalism and the emerging social sciences at that time.

They are not there to play that role anymore. Tens of thousands of educated or well-to-do Jews left for the West in the 1930s, with millions left behind to perish in the Holocaust. After World War II all ethnic Germans, including gifted businessmen, agricultural specialists and farmers, were accused of collaboration with the Nazis and expelled from their homelands in Poland, Czechoslovakia and Hungary. Finally, escaping from communism, most of the Jews of east-central Europe who survived the Holocaust have since moved to the West or settled in Israel.

There is now a pressing need for a new entrepreneurial class. Western-sponsored business schools can and to some extent already do compensate for the lag. Judging by the past, however, only a calm political environment free of ethnic and religious discrimination would prompt talented people, whether they belong to a minority group or not, to stay in their homelands (rather than emigrate) and provide professional leadership to the ongoing processes of transformation.

The third circumstance, of course, is the legacy of communist economics, which has instilled patterns and expectations altogether different from those present in market economies. The list of such patterns and expectations is endless. A simplistic summary of communist economics is that the state decides everything: which factory to build and what it will produce, who will run it and how many will work there and how much they will be paid; the state sets the price of whatever it has decided the factories will make. The people, in turn, are guaranteed a job that does not pay well, and thus they have no reason to work hard, and so forth. In the end the state is unhappy because socialism is "bankrupt"; but it takes comfort in the knowledge that it controls the (nonexistent) bankruptcy court.

This caricature of communist economics is meant to suggest not only the enormity but the uniqueness of the tasks ahead. Such radical institutional, as well as social and psychological, changes as are needed lack both precedents and guides. As many have noted there are no textbooks on what steps to take to get from a communist to a market economy—on how to convert one into the other. It might be easier to erect a market economy from scratch than to build one from shambles.

The conclusion is self-evident. The pervasive condition of backwardness, the absence of a strong entrepreneurial middle class and the economic ruin that communism has left behind present formidable obstacles to economic recovery and renewal. In the absence of a more tolerant political culture, chances for economic progress are poor; without economic progress, chances for the new democracies to take hold are equally poor.

Because east-central Europe had expected the United States to do far more to assist the transition, there is immense disappointment now, a feeling of blighted hope approaching a sense of betrayal.

The change is remarkable because for so long in times past America could do no wrong. After all, it was—and was seen to be—properly sympathetic to the Hungarian war for independence in the middle of the nineteenth century, generous toward Polish immigrants seeking freedom and prosperity here at the turn of this century, supportive of ethnic justice in the Balkans after World War I, and resolute against fascism during World War II and against communism afterward. Moreover the people of east-central Europe always admired everything American, notably U.S. technological prowess. The region's industrial workers heard that American factories were ultramodern, and peasants heard that farming was highly advanced. Scientists believed America was the world's most inventive laboratory, the place where Nobel Prize winners made stunning discoveries. Products "Made in America," from cars never driven to cigarettes occasionally smoked, were synonymous with high quality.

During the early phase of the Cold War especially, these views and sentiments were reinforced by America's anticommunist stance. Which country sought the liberation of east-central Europe from Moscow's oppressive tyranny? Which country stood up to communist aggression in Berlin and Korea? Which country defended western Europe against a potential military onslaught, and which one financed Radio Free Europe to keep hope alive in the other Europe? For most people of east-central Europe the political equation was simple: as the communists were known to be bad, Americans must be good. Perhaps only after President Kennedy's assassination did perceptions of the United States begin to reflect some familiarity with complexities.

Now, feeling abandoned, people are more critical, their judgments less favorable about the United States. It is a measure of their current mood that populist demagogues can seek popular approbation by blaming America for some of the region's historical misfortunes. Hinting at conspiracy revives old questions: Did President Roosevelt sell out east-central Europe to Stalin at the 1945 Yalta summit? Did Washington send word to Moscow during the 1956 Hungarian crisis saying it did not favor governments unfriendly to the Kremlin near Soviet borders? Did President Johnson convey a similar message to Moscow during the Prague Spring of 1968? But the worst may be the latest one: Is present U.S. indifference toward the region due to a Bush-Gorbachev secret pact at the 1989 Malta summit that confirmed Moscow's sphere of influence—as decided in Yalta? From Yalta to Malta!

The conspiracy theories are false, and most people in east-central Europe know it. Yet these people have plenty of reason to feel misled. Early American rhetoric about liberation and the practice of prayers during Captive Nations Week aside, successive U.S. administrations missed few opportunities to challenge the communist dictatorships and press for change and human rights, declaring repeatedly that Europe must be "whole and free" again. The very aim of American foreign policy was to replace the "evil empire" with democratic states, on the correct assumption that democracy was the best guarantee for lasting peace. If the aim was only to create tension in the bloc and thus put Moscow on the defensive, as the communists used to charge, how could the people of east-central Europe know? Henry Kissinger put it well: "It is hardly to the credit of the West that after talking for a generation about freedom for eastern Europe, so little is done to vindicate it."

What could the United States do, then, to meet some of the

region's expectations, fulfill some of its own moral obligations
and mitigate some of the problems of transition?

—*Recognize that the expected proliferation of small wars and conflicts in Europe calls for new thinking about security.* At issue now is the
stability of Europe, East and West. It is a problem completely
different from, but potentially as serious as, the Soviet threat to
western Europe, because the peace of Europe is not divisible. In
the former Yugoslavia, proliferation began with the almost peaceful separation of Slovenia from the rest of that country, continued
with a civil war between Croats and Serbs and turned into a
bloody nightmare in Bosnia-Herzegovina.

Let us hope that the hostilities end there, but it is more likely
that they will spread to other parts of the region. Then, as the
flood of refugees seeks food and shelter abroad, various xenophobic and populist movements in western Europe are bound to
gain new strength and new supporters. Might they even succeed
in undermining that most promising trend of the postwar era that
the United States has so vigorously and unselfishly promoted for
over four decades—the trend toward European integration and
unity? Surely the most important task for U.S. foreign policy in
the 1990s is to prevent the Balkanization of Europe.

—*Clarify what the United States will do and what it cannot do.*
Clearly there are, and should be, limits to what the United States
can do. Aside from simulating private investment and granting
modest sums for specific purposes, it should not assume responsibility for the region's economic reconstruction. The United
States should invest most of its attention in countries with some
geopolitical significance and in those with the best prospect of
carrying out a successful transition to democracy. This means the
central European states that lie between Russia and Germany
(Poland, Hungary and the Czech lands) and possibly Slovenia.
The United States should press NATO and encourage the European Community to accept these countries as full members—as
soon as possible, but certainly before the end of this decade. Both
NATO, thus given a new lease on life, and the EC should offer a
fixed date for membership, provided their conditions for such
are fully met.

—*Mobilize private investment in east-central Europe.* Contrary to
the received wisdom of the moment, a vast assistance program on
the pattern of the Marshall Plan would not do much good. Privatization has not yet gone far enough for the region's economies to
absorb large amounts of foreign funds. What is needed is small-

scale private investment that is less likely to be wasted. If the White House and the Department of Commerce were to hold frequent consultations with American bankers and industrialists, and advise them of profitable business deals to be made and the U.S. national interest to be served in east-central Europe, it would make a difference. If politically stable the region is a potential gold mine for small- and medium-sized American companies. There is probably no other place in the world, for example, where so many educated people are unable to make good use of their skills and talents.

—*Pursue preventive diplomacy before the next conflict erupts.* In 1991 Washington engaged in verbal acrobatics by stating its preference for Yugoslav "unity and democracy," a statement the Serb leadership chose to interpret as a green light to make Croatia stay within a united Yugoslav federation. It took 11 long months and tens of thousands of deaths for the United States to mobilize the international community. Even then, for reasons having to do with American domestic politics, the issue was still presented as one of "humanitarian" concern rather than a threat to European stability. If the United States had done in mid-1991 as much as it is doing in mid-1992, the Serbians in Belgrade and in Bosnia-Herzegovina might well have been deterred from proceeding as they have.

Sadly, European and U.N. warnings have gone unheeded without American-backed initiatives. Even the opening of Sarajevo airport, however temporary, was due to U.S. warships making their presence felt in the Adriatic. The lesson for American diplomacy elsewhere in east-central Europe, then, is to clarify U.S. preferences early and state them without equivocation and without worrying about charges of interference in a country's or the region's internal affairs. While some politicians will undoubtedly resent such interference, most will welcome it. President Árpád Göncz of Hungary has publicly challenged the West in general and the United States in particular "to give frank answers to central Europe's agonizing questions."

Celebrating the defeat of communism while underestimating the dangers ahead, America is turning inward. Europe lacks leadership. In the midst of domestic chaos Russia faces upheavals both at home and in the other successor states of the former Soviet Union. From the United Nations to the Conference on Security and Cooperation in Europe, international organizations are engaged in defining their new role after the Cold War. Given a recessionary economic environment, too, international circumstances favoring the rise of a democratic east-central Europe and the perdurability of a stable Europe are thus less auspicious than previously assumed. Sarajevo is back to haunt the last decade of the century, as it did the generation of 1914.

The key missing ingredient is domestic pressure in the United States for a more active engagement in the region's future. Such pressure is absent because the issue is invariably, if mistakenly, identified in terms of new expenditures, and because American political intellectuals who shape public opinion have been so strangely silent. Where are the conservatives who used to speak out on behalf of the "satellite nations"? Where are the neoconservatives who tried to make the struggle against communism part of the liberal agenda? Where is the whole liberal community with its insistence on a pro-democratic foreign policy? With due respect to some notable exceptions, the silence of American political intellectuals is deafening. Yet, in the absence of an American-led international effort, postcommunist Europe may get no further than the gates of the promised land.

GERMANY AND THE NEW EUROPE[2]

When the Berlin wall came down in November 1989, few could have predicted the speed of German unification. In outlining a ten-point program for German unity just three weeks later, Chancellor Helmut Kohl envisioned a long period of transition—perhaps five to ten years—a transition that would involve cooperation or at most confederation between the two German states. But by early 1990 it was clear that the momentum behind unification could not be stopped—street politics in eastern Germany, interacting with electoral politics in both Germanys, denied the luxury of a gradual transition.

[2]Article by Gregory F. Treverton (a senior fellow of the Council on Foreign Relations) and Barbara Bicksler (a member of the research staff of the Institute for Defense Analyses)—this article is a condensed version of Mr. Treverton's forthcoming book, *America, Germany and the Future of Europe,* from *Society* 29:48–56 Ja/F '92. Copyright © 1992 by Transaction Publishers, Inc. Reprinted with permission.

In October 1990, less than a year after the opening of the wall, unification became a reality. Still, history casts its shadow, and with unification came the question whether the world can live easily with the new Germany. For the first time in German history, unity was the result of democracy—a peaceful revolution, not iron and steel. Germany today is hardly the country it was in the 1930s. It is domestic, prosperous, and has a fair degree of domestic consensus about foreign policy.

Events did not stand still after the fall of the wall while Germany got on with nation building. Just as the euphoria of 1989 was giving way to sober second thoughts in Germany—in the East about the pain of transition and in the west about its costs—external issues intruded, especially the Gulf War, but also the failure of the latest round of international trade talks held under the auspices of GATT (General Agreement on Tariffs and Trade). The timing could not have been worse. The immediate issues were reminders of the external challenges that press upon the newly reunited Germany: Germany's commitment to the European Community, to the North Atlantic Treaty Organization (NATO) and the trans-Atlantic connection, to rebuilding Eastern Europe, and to reshaping its relations with the Soviet Union.

The Gulf War and GATT were also reminders of how strange the United States and Germany still remain to each other despite forty years of alliance. The process of unification had been a high-water mark in German-American relations; unwavering American support was a virtuoso performance managed through constant contact at the top of government. However, once German and American attentions were turned away from each other, Washington to the Gulf and Bonn/Berlin to itself, their leaders quickly diverged. So did their politics. The episodes stand as a caution against expecting too much from each other and against paying too little attention to how expectations are created.

The German Elections

Germany held its first nation-wide elections in fifty-seven years on December 2, 1990. The result was a vote against the political extremes and for unification and economic success, juxtaposing the optimism of the governing coalition with the pessimism of the opposition. It was also a tidy result, perhaps misleadingly so, contradicting predictions that unification would cause political fragmentation. Instead, unified Germany remained a three-party state.

The victory of West Germany's governing coalition, Chancellor Helmut Kohl's Christian Democratic Union (CDU) and its sister party in Bavaria, the Christian Social Union (CSU), plus the Free Democratic Party (FDP), a victory in the East as well as the West, was first and foremost a positive referendum on Kohl's determined push toward unification and, second, on the coalition as the best manager of economic reconstruction. The German public gave Kohl high marks for seizing the moment of unification and negotiating it into reality with both the Soviet Union and Germany's western allies, especially the United States.

The electorate punished those parties who were not committed to unification—the Alliance '90/Greens—but even more profoundly the coalition's major opposition, the Social Democratic Party (SPD), which appeared divided and confused at the historic moment. Much of the former German Democratic Republic had been Social Democratic territory before 1945, but in 1990 it turned out that its citizens wanted that which was least like what they had for forty-five years, and so voted conservative.

For the SPD, the election results created a dilemma and signaled the need for change in the party, which faces a crisis of its political elite due to a problem of recruiting qualified new blood. Germany's economic success has eroded the SPD's working class base, and the party is run by activists who are less and less representative of the people. The appeal of its candidate for chancellor, Oskar Lafontaine, who suffered a near-tragic knife attack mid-campaign, was mostly limited to younger voters. Given the CDU's image as a solid economic manager, Lafontaine's pessimism about the economic travails of unification probably served to help the CDU more than his own party.

Both the Greens and the "Reds"—the former East German communists, renamed the Part of Democratic Socialism (PDS)—lost. Only some support from eastern Germany kept the Greens in the Bundestag, and the PDS got in because a special, one-time pre-election deal gave seats to any party that earned the 5 percent threshold in either East or West. On the right, the Republicans were erased from the Bundestag.

However, even on the heels of unification, the Christian Democratic vote was the party's weakest since 1949. The CDU came nowhere near achieving an absolute majority of the vote. One reason was distrust for Kohl's promise not to raise taxes to finance unification. But more important was the success of the other pro-unification party, Foreign Minister Hans-Dietrich Genscher's Free Democratic Party, which did well nationwide. Genscher, identified with the diplomacy of unification, ran well both in his native East and in the West. As in the past, a vote for the FDP represented a vote for continuity, but not for the CDU.

The vote for the CDU was more a retrospective affirmation of Kohl's stewardship of unification than a clear mandate for the future. What was for Germany a low election turnout—78 percent in the west and 75 percent in the east—may signal a certain political disillusionment among the electorate. The young generation, brought up on stories of his Gerald Ford- bumbling and less than piercing intellect, is skeptical about Kohl.

So, too, the tidiness of the result may be misleading. Economic turbulence, a backlash against immigration, and a stronger, more organized eastern Germany may break down coalition support. Poll results suggest that three-fifths of the German people see a future of hopes, the other two-fifths a future of fears.

For now, though, the SPD's role remains in question, and it represents no plausible threat, its turnaround yet uncertain. It holds out little temptation for the FDP to switch coalition partners again (the SPD and the FDP governed West Germany from 1969 until 1982). Moreover, the FDP remains the creature of Genscher and so its own future as a vote getter is constrained. In none of the parties is the new generation stepping into positions of leadership yet.

German Domestic Preoccupations

The most immediate issue facing the coalition government is economic reconstruction of eastern Germany. Salvaging former East Germany will be a drain on the German economy, its costs still largely incalculable. Each day brings higher estimates, as requirements for new telecommunications, roads, buildings, for agricultural and industrial rebuilding, and for social services become more apparent. It will be years before the exact costs of unification will be known.

Yet Germany's economy is strong—strong enough to be confident that the costs of unification can be met until the economy in eastern German begins to grow. At unification, Germany's GNP was 1.7 trillion dollars after eight years of economic expansion; its trade surplus was 80 billion dollars and private savings amounted to 140 billion dollars. Demand for western products by the East has already pushed up growth rates in former West Germany, and there is little doubt that united Germany will be a raging success in the long run. At some point, the deterioration in eastern Germany will reverse, to be followed by spectacular growth rates, perhaps approaching 10 percent. The question is when will this point be reached, in several years or longer?

If unification was a friendly takeover of the east at bargain-basement prices, the immediate burden of unification will nonetheless be heavy and will be felt both within Germany and outside. In Germany, financial pressure has already forced Kohl to renege on his virtual "read my lips" campaign promise. The first all-German budget included expenditures of 255 billion dollars with 50 billion dollars allocated to unification costs. The budget also included a tax increase of 31 billion dollars on personal and corporate income taxes, gasoline, and other sales taxes. The tax increase was blamed partly on German outlays for the Gulf War and for the Soviet Union, but the main culprit was unification.

If these tax hikes are not sufficient, the government may be compelled to cut back further on other public expenditures, including the social services to which Germans are now accustomed. Germany runs the risk of a Reagan-like economic cycle, with rising budget deficits and interest rates. Its fiscal deficit will increase from 30 billion dollars in 1990 to 45 billion dollars in 1991. Interest rates in Germany rose already earlier this year.

The most serious consequence will be rising unemployment in the East, where unemployed and forced short-time workers comprised more than one-fifth of the workforce in January 1991 according to official statistics. It will get worse before it gets better, and parity with western Germany in employment, not to mention income or living standards, is years away. Meanwhile, the East Germans' sense of being colonized by their western brethren grows, and emigration westward remains high. Protests have been breaking out throughout eastern Germany.

The impact of unification costs outside Germany will be mixed. Despite a high savings rate, German demands on the world's capital markets will be very high. Germany has been the second largest capital exporter after Japan. These exports will reverse as Germany's surplus is erased by its own internal spending; short-term capital exports fell dramatically in 1990 to 17 billion dollars from 67 billion dollars the year before. A continuation of this trend will put upward pressure on global interest rates, and leave open the question of who will finance the American deficit and provide needed capital to eastern Europe and the Soviet Union.

On the other hand, Germany's increased demand for imports from the rest of Europe and the United States, will stimulate those economies, reducing the existing German trade surplus and perhaps offsetting the deflationary impact of the slowdown in German capital exports. In January 1991, Germany's trade balance dropped to 800 million dollars—compared to a 6.8 billion dollars surplus a year ago—the result of strong demand in eastern Germany for everything from cars to clothes.

Americans and Europeans alike worry that Germany will become too inward-looking during this period of transition. Of particular concern is the impact of German unification—and the resulting fiscal and monetary policies—on European integration. Germany has been a leader in the European integration effort, and in the run-up to integration Bonn stressed that it would not be diverted from its European vocation.

Given the central role of the Deutschmark and the German *Bundesbank,* a critical index is European Monetary Unification (EMU). The European Community agreed on an ambitious plan for EMU in December 1990, but there were grounds for uncertainty about the timing of its implementation. The inflationary impact of reconstructing eastern Germany is bound to make the German government more inflation-phobic and the *Bundesbank* still less willing to share authority with other nations in a truly European central bank, or *Eurofed. Bundesbank* President Karl-Otto Poehl went public with these concerns in March 1991 and criticized the Kohl government's handling of German monetary unification in 1990 and thus arguing against any hasty move toward monetary union at the European level. . . .

Eastern Europe and Migration

Eastern Europe confronts a nest of problems—economic restructuring, democratization, and migration. The stability of democracy there is bound up with the success of economic reconstruction. If economies fail, a reversal to autocratic regimes cannot be ruled out. Nor can a reemergence of nationalities issues and ethnic problems. Germany, once the cold-war front line, is now the country on the frontier of Eastern Europe, and its role there raises similar questions about the strength of the European framework and the role of the United States.

How the European Community responds to the economies in Poland, Hungary, and Czechoslovakia is critical. Germany has taken the lead in supporting eastern Europe and is urging collective support by the European Community. The reach of the Community eastward raises the old debate over deepening versus widening. If the two are not necessarily mutually exclusive in principle, the practical questions are real. Should existing Community members press for deeper integration, beyond economic integration to monetary, political, and even security union before it widens by accepting new members?

In principle, deepening now could give the Community a stronger basis on which to widen later. While it is too early to talk about Eastern Europe's entry into the Community, an "association" with the Community could give these countries financial help, markets for exports, and incentives to remain on the path to democracy. So far, the European Community's Common Agricultural Policy (CAP) has been no more generous to agricultural imports from Eastern Europe than to those from any other parts of the world.

Economic conditions would be the main catalyst for massive migration from east to west—from eastern European countries and from the [republics of the former] Soviet Union. Germany is preoccupied with this prospect—especially with the three million ethnic Germans remaining in Eastern Europe and the Soviet Union. New immigrants will compound the existing strain. By year's end some four million former East Germans will be out of work while only about half a million new jobs a year are expected, and only half of those in the East.

Immigration is already a major issue in German domestic politics, an issue that is both divisive and sensitive. Currently, Germany's constitution grants liberal political asylum, and Germany will insist on retaining this policy. But the migration issue is now one of economic asylum. The FDP supports a liberal immigration policy, the CDU lacks the majority to set the agenda alone, and the position of the opposition is uncertain. This debate will take place against the background of the moral issue confronting all western nations, which have won an objective dear to them— the freedom of movement, the right to emigrate. The United States is used to granting economic asylum to East Asians and to Latin Americans—Germany is not. Freedom to emigrate does not necessarily mean the right for everyone to change citizenship. Yet, now that freedom to migrate has been won, the problem cannot be wished away.

Many countries are tempted to close their borders, erecting new borders now that those of the Cold War are down. . . . The United States may put up its own barriers. Shared problem solving is in short supply, as are innovative solutions. Talk of forestalling emigration by improving conditions in eastern Europe and the [former] Soviet Union only re-raises the question of how to accomplish this end.

GATT and the Gulf

Thinking about the post-cold-war world, and about German and American roles in it, has been sharpened by two recent episodes.

The latest round of GATT (General Agreement on Tariffs and Trade) negotiations aimed at opening the international system—dubbed the "Uruguay Round" because the meetings began in Punta del Este, Uruguay, in 1986—was scheduled to conclude at the end of 1990. Instead it collapsed. An impasse over agriculture was the most visible culprit. The United States has long objected to the European Community's agriculture policy as protectionist—a restraint on international trade—but in the past has yielded on the issue in exchange for European support on other trade questions.

This time Washington held firm. It judged the Community's negotiating proposal as meager: a 30-percent cut in overall farm supports over the ten-year period from 1986 to 1996 (and so only a 15-percent cut from 1991 to 1996), with no assurances on lowering export subsidies or providing access to its markets. The United States and other farm exporters wanted a 75-percent cut over ten years, with a 90-percent cut in export subsidies, but would have compromised, as a start, on 30-percent reductions in export subsidies and domestic supports over a five-year period. The talks ended abruptly on December 7, 1990, when the European Community reverted to its even less forthcoming original position.

The breakdown of the "Uruguay Round" seemed to confirm fears that economic issues will become more contentious as the shared imperative of security wanes. Americans, not least the Bush administration, seemed to feel Germany "owed" the United

States one on agriculture after the American role in unification. To them, Chancellor Kohl's failure to act represented a turn toward France and away from the United States. Perhaps Europe was turning toward its own interests at the expense of the United States.

Was Germany abandoning its role as the chief trans-Atlantic pillar of the Europe-American relationship? Americans were left fearing that the breakdown would abet its own temptations for more bilateral agreements and greater protectionism and pointing to Germany to take the lead in resurrecting GATT. The failure of GATT seemed a serious blow to multilateralism across the board, including in the Gulf where the Bush administration argued it was defending economic interests not only for the United States but for Europe as well. Would the United States be more wary of leadership sharing?

This American argument surprised many Germans, who thought the United States had put too much emphasis and pressure on agricultural issues. They cautioned against linking trade issues to other issues, like the Persian Gulf war, or allowing the GATT failure to contaminate German-American relations. The failure of GATT was not an act of defiance against the United States but more the result of overload in both Germany and the European Community. Germany was preoccupied internally, not up to a fight over the issue, either with its own farmers or with France. Clearly, trade friction is not a good omen. Both sides stand to lose if there is no movement on agricultural subsidies. But it is not the only or even the most important issue.

Still, the entire trading system may unravel. GATT negotiations have resumed, but some way of dealing with the agricultural issue is still needed, as well as attention to other outstanding Uruguay Round topics, like trade in services. Perhaps it is time to think of new forms of economic cooperation, from more explicit trilateral American-European-Japanese management to the Organization of Economic Cooperation and Development (OECD)—the score of most industrialized nations in the world—or even converting GATT into a global world trade organization, the hope of the late 1940s.

The Persian Gulf crisis, which began when Iraq invaded Kuwait on August 2, 1990, too, caught the German government off guard, leaving it to confront both constitutional and financial problems, all compounded by the symbolism of past German involvement in selling chemical and other lethal facilities to Iraq.

The timing could not have been worse, competing as it did with the immediate domestic pressures of unification and preoccupation with the upcoming German election. If there was an implicit "deal" it was that Germans thought at first that Germany would take care of eastern Europe and the Soviet Union while America would tended to the Gulf.

Belatedly, Germany recognized the importance of the Gulf, not least to George Bush who had staked his presidency on it, and provided significant financial assistance (nearly 11.4 billion dollars). Germany agreed to contribute 9.7 billion dollars in military hardware, services, and cash payments to the allied coalition and Israel, and 1.7 billion dollars in economic assistance to Egypt, Turkey, Jordan, and other neighboring Arab states. About 5.5 billion dollars were earmarked for the United States. Germany also sent Patriot missiles to Israel and Fox chemical warfare detection vehicles to the coalition in Saudi Arabia.

Bonn followed the United Nations resolution for a total embargo against Iraq and worked throughout the crisis to close remaining holes. Germany was also committed to the American presence in the Persian Gulf and was aware that military force was an option; it, like the other Europeans, gave Washington permission to use European bases and European-based troops for Gulf purposes. Indeed, Americans and Germans were somehow resigned to the fact that many American GIs who were sent to the Gulf would not resume their stationing in Germany after the war.

In early January 1991, Turkey, a NATO ally, asked for treaty protection against Iraq. Bonn/Berlin responded clumsily, treating its allies to a Bundestag debate over whether Iraqi Scud missiles were a threat under the NATO treaty and whether Turkey had somehow provoked the threat by letting coalition aircraft use its bases for attack on Iraq. In the end, though, Germany did send planes, eighteen Alpha jets with several hundred German personnel.

Fortunately the war ended quickly—just over a month after allied bombing raids began on January 16, 1991, with few casualties for the United States and the coalition. Had the war been longer and bloodier, there would have been more arguments in the United States Congress against spilling "American blood for European oil." There would have been more pressure on the awkwardness of Germany's position, past troublemaker as a source of technology for Iraq but present sitter on the sidelines.

The possibility of a military role "out of area" is a divisive issue for Germany. The constitution, which to an outsider would permit anything, has been interpreted to prevent German forces from being deployed outside German or NATO territory. Germany was also concerned about the consequences of military actions in the Gulf—the implications for regional security, for oil resources, and for Israel (especially if German soldiers were involved). The debate in Germany first pitted those opposed to any involvement by the German army, the *Bundeswehr,* outside Europe against those who would limit such a role to "blue helmets"—United Nations peacekeeping forces.

As with GATT, it would be a mistake to make the Gulf a litmus test of German-American relations or of Germany as a responsible new world power. Clearly, Germany will have to deal with the question of using forces out of area; the Kohl government seeks a role not limited to UN peacekeeping, one that might include, for instance, German contributions to a Western European Union force. But the issue could not have been resolved in the heat of the crisis, nor would it have made sense for the United States to have forced the Germans to accelerate their debate.

Germany cannot hide behind history, but the Gulf war occurred too soon for Germany to come up with a politically cohesive military response. Moreover, Germans have become accustomed to forty years of thinking of their country as the likely battleground; defending someone else was not a question. In the end, it probably would have suited no one to have German soldiers in the Gulf in large numbers.

For now, the Persian Gulf War probably raises more questions between Germany and its European partners than between Germany and the United States. Progress toward political and eventually security union will be slowed, and it was not moving fast before. Who in Britain or France would want to tie their country's policy to Germany's? At the same time, the European Community's failure to get together in the short run probably will increase pressure to do better in the long run. If the Community does not get its act together, the next crisis will be a replay of this one, with little European influence on American decisions but considerable American pressure on Europe to help out once decisions are taken.

Do GATT and the Gulf suggest that Germany and America are headed down a tit-for-tat path of litmus tests and escalating mistrust? The German connection is important to the United States, politically, economically, and militarily now more than ever, not least in building the new Europe. As interests and institutions in Europe are redefined, America will want influence in the process. Litmus tests and a bookkeeping mentality will not serve that purpose.

Reshaping European Security

In one sense, the Gulf crisis was a preview of coming events for European security. Western Europe is an island of stability in a sea of uncertainty. While Europe is militarily more stable because of the [absent] Soviet threat, economic instability could heighten political instability, immigration, and ethnic conflict, not only in the east but in the south as well. New military threats may emerge in the south—a nuclear Hussein, for instance. . . .

No new order in Europe will emerge full-blown soon, but some elements can be outlined. Western economic assistance will not make eastern Europe rich but can help smooth the transition to democracy by offering some hope. The European Community will serve as an incentive for good behavior by eastern European countries; it is a "club" to which those nations aspire but one whose prerequisites are democratic politics and peaceable foreign policies.

Arms control has an important role to play. . . . It needs to move to a wider forum that will include both the eastern Europeans, now that the [Warsaw] Pact is dead, and Europe's neutral countries as well. At the same time, this wider forum should not preclude a range of agreements that smaller groups of states may wish to make.

As Europe widens arms control and begins constructing pan-European collective security arrangements, the Conference on Security and Cooperation in Europe (CSCE) is a hopeful development, though still in embryo [. . . .] But no illusions should be harbored about its near-term effectiveness. It is no more than an embryo, despite last year's agreement in Paris to give it some institutional strength in conflict resolution and election monitoring. NATO remains as an insurance policy during the period of transition, perhaps a long one, and a building block toward a wider European security system.

It also seems time to think about fashioning a new bargain with regard to out-of-area issues. For their part, Europeans might do explicitly what they have tiptoed toward over the last decade: recognize NATO as a forum for such issues. In return, the United

States could commit itself to consultations that are real and signal its readiness to have the Europeans consult with each other first through the Western European Union or ultimately the European Community.

It would be a mistake for Germany to take a narrow approach to these issues in its internal debate. For now, Germany is a civilian nation with pacifist leanings (a product of history). But neither history nor position nor size will permit Germany to be a large Switzerland in the middle of Europe. Nor can Europe be a purely civilian power in a new world order. The Gulf war underscored that fact, as well as demonstrated the differences between Germany and its European partners, especially Britain and France.

For German, the task is to contemplate changing its constitution to permit actions under "blue helmet" or other collective security operations. The risk of not doing so is being marginalized in a new European security structure. For Germany's European partners and for the United States, the task is finding ways for Germany to take responsibility commensurate with its economic and political weight, ways that do not force questions on the German body politic that would be in no one's interest to see answered.

The United States has a continuing military role to play in Europe. Its troops are a stabilizer, and there seems to be consensus that some level of American military presence should stay in Germany. The United States also plays an important role in arms control. Building a new security order beyond the Cold War still calls for a close relationship between Europe and America, and Germany and America as well.

European Integration

The European Community will be central to America's European connection. Integration has made impressive progress in recent years, and, for all the doubts about European monetary unification, Germany is committed to the continuing process. By 1992, the European Community will be the defining force for economic activities in Europe, with monetary and political union at the top of the agenda.

As the member countries of the European Community develop common foreign economic policies—for instance with regard to eastern Europe and the [former Soviet republics]—they will inevitably begin to develop common foreign policies, whatever the direction of formal European political cooperation. Adding security to the Community agenda, at some point, will become inevitable in the course of further political cooperation.

Yet, today the Community is central business for no part of American officialdom, and consultation is haphazard despite recent agreements to improve it. The State Department concentrates on bilateral relations, Defense looks to NATO, the Treasury to the group of seven industrial countries. As security relationships decline, it is in American interest to further its relationship with the European Community, and Germany can play a central part in developing this partnership.

The Trans-Atlantic Connection

The Gulf and GATT, coming on the heels of German unification, have raised old questions about Germany's role. Will it turn inward, or toward Europe and away from the United States, or eastward?

All of these are possible. Yet, most likely Germany's orientation will remain fundamentally westward, with the trans-Atlantic connection an important element. More than 90 percent of the German economy is directed west and will remain so. Until 1990, less than 5 percent of the Federal Republic's trade was with eastern Europe and the Soviet Union; adding eastern Germany only increases this share to 10 percent, perhaps slightly more for a time. . . . Germany's largest companies are already "European." Soon this will be the case for medium-size companies as well. Nor is it in Germany's interest for economic reconstruction in eastern Europe and the [former] Soviet Union to be too much "made in Germany"—yet another shadow of history. Partners would certainly be welcome.

Germany will seek for some time a low profile and subordinate foreign policy to its domestic agenda. In part, that profile will be a response to residual fears of German militarism among its neighbors. To assuage these concerns, Germany seeks to define its global role within larger multilateral processes—the United Nations, the European Community, or CSCE. Unified Germany will become more assertive, and it may be given to bouts of tactlessness from time to time, but it is not now moving to become a "great power." Notice how quickly the subterranean fears of unified Germany on the march turned into criticism of Germany for doing too little during the Gulf war.

Germany will try to develop multiple "special" relationships, balancing its interests between the United States, Western Europe, Eastern Europe, and the [republics of the former] Soviet Union. This multifaceted approach to foreign policy is not, in the minds of most Germans, a means of avoiding choice but a means of exercising economic and political leverage across a broad range of German interests. However, to Germany's partners, not least the United States, the balancing act risks looking like a way of avoiding choices or even of weakening Germany's links westward.

German-American relations were so good during unification that they were bound to get worse. Expectations were high on both sides. The United States, for instance, wanted a unified Germany to take the lead in developing the European Community as a reliable partner for America; in reconciling European political integration and the Atlantic Alliance; in fashioning a new security order in Europe that would be compatible with NATO; and in reforming GATT.

The risk of a disconnection between the United States and Germany over what each expects of the other, a gap leading to disappointment and frustration, was there, and still remains. Each country has disappointed the other's expectation—the United States in its niggardly role in eastern Europe and the Soviet Union, Germany over the Gulf and GATT. Future progress over agriculture in GATT is bound to be less than the United States would like, and Germany's arguing over its constitutional limits is likely to produce ragged results. More fundamentally, the question of whether German and American interests in Eastern Europe are different, in intensity if not in kind, is still an open one.

In these circumstances, the watchwords for the future should be: Don't expect too much and especially do not turn expectations into litmus tests that then breed distrust. Germany is bound to be self-preoccupied, and the United States has its own domestic business to tend. The waning of the Soviet threat does diminish the need for close attention to defense arrangements, Saddam Hussein to the contrary notwithstanding. And so expectations can safely be diminished accordingly.

The Gulf and GATT also underscore the need for constant tending of the relationship—through private, public, and official channels—lest diverging expectations take on a life of their own in the respective domestic politics. When the Gulf crisis intervened, Bush's telephone calls turned to it and away from Germany. Germany's attention quickly turned as well, to problems closer to home. The two governments soon moved in very different directions, with sharply diverging expectations. By comparisons to German-American relations, the Anglo-American connection almost seems to tend itself.

DATELINE TASHKENT: POST-SOVIET CENTRAL ASIA[3]

At the end of the twentieth century, with a once-wide world shrunken into a global village, it seems astonishing that America should be called upon to establish relations with a virtually undiscovered region of the world. But following last year's breakup of the Soviet Union and the release of its Central Asian republics into the world political arena, the United States has encountered perhaps its biggest and least-known new diplomatic partner since Commodore Perry sailed into Tokyo Bay.

The steppes and deserts of Central Asia had been locked behind the walls of the Russian czarist and Soviet empires since around the time of the U.S. Civil War—long before America had become a power with global interests. Now America's interests in Central Asia's stable development are vital. The region holds vast energy resources as well as ex-Soviet nuclear weapons and facilities. Its stability will be important to the other former Soviet republics and its direction may greatly affect the Asian and Islamic worlds it is now rejoining.

Yet few Americans have considered a U.S. relationship with Central Asia. Many presume that the reportedly strong Islamic fundamentalist movement there and influence from neighboring Iran make it hostile territory for U.S. diplomacy. But there is no broad fundamentalist movement, and any hostility is largely imagined. Indeed, eight months of travel and interviews in the region, and discussions with U.S. specialists and diplomats, suggest that it is Washington rather than Central Asia that is unreceptive to a productive relationship.

[3]Article by James Rupert, assistant foreign editor at the *Washington Post*, from *Foreign Policy* 86:175–195 Summer '92. Copyright © 1992 by the Carnegie Endowment for International Peace. Reprinted with permission.

As a shorthand, it is useful to think of Central Asia as a region now beginning the processes of decolonization and nation building that have driven the turbulent politics of the Arab world since its independence in the decades following World War II. After more than a century of Russian rule, Central Asian Muslims face the same tasks as did the newly independent Arabs: They must define cultural and political identities scrambled by colonial power; choose from among Islamic and Western models of governance that they poorly understand; and manage internal conflicts once arbitrated by an outside ruler. They must especially meet the basic needs and rising expectations of impoverished, expanding populations. They face these challenges with authoritarian political systems rife with patronage and corruption and a shattered, dependent economy that is destroying the environment of the Aral Sea basin. While there is no strong Islamic political or "fundamentalist" movement now, the soil for such a movement is as fertile in Central Asia as it was earlier in Algeria, Jordan, Tunisia, and other countries where such movements now complicate movement toward liberal democracy. It is difficult to say how long the Central Asians have to make significant progress on the tasks they face before political desperation and radicalism set in.

In Central Asia, officials and citizens alike are eager for close relations with the United States; America could offer critical influence, resources, and technology. But Washington's attention to foreign affairs is substantially limited by an election-year rise in isolationism and stretched over a broadened range of difficult issues. Central Asia has no political constituency in the United States. The only voices that could draw attention to the region will be those of strategic thinkers and area specialists who understand its importance to U.S. interests. But, as numerous scholars and policy analysts have pointed out, the Bush administration tends to concentrate key foreign policy decisions at the top, muffling the voices of area specialists and limiting its own ability to work on important issues that are not in the headlines.

Even a rudimentary U.S. policy in Central Asia was delayed by Washington's unpreparedness for the Soviet collapse. As early as the mid-1980s, scholars on Soviet nationalities and Central Asia had hinted at the possible breakup of the Soviet union, but officials did not plan for it. When the collapse came, Washington acted reflexively, attempting to shore up Mikhail Gorbachev's position long after he had lost any realistic hope of keeping power, rather than recognizing and accommodating the aspirations of the republics.

In particular, Washington moved warily toward the six cultur-ally Islamic republics—five in Central Asia plus Azerbaijan across the Caspian Sea. It might have congratulated them on their inde-pendence and offered to open a broad relationship that would help them achieve their own aims while addressing a strategic, long-term U.S. agenda in the region. Instead, out of the six Mus-lim republics, the United States immediately recognized only two: Kazakhstan, the sole Central Asian republic with nuclear weap-ons; and Kyrgyzstan, the republic ostensibly most committed to reform. In a narrow opening seen by many in Central Asia as a condescending and vaguely biased against Muslims, Washington delayed establishing relations with the four remaining Muslim states, demanding their adherence to basic rules of international conduct, human rights, and democracy. While the intent may have been laudable, it ignored two points: The United States maintains relations with countries that routinely violate such rules; and America would ultimately have no choice but to estab-lish full relations in the region, if only to avoid leaving Iranian diplomacy uncontested. In February 1992, Secretary of State James Baker reversed the policy and settled for promises by the Azerbaijan, Tajik, Turkmen, and Uzbek leaders to observe the U.S. principles. Although his explanation to Congress—that the United States needed to open relations with these states because Iran was doing so—was forthright, it bolstered the message that the United States does not consider the Central Asian states im-portant in their own right. The State Department did manage to defuse the situation somewhat by scrambling to open embassies—two in hastily prepared hotel suites—in the republics.

Except for the Tajiks, who are ethnically Persian, the ex-Soviet Islamic belt is formed of Turkic peoples: Azeris, Kazakhs, Kyrgyz, Turkmens, Uzbeks, and others. The broadly uniform Turkic cul-ture and language that gave Central Asia its earlier name—Turkistan—was blended over a millennium from among the orig-inal nomadic Turks who migrated to Central Asia from the east, and the Arab, Persian, and Mongol conquerors who followed. Pre-Soviet Central Asia was a land of feudal or nomadic emirates whose people had little or no concept of political participation. The Soviet Union worked harder to remold the traditional Islam-ic societies it ruled than any of the European colonizers except perhaps the French in Algeria. Many of the changes that Moscow wrought deeply affect Central Asia's politics today.

Most significantly, Soviet policy firmly established the "nation-alities" into which Central Asia is now divided. In pre-Soviet

Turkistan, people had defined themselves primarily as Turkic or Tajik Muslims, identities that could have permitted the evolution of a unified polity across the region. The Soviets sought to prevent that by establishing five Central Asian republics, forcing on each a distinct "national" language and culture. It appears that strategy was a success. In hundreds of interviews in recent months, both city and village dwellers have expressed loyalty to their supranational identities as Muslims or Turks and to local identities of clan or region, but most often they have made clear that their strongest sense of affiliation is with their "national" group. National identities may have grown partly from the "national cultures" of literature and folklife that Moscow promoted to applaud and justify its rule, but mainly because each republic has become an institution serving a constituency within which it has built common interests.

Pan-Turkism, the idea that the Turkic peoples stretching from Turkey to the Xinjiang region of China must develop their common destiny, is a cultural force but has no visible future as a regional political movement. It is most popular among the more than 16 million ethnic Uzbeks, who would dominate any unitary Turkic structure in Central Asia. Turkic political unity would threaten the Russians who dominate northern Kazakhstan; therefore Kazakhs shy away. The roughly 4 million (non-Turkic) Tajiks and the Kyrgyz and Turkmens (each group with about 2.5 million people) would fear being swallowed up.

Islamic Revival

Recent reports suggesting that the vital factor in Central Asia is rising Islamic "fundamentalist" power, perhaps with Iranian or Saudi support, are simply not correct. Central Asia's Islamic revival is an indigenous movement and more cultural than political. The region's essential problem is that the Soviet collapse has left it with great aspirations but without political institutions for expressing them or a political model within which to pursue them. The Islamic revival rises from the Central Asians' most powerful aspiration: to assert the identities that Moscow suppressed for decades. Mainly, the revival does not seek state power; most people at newly crowded mosques and Islamic bookstalls say they seek Islamic influence in government by electing "good Muslims" rather than by installing a theocracy.

In 1991 and early 1992, Iran, Pakistan, and Saudi Arabia

sought to influence the revival. But their roles are new and, given that revived nationalist feelings also spring from Central Asia's search for identity, their prospects seem limited. Saudi Arabia made the most obvious efforts, receiving the senior Central Asian clerics on pilgrimages and donating cash, computers, and Korans to the clerics' hierarchies, or "spiritual boards." Those institutions, once Soviet controlled but now largely independent of republic governments, seem focused on training mullahs, building mosques and Islamic schools, and improving people's hazy and rudimentary understanding of the Islamic faith.

Iran's visible diplomacy has been cautious. It has sent trade delegations and opened embassies in an apparent effort to build a broad relationship. Nongovernmental organizations have sent Korans, but diplomats have avoided statements that could be construed as having direct religious content. Officers of Central Asian security organs and Western intelligence reports allege Iranian financial support for some Central Asian groups with nationalist-Islamicist aims. While that support is likely, it has not yet manifested itself in either the strengthening of such groups or expressions by them of loyalty to Tehran. Pakistan has offered positions in religious colleges to Central Asian student mullahs, and delegations of mullahs and lay leaders from India, Libya, Malaysia, and Pakistan have visited local congregations.

Islam's revival has already sprouted grassroots political movements that will recruit the disaffected if Central Asian governments fail to meet basic aspirations. Such movements now find mass support only in Tajikistan and the Fergana Valley, which is divided among Kyrgyzstan, Tajikistan, and Uzbekistan. Tajikistan's Islamic Renaissance party mobilized thousands of people during anticommunist street demonstrations in fall 1991 and spring 1992; and Central Asia's most locally powerful Islamic political movement is in the Fergana Valley. There, in Uzbekistan's Namangan province, an organization called *Adalat* (Justice) seeks to enforce Islam-inspired law in villages and neighborhoods with religious remonstration, social pressure, and brute intimidation. For now, secular rule is well-rooted in Central Asia, and the Islamic movement suffers splintered leadership and a lack of institutions. But Islamic political activists already challenge government in Fergana and Tajikistan—and 5 or 10 years may well permit the development of an institutional Islamic rival for power there. If a generation is left frustrated by a failure of the secular model, all of Central Asia will likely face a challenge like that in Algeria today, 30 years after its independence.

Violence in Central Asia is manifested regularly in riots and ethnic clashes. Rather than springing from religious militancy, though, violence has generally occurred where economic frustration—often from price rises or lack of land, housing, or water—has coincided with ethnic tensions. Such violence is never far from the surface in the Fergana Valley, where Uzbeks clashed with minority Meskhetian Turks in June 1989, killing at least 100 and forcing the evacuation of more than 16,000. In June 1990, Uzbeks and Kyrgyz fought over land rights in the Fergana Valley city of Osh, killing more than 200, and villages in the valley have also fought repeatedly over water rights. Residents of Dushanbe, the capital of Tajikistan, also rioted in 1990 following rumors that refugees from the Armenian earthquake were to be given apartments while Tajiks continued to suffer a housing shortage.

Economic dissatisfaction is intensified by the universal realization that life is better elsewhere. Soviet Tajiks and Uzbeks, for example, appear more attuned to the outside world than do their respective ethnic brethren in northern Afghanistan. Generations of Central Asians have seen the broader world through Soviet education and military service. The electronic revolution has brought pirated tapes of Michael Jackson and Madonna to urban bazaars. Possibly the best-known American among young boys is Arnold Schwarzenegger, whose boot-legged movies are played at ubiquitous "video salons." While governments that won independence in the 1950s or 1960s may have had mass populations that knew only of their traditional, village-based lives, Central Asians' glimpses of foreign affluence are likely to accelerate demands for change.

One frequent burden of decolonizing economies, rapid urbanization, has not yet begun in Central Asia. Thus far, the rural population seems firmly rooted and little inclined to flock to cities in a way that has produced impoverished, politically explosive shantytowns in many African, Asian, and Arab countries.

The political structures that must start meeting the Central Asians' aspirations are, for the most part, repainted communist bureaucracies. For decades those bureaucracies implemented Moscow's policies while they also discreetly struggled for power in what resembled a guerrilla war. With overweening force at its command, Moscow was able to win battles over who would govern and how; but it could not prevent local elites from building political patronage machines on the basis of regional, tribal, or clan ties. Those political machines largely remain in power.

The collapse of the Soviet Union was a European event, driven mostly by Balts and Russians and, finally, by the voters of Ukraine. In the European republics, the people forced political change from below with what became mass demands for national sovereignty and democratic participation. In the culturally Muslim republics, political change has typically been demanded only by small groups of intellectuals who have almost never been able to generate mass followings. The one notable exception is outside Central Asia, in Azerbaijan, where the Popular Front built a fractious yet powerful coalition that forced the government to take a tough, nationalist stance insisting on continued control over Nagorno-Karabakh, the predominantly Armenian enclave controlled by Azerbaijan.

While Europeans escalated attacks on the very legitimacy of the Soviet government, the leaders of the Muslim republics sought only to use Moscow's weakness to assert nationalist claims—control over resources and a greater degree of national identity—that they had long sought from the center. But they also fought to maintain the Soviet structures, which preserved their power as apparatchiks, cradled their dependent economies, and provided a bargaining table at which to regulate their relations with the dominant Russians. The non-apparatchik exception was Kyrgyzstan president Askar Akayev, a physicist who unexpectedly came to power amid a feud between factions of the Communist party. Aside from Akayev and Kazakhstan's Nursultan Nazarbayev, Central Asian leaders showed at least qualified support for the August 1991 hard-line Communist coup attempt. When the coup's collapse doomed the Soviet structure, leaders of five of the six Muslim republics simply abandoned it, claiming political legitimacy as spokesmen for national independence, or as the only people who could maintain order. (Nazarbayev could not call for Kazakh secession from even the lame-duck USSR for fear that the ethnic Russians who dominate Kazakhstan's northern regions would themselves secede.) Central Asia's leaders have sought to legitimate themselves through popular elections, few of which (except in Tajikistan) had attributes of democratic voting or were viably contested.

As in all the former Soviet republics, the bureaucracies of the Central Asian states have little experience in responding to popular will or mobilizing popular support for policies. While the republics' leaders have met some popular demands for a reassertion of traditional and national identities, they will not be able to rejuvenate their economies without giving up essential levers of power, such as state ownership of land and industry. Even where top leaders are pressing for rapid privatization, as in Kazakhstan, entrenched elites within the administrative apparat have impeded implementation or directed new business opportunities to their relatives and political clients. Official corruption has worsened as the collapse of central Soviet authority removed the main control on republic-level officials.

The economic development required for political stability will be complicated by booming populations—more than 3 per cent annual growth in many areas—and a disastrous environmental legacy. Ignoring the fact that the Aral Sea is a closed, finely balanced watershed, Moscow designated the regions surrounding the Syr Darya and Amu Darya as a vast cotton plantation. Even nature was forced to yield to the plan. By diverting the two rivers to irrigation, the Soviets dried up their flow to the sea. Environmental specialists offer no hope for restoring the Aral Sea in the foreseeable future or even for halting its shrinkage. Windblown salt from vast stretches of exposed seabed has ruined farmland. In over-irrigated regions, rising water tables carry underground salts to the surface, with the same effect. Irrigation runoff, rich with fertilizers and pesticides, serves as drinking water for rural populations. High rates of typhoid, hepatitis, and throat cancer result. Near the Aral, mothers' milk is contaminated with pesticides and infant mortality is shockingly high—roughly 100 deaths per 1,000 births.

Central Asia must reduce its population of cotton, one of the chief sources of its hard currency, to grow enough food to feed itself and to help free water to allow recovery of the environment and economic development. Unfortunately, one of the most logical replacement crops for impoverished farmers will be opium— especially since corrupt officials, inaccessible terrain, and nearby borders will offer prime conditions for hiding and moving narcotics.

In de-Sovietizing Central Asia's economy, industries—which are concentrated in Kazakhstan—will suffer most because of their gross inefficiency and the need in many cases simply to abandon them. Unemployment was already severe in Central Asia during the 1980s and is growing. It appears to be worst in Fergana, and it can hardly be a coincidence that that valley has been the most consistent scene of violence. Central Asia's education and job-training systems were the poorest in the Soviet Union, so many of its unemployed are also undereducated. The shortage of skills has intensified as tens of thousands of relatively skilled European minorities—Germans, Jews, Russians, Ukrainians—have been leaving to escape nationalist tensions.

It has been in economic relations that Central Asia has most enthusiastically embraced its southern neighbors. While all ex-Soviet republics are desperate for development capital and any kind of productive trade, Central Asia has little hope of substantial help from the West except in the extraction of oil, gas, selected minerals, and cotton. Asian countries are not the economic engines that the West is, but Asian firms outnumber Western ones in the region, investing in tourism, cotton, leather processing, and other light industries. India, Iran, Pakistan, South Korea, and Turkey have actively sought business, hosting Central Asian presidents and trade groups. Notably, Japan for the most part has kept its distance from Central Asia, as it has from the rest of the former Soviet economy.

With budget pressures and competing demands on U.S. foreign policy, it is unrealistic to expect significant new aid for a region that lacks a political constituency in Washington. But the United States can play an important though relatively inexpensive role in promoting Central Asian stability.

The first requirement for such a role will be to respond to the basic aspirations all Central Asians share: full stature as states, practical independence, and economic development. An effective policy must express these aspirations as central goals, rather than suggesting condescendingly that America's main concern is to block the influence of Iran. Such a policy should understand that the Central Asians will naturally seek relations with Iran as a neighbor, just as two long-time U.S. allies, Pakistan and Turkey, have done for years.

Within a broad relationship stressing the Central Asians' goals, the United States should also promote its own interests. For the foreseeable future, the primary interest will be a sustainable stability that can allow an impoverished, fractious region to begin implementing economic development and political pluralism. That, of course, must go beyond the brittle stasis of conservative ex-communist bureaucracies keeping control through renamed Communist parties and KGBs. Along with those general principles, the United States will have particular interests and face particular challenges in each republic.

Uzbekistan. With close to 20 million people, most of the troubled Fergana Valley, and a border on each of the other Central Asian states, Uzbekistan will be the key to the region's stability. Largely because of Fergana, however, its stability is fragile.

Uzbek politics is a contest among five regions—Fergana, Khorezm, Samarkand/Bukhara, Surkhandarya/Kashkadarya, and Tashkent—with Fergana and Tashkent the most powerful. President Islam Karimov, from Samarkand, appears to balance the regional rivals within the former Communist party (now the People's Democratic party), which retains power as it did under Soviet rule: through patronage, repression, and price controls. Karimov stresses Uzbek nationalist symbolism but also wins support from the 11 per cent Russian minority by casting himself as the man to assure their continued security in the republic.

Karimov has expressed a desire to follow the Turkish economic and secular model, but he has had to be pushed by Tashkent elites seeking economic liberalization. Privatization of land and business has been limited. Direct American economic interests in Uzbekistan for the near future will probably be limited to cotton trade and possibly oil and gold extraction.

Karimov has allowed only symbolic political freedom in legalizing the Erk Democratic party, an intellectual-based opposition party as yet too small to challenge him. Birlik, which has (but may not control) mass political support in the Fergana Valley, and the Islamic Renaissance party, whose strength is unclear in Fergana but negligible elsewhere, are repressed. Tashkent cannot prevent opposition rallies in Fergana, however, and occasionally it has had to rely on clerics, headed by the Tashkent mufti, to help dampen periodic violence there.

Kazakhstan. With 16.5 million people, weapons facilities, nuclear missile bases, and large fossil fuel and mineral deposits, Kazakhstan is the other heavyweight of Central Asia. It is also the most distinct republic. Islam, which served for more than a millennium as a cement for the other Central Asian Muslim societies, is diluted among Kazakhs, who as nomads preserved traditional animism and ancestor worship almost intact until about 200 years ago. While Kazakhs regard themselves as Muslims, Islam must compete with their nomadic and Mongol culture and value systems. Kazakh society remains divided along regional and clan lines. Northern Kazakhstan is mostly Russian, the south mainly Kazakh.

With a delicate ethnic balance of around 40 per cent Russians and a nearly equal number of Kazakhs, Kazakhstan forms a political and cultural bridge between Russia and the core of Central Asia. President Nazarbayev envisions building Kazakhstan's economy largely as Russia's bridge to China and East Asia, and has begun reopening rail, road, and air links to China. The tie to China is political, too: A million Kazakhs live in Xinjiang, and more than 185,000 Uighurs, the main ethnic group of Xinjiang, live in Kazakhstan, where they are permitted to press quietly for Xinjiang's independence. While Nazarbayev is a pragmatist who understands the need to accommodate varied groups and permit at least formal political activity, it is not clear that he holds solid democratic convictions. He has kept the formerly communist administrative apparat largely intact, citing the danger of instability if he were to uproot it quickly—but in so doing he has allowed his economic reforms to be weakened.

Nazarbayev is backed by Russian and Kazakh political groups as an honest broker who condemns militant nationalism. He quit the Communist party and has encouraged the registration of numerous, though minor, political groups. Fears of ethnic conflict remain, however, in part simply out of recognition of the disastrous effects such conflict would have on Kazakhstan. There has been virtually no political melding of the two communities.

Although he has used missiles as bargaining chips to enhance Kazakhstan's position with Russia, Nazarbayev's commitments to secure Kazakh nuclear systems initially met with American approval. Still, in April 1992 the Bush administration declined to certify Kazakhstan as eligible for U.S. aid for dismantling nuclear arms following conflicting Kazakh public statements about the disposition of those weapons.

U.S. economic interests could grow with U.S. oil firms helping in the development of Kazakh oil fields, and Kazakhstan's considerable mineral wealth could draw Western investment. Encouraging stability in Kazakhstan will necessitate discouraging conflict between Russians and minority Muslims within Russia, a possibility that appeared likely in late 1991 when Russian president Boris Yeltsin seemed ready to crack down on Muslim separatists in the North Caucasus.

Kyrgyzstan. Kyrgyzstan will likely be the most important to the United States as a model of the possibilities of democratic, pro-Western development for the rest of Central Asia. Islam was adopted late by the nomadic Kyrgyz, so its influence is limited, although it is stronger in the Fergana Valley in southern Kyrgyzstan than in the rest of the country. A relatively tolerant tradi-

tion, an ethnically European population that constitutes a quarter
of its 4.3 million population, and President Akayev's commitment
to democracy have helped contribute to what is Central Asia's
most vigorous democratic movement. But the Kyrgyz-European
divide also poses the greatest threat to democratization as Kyrgyz
nationalist sentiment grows and minorities flee. Akayev tries to
mitigate conflict by balancing political appointments among regional, ethnic, and political groups.

After the August 1991 coup attempt, which also threatened
his ouster by hard-line Communists in Bishkek, Akayev banned
the party and seized its property, ending its political role. He has
gone further than any other Central Asian leader in attacking the
power of old elites, reforming local government bodies, and even
ordering the government to cede control over the press.

Economically, Kyrgyzstan is even more dependent on its
neighbors than other republics—it does not even have an oil re-
finery, for example. More than any other Central Asian leader,
Akayev has pushed for land reforms, claiming in February 1992
that half of his country's farms had been privatized or converted
into cooperatives. Kyrgyzstan has been aligned with Kazakhstan
and Russia and more distant from more conservatively communist Uzbekistan, Tajikistan, and Turkmenistan.

Turkmenistan. Central Asia's most politically primitive republic, Turkmenistan will have the longest road to any form of democratic pluralism. Power is concentrated in the hands of the Teke,
the largest of the republic's three main tribes whose rivalry forms
the basis of political contest. President Saparmurad Niyazov is
highly Russified and was educated in Moscow. His wife is Russian
and his children speak Russian rather than Turkmen, facts that
contribute to disapproval among many Turkmens who feel that
Niyazov is a cultural outsider. His administration still relies heavily on Russian bureaucrats and the republic holds many ex-Soviet
troops and sensitive military installations. Repression here is the
tightest in the region: Two tiny, secular opposition groups are
banned, and their members are periodically arrested or harassed.

Like Kyrgyzstan, Turkmenistan is one of the most economically primitive republics and is thoroughly dependent on Russia.
But considerable gas resources and its small (3.5 million) population offer it more hope than others have for quick economic
development that might reduce poverty and promote the stability
necessary for political change. Although Turkmenistan has
turned to neighboring Iran for help with gas development, it

would welcome a U.S. role. Few Turkmens see Iran's Shiite theocratic regime as an appropriate model for development. Further, Iran has neither particular influence nor a good popular image in Turkmenistan, largely because of longstanding conflicts between Turkmens and Iranians and because Tehran's relations with its own Turkmen minority are difficult.

Tajikistan. Tajikistan (population 5.1 million) is the most immediately unstable republic. Many young, unemployed village men are deeply traditional and impressed by the symbolism of Iran's Islamic revolution. They demonstrated in fall 1991 and spring 1992 for the ouster of the ruling Communists. Their protests appeared to be succeeding in early May as a coalition of nationalist, Muslim, and reformist groups was gaining power in Dushanbe at the expense of Communist president Rakhman Nabiyev.

Tajikistan, like Fergana, was a center of the anti-Soviet Basmachi guerrilla movement during the 1920s and 1930s. That history indicates a fierce adherence to tradition and resistance to cultural imports—one that has helped form the base for an Islamic political movement in the two regions. Tajikistan's most visible element of this movement is the Islamic Renaissance party (IRP), whose factions seek a *shariat*-ruled Islamic state but dispute how far to cooperate with the more moderate mufti, or senior clerics. Mufti Akbar Turadzhonzada is a leading Tajik political personality. He tells foreigners that he wants a structurally secular, spiritually Islamic state that adheres to international human rights standards. He cites Iran's violation of those standards and its political isolation from the West as mistakes to avoid. But he does not mention that vision publicly to the Islamic movement, which would firmly oppose it.

Nabiyev, a Communist leader from the Brezhnev era, had won what appeared to be rather free elections in November 1991 despite broad signs of his unpopularity. The victory illustrated the fears among European residents of an opponent backed by the IRP and the Tajik nationalist movement, Rastokhez—fears likely to be worsened by the May uprising.

Regional rivalries—born of the topography of isolated valleys—form the basis of Tajik politics. The Fergana Valley region of Khodzhent (formerly Leninabad) has dominated the power structure since the advent of Soviet rule. In the rest of Tajikistan, across a mountain divide, residents, including those of Dushanbe, have expressed resentment at what they feel is underrepresentation.

Tajiks view Iranian culture as a major resource for the strengthening of their own identity, one different from that of their Turkic neighbors. Yet, relations with Iran are ambivalent: Tajikistan's Sunni religious leaders express wariness of Iran's Shiism and have strained relations with their own Shiite minority.

No matter what direction political changes in Afghanistan now take, many Tajiks will continue to worry about possible efforts by militant Afghan fundamentalists to export their ideas. *Mujahedeen* guerrillas in recent years crossed into Tajikistan, sometimes with Islamic literature for distribution. The Tajik KGB has charged the *mujahedeen* with armed subversion, but there has been no independent evidence of significant arms flows. Tajikistan has an interest in close security ties with Russia, both for help to secure the Afghan border and as a counter to its Turkic neighbors.

The main U.S. interest in Tajikistan will be a return to political stability, under continuing threat from the republic's cultural, regional, and economic divisions. The United States also will want to ensure that the deeply corrupt bureaucracy does not seek to profit by producing opium or selling uranium supplies.

Throughout Central Asia, direct tools of U.S. policy will, of course, be limited. Currently available bilateral aid funds will have to be targeted carefully. Particularly useful U.S. roles might include providing technology and skills—especially in dry-land agricultural techniques such as drip-irrigation—that could reduce water use and help farmers shift from cotton production to a more balanced agriculture. Vocational and rural health education and water management reform require basic, low-level technology assistance that might be provided by the Peace Corps. One of Central Asia's most critical needs is to train experts who can play central roles in the transition to market economies and democratic political systems. Unmatched U.S. capacities in higher education could be especially helpful.

Perhaps the most obvious single U.S. policy instrument in Central Asia is Radio Liberty. In casual conversation, Central Asians cite the U.S.-funded service often enough to make clear that it is a major source of news about their own countries. Central Asian presidents, groping to understand the international arena in which they now work, have sought advice from their compatriots at Radio Liberty. The station is becoming a surrogate journalism institute for the former Soviet Union, training reporters from the republics at its Munich headquarters. Although Radio Liberty has faced temporary staffing inadequacies, increasing its broadcasts to Central Asia could be a relatively low-cost way to promote the stability and development that serve U.S. interests.

Given the limits on its foreign aid, Washington will have to encourage its European and Asian partners to take leading roles. Germany and South Korea have a special interest in aiding Central Asia because more than a million ethnic Germans and roughly half a million ethnic Koreans live there. The two communities were deported there from the Volga region and the Soviet Far East during World War II because Stalin distrusted them. Germany has already begun an aid program to encourage ethnic Germans to remain in Kazakhstan rather than emigrate to Germany.

Regional powers can also play constructive roles in Central Asia. The State Department seems to have heeded suggestions to promote Turkey's role in the region. Turkey's market economy and relatively democratic system can serve as a model, and its natural ethnic and cultural links to the Turkic peoples assures its interest. India's large economy, experience with the former Soviet Union, and technical skills can offer investment and development expertise. Russia should be encouraged to keep those roles that are consonant with the Central Asians' own interests, but the United States should be especially careful to not be seen as encouraging vestiges of Russia's Soviet-era "big brother" role, supervising its former colonies.

The Arab states along the Persian Gulf are particularly interested in helping their fellow Muslims in the former Soviet Union—and most of their aid appears targeted at religious development. A creative policy might seek their help in a multilateral Western-Islamic effort to provide aid and investment to address basic Central Asian economic and health problems. Such cooperation might mitigate unconstructive arguments that an inevitable and universal conflict exists between the Western and Islamic worlds, or that the two must scramble to control Central Asia's future. Recent American oped page discussions have even suggested that such a conflict might replace the Cold War as a crusade around which American foreign policy can define itself. Such a thrust to U.S. policy would be disastrous; Americans must understand that it is possible to encourage democracy in the Islamic world without casting themselves as enemies of Islam.

One effect of seeking partners is that many other U.S. policies indirectly become more relevant to Central Asia. Anything America does to enhance stability in Russia, democracy in Pakistan and Turkey, or economic liberalization in India is useful in Central Asia. So, of course, is any step to moderate Iran. The single most important element of indirect policy—especially for Tajikistan— will be efforts to stabilize Afghanistan. The Afghan war has provided a bazaar of weapons and a source of instability on Central Asia's borders, and it has blocked what is, for much of Central Asia, the most direct route to a warm-water port.

The first challenge for a constructive U.S. role in Central Asia will be to bring American attention to the region. That is hampered by a mood of isolationism and by a unique sense of futility about dealings with the Islamic world. The cycles of America's frustration and trauma in the Islamic Middle East collectively haunt U.S. policymakers as nothing else since the Vietnam war. Living room images of hostages, hijackings, and bomb wreckage have forged the attitudes of a generation of Americans. Most probably fail to understand the extent of the U.S. role in fostering the rage behind such violence and assume it is characteristic of Islam. Since most Americans have difficulty distinguishing among Muslims, the frustrations of Iran and Lebanon will obscure the potential prospects of Kazakhstan and Kyrgyzstan.

The case for U.S. attention to Central Asia will be made by foreign policy specialists rather than by public forces. Even within the American foreign policy and scholarly communities, though, only a relative handful specialize in Central Asia. They will need allies from the larger circle of specialists on the Arab and Islamic worlds. They also will need to gain the attention of key decision makers. Their difficulties were underlined by the December 1991 resignation of Paul Goble as State Department special adviser on Soviet nationalities and Baltic affairs, who, despite being the only prominent Central Asia specialist in a key policy position, expressed frustration at the lack of attention given to such issues.

Precisely because the world has become so small, the United States must attend to the troubled lands of Central Asia: vast, nuclearized, rich in resources yet mired in poverty. Political leadership must not ignore them, even if the popular mood does. America remains the worldly power; Central Asia is the long-isolated newcomer. But unlike Commodore Perry's arrival in Japan, it is now Asians who knock and Americans who must answer.

WHY NOT TRY DEMOCRACY?[4]

Hidden and neglected amid the fanfare of the Yeltsin team's ascension to power following the failed coup . . . has been a startlingly expeditious shift in the thinking of Russia's new rulers. The leaders and ideologues of the self-described democratic movement, many of whom now occupy government posts in the Russian federation, ardently defended the separation of powers [not too long] ago. But now that they are in power their perspective is changing. After years of criticizing the slogan "All Power to the Soviets," they now proclaim "All Power to Us."

A newborn faith in executive power—and a concomitant skepticism of the legislature—is found everywhere, from the Russian President's office down to the sprawling government bureaucracies to the unmanageable offices of city mayors and Yeltsin's appointed representatives in the provinces. Elected representative bodies have either been disbanded to the jeers of the public, as was the case with the U.S.S.R. Congress of People's Deputies and the Supreme Soviet, or turned into the butt of jokes, as were the Moscow and Leningrad city councils.

The passion for executive dominance seems to be the fulfillment of Russian political scientist Andranik Migranian's controversial argument of two years ago that authoritarian rule was "unavoidable during the transition from totalitarianism to democracy" and essential for the transition to a market economy. The idea fell on fertile soil and is gradually becoming received wisdom among the new "democratic" establishment in Russia. As people become increasingly disenchanted with the newly elected legislatures, these ideas gain wider currency.

Elected bodies in Russia have provided ample reasons for disillusionment: In adopting reforms they have been paralyzed by constant bickering over procedural points and always ready to amend or disregard laws at the behest of those in command. Despite these inadequacies, however, to call them obstacles to change stands recent history on its head. In the Gorbachev era the Russian Parliament's reforms were obstructed by opposition

[4]Article by Tatyana Vorozheikina, senior researcher at the Institute of World Economy and International Relations in Moscow, from *The Nation* 254:594–596 May 4 '92. Copyright © 1992 by The Nation Company, Inc. Reprinted with permission.

from central and local government agencies, not from local legislatures or soviets. The resistance came from the Communist Party, industrial managers and administrative functionaries at various levels.

Less than a month after the coup attempt Yeltsin's chief aide,
Gennadi Burbulis, let the Russians know that their elected representatives would no longer be needed. "Most representative bodies have become a hindrance to our reforms," he announced on
government television. "These bodies were needed to destroy the
totalitarian system but now they have accomplished their mission.
Russia hungers for a vertical power structure," a vertical chain of
command to "enforce the President's will and policies." The ultimate goal was to "eliminate opposition to the President in the
executive branch of government."

Yeltsin and his aides argued that local governors should be
appointed rather than elected so that the "right people" would be
installed. "The uncertainty about the election's results in some
regions requires appointment as the only possible procedure under the circumstances," wrote People's Deputy Stepan Sulakshyn
in *Izvestia*. Thus an ideological rationale to clothe the bare "logic
of power" was being woven. The Russian Congress approved an
amendment recommending that Yeltsin remove his handpicked
local administrators. "In all times, in all countries, drastic reforms
and reformist breakthroughs were effected only by reasonably
authoritarian leaders. Never have societies transformed themselves at a time of flourishing parliamentary systems," argued
Yeltsin adviser Sergei Stankevich.

It would be wrong to ignore the real problems behind these
strikingly frank statements. The Russian Congress of People's
Deputies has been, until [early 1992,] an ineffective body that
stalled the adoption of many urgently needed laws, and local
executive authorities have often obstructed their implementation. The disintegration of the old Communist system brought
about the collapse of the government hierarchy that had constituted the backbone of the state and society. There is now chaos
because a civil society and market economy regulated by law have
not yet been put in place. But attempts to create a new vertical
power structure with a strong executive at the top, unchecked by
legislative and judicial restraints, can lead only to the revival of
the old statist mechanisms of power under a new name. There is
no other system of authority to hold this amorphous society together.

The proposals for a new authoritarianism are doomed to failure. The central government has been too successfully presented as the main culprit for the population to welcome enthusiastically a revival of it by Yeltsin's appointees. Attempts to rule by force would only further destabilize the situation. The clearest example of this is the attempt by Russian authorities to place a Yeltsin appointee in control of the Chechen-Ingush autonomous region and declare the presidential elections were illegal. The result was the consolidation of the opposition around Chechen President Gen. Dzokhar Dudayev and further destabilization in the already precarious Caucasus region.

Paradoxically, it is decentralization that could become a key element in the strengthening of civil authority in Russia. Decentralization is not synonymous with disintegration; indeed, disintegration is the consequence of the supercentralization that suppressed all other mechanisms of self-regulation in society. To create a new political fabric and therefore a stable authority, the development of self-government from below, even with its inevitable risks and mistakes, is necessary.

It is difficult, of course, to face the messy reality that elections may bring to power not only the "right guys" in the eyes of democratic leaders but some "bad guys" as well. Representative government—fully enfranchised legislative and judicial bodies and elected executive bodies—is the only thing that can make society responsible for the power wielded in its name. In the long term this path will also eliminate the deeply ingrained and essentially destructive opposition to all authority that flourished in the former U.S.S.R.

The advocates of authoritarianism believe that central control is essential for the establishment of a market economy, which in turn is the key in their eyes to the creation of a successful civil society and democracy. They support this contention by pointing to countries, from Chile to Singapore and South Korea, that employed authoritarian methods to modernize their economies successfully, thereby laying the groundwork for democracy. But the governments of Singapore and South Korea are far from democratic. The return to democracy in Chile resulted not from Pinochet's authoritarian economic modernization but from the deep-rooted democratic tradition in the country, which had had one of the most European political systems in Latin America. Besides, the experience of other countries isn't necessarily relevant to Russia. There is no guarantee that an authoritarian regime would be willing to create a market economy. What motives would it have to overcome the inertia of state power built up over decades? Would the pro-market views of the present political leaders be any more long-lived than their democratic beliefs? Can we really expect that, driven by the ironclad logic of expediency, especially amid chaos and disintegration, they would not grasp the old familiar administrative levers? Wouldn't it be safer, and more beneficial to the market economy itself, to preserve the representative checks that have already started to erode the market-hostile monopoly on power of the former state institutions?

On the other hand, it is pious faith in the market that underlies the current "authoritarian-democratic" aspirations, including the desire to prevent the election of local governors. Today, they argue, the people are "wrong" and they will not elect "us." Therefore, let us appoint "our" people to carry out "our" reforms and install a market economy. Once this is in place a middle class will emerge, and then "we" will be able to hold elections because the people will make the right choice and elect "us."

The proponents of the new authoritarianism make a familiar and notorious claim to a monopoly on truth. There is a striking affinity between their interpretation of the middle class and the "new man" we were trying to develop during one stage in the construction of Communism. But there are more fundamental weaknesses with their arguments.

The notion of authoritarian modernization for the sake of future democracy completely ignores the fact that the economy has never been the determining factor in our social system. The logic of economics in Russia has never defined the logic of power—it has always been the other way around. The chances that the latest economic reforms, if carried out, would destroy this pattern are very slim both in the short and in the long term. In Russia, no automatic linkage can be expected between economic systems of ownership and the proprietors' political sympathies. But it is this belief in an emerging "market-oriented" middle class that obscures the significance of the already existent, if weak, elements of civil society that emerged during the most intellectually productive postwar period—1965–1985. During the "period of stagnation" under Brezhnev a new generation was formed that gradually jettisoned the blind ideological faith and deep-seated and visceral fear that pervaded Soviet society, an aftermath of the years of repression. This generation of intellectuals, professionals, skilled workers and people in independent professions made the reforms of *perestroika* possible. It is these groups, through their participation in elected bodies, that are most capable of opposing any tendencies toward an anti-market monopoly of the executive branch. And none of these groups are directly linked to the market economy.

"Our fear of the coming winter does nothing to change Nature. The winter will set in all the same," wrote Leonid Nikitinsky in *Komsomolskaya Pravda*. This analogy is used to prove that authoritarian rule is inevitable. Such sentiments are very common among the majority of our intelligentsia, who are motivated by an understandable human desire for stability (it's better to have an authoritarian regime than a civil war).

But society is different from nature; it needs an alternative. A society without alternatives is a society of "historical necessity," inexorably heading for another blind alley. The lack of political alternatives to the "party of power" (i.e., Yeltsin's government), along with growing social apathy and destructive tendencies, makes the future of democracy and the authority of the current government ever more precarious.

And if "winter" does come, the pressure for an alternative will become increasingly urgent because, unlike nature, society cannot expect the automatic arrival of spring. Whenever people who call themselves democrats embrace the "objective necessity" of an authoritarian regime, democracy is dead.

SPECULATIONS ON THE NEW RUSSIA[5]

The breakup of the Soviet Union shouldn't have been as surprising as it obviously was for the West. As long ago as 1945, the argument that there actually were 15 republics banded together carried enough weight that the U.S.S.R. was granted three seats in the United Nations General Assembly. Most Americans never got it straight, mixing up Russia with the Soviet Union and Georgia the Soviet Republic with Georgia the U.S. state.

Despite the euphoria in the West during the last few months, there still are many directions that events in the former U.S.S.R.

[5] Article by Llewellyn D. Howell, international affairs editor of *USA Today*, from *USA Today* (Magazine) 120:31 Mar '92. Copyright © 1992 by the Society for the Advancement of Education. Reprinted with permission.

could take, few of which really would be beneficial to the U.S. Russia remains a state that will be at the center of international events and any New World Order.

Let me suggest a few scenarios for 2017, 25 years into our future (remembering that, just 25 years ago, we were at the height of the Vietnam War). They're put forth to stimulate thought, but perhaps one will hit near the target.

Scenario one (49% probability): The Confederation of Independent States (CIS) was abandoned totally in the late 1990s. Belarus, Moldava, and Ukraine have forged strong links with the central European states of Poland, Slovakia, Hungary, and Romania. Kazakhstan, Uzbekistan, Kyrgyzstan, Tajikistan, and Turkmenistan have formed a loose, Islam-based federation with Afghanistan and Pakistan following their successful joint war against India. Kashmir is occupied by joint troops of the seven nations, but is controlled politically by Pakistan. Russia remains a right-wing authoritarian state (compared with the West), but has become economically very successful due to "coastal" development—the Germans have invested heavily in technical manufacturing west of the Urals, while the Japanese, Koreans, and Taiwanese have shifted their heavier industries out of their own countries to Russia's Pacific coast. Strong migration is making Russia as much a Pacific country as a European one. Agriculture was the first industry to catch the capitalist train, and Russia now outproduces the U.S., Canada, and Australia combined with grains that continually undersell those of the West. As a result, most small Western grain farmers have gone under. The Western Europeans remain more prosperous, but Russians are wealthy enough to spend leisure time dabbling in politics and are agitating for abandonment of the Singaporean political model and for the involvement of more than one party in the governing process. The army still is large and remains stationed primarily along the Chinese and Kazakhstan borders. The U.S. suffers from both agricultural and manufacturing competition as the major economic powers, Japan and Germany, tie themselves to the rising Russian star.

Scenario two (30% probability): The CIS was abandoned totally in the late 1990s. The Russian military government that formed at the height of the decade's economic depression remains in power after the successful war against Ukraine, which now is controlled directly by Russia. German-led Europe still seems to be Russia's greatest threat, so strong bonds have been forged with politically neutral Japan, which has been given special economic privileges throughout the country in return for economic aid and beneficial investment. The Islamic republics of the former U.S.S.R. remain economic hostages of Russia. Sporadic fighting continues with the Chinese over lands in the Pacific east that have become increasingly important as Japan expands economically and militarily, but that conflict primarily remains a nuclear standoff. Population expansion is the greatest preoccupation of the Russians as they seek domestic market growth, an increased European population base, and a larger labor pool for their competition against the United States of Europe.

Scenario three (15% probability): The CIS was abandoned totally in the late 1990s. After the disaster of the attempt at a Russian free market economy, the former Communist Party membership reasserted itself as a socialist political organization and took control of the government. Happy with the reestablishment of order, the Russians gladly accepted this familiar configuration, the increased importance and opportunities of military life, and the calls to nationalism. Ukraine and Belarus have been brought back into the Russian domain, but the Islamic republics were abandoned to the chaos of the Greater Middle East. Military powers China and India pose the largest threats, while isolationist America has succumbed to industrial and agricultural doldrums.

Scenario four (five percent probability): The CIS was abandoned totally in the late 1990s. Muted efforts to establish a free market economy in Russia faltered in the face of food shortages, the ravages of harsh winters, and the eruption of violence among the 39 ethnic groups that composed the population of the Russian federation. Russia is on the verge of breaking into its racial and cultural components, with China, Kazakhstan, Ukraine, and Finland all making claims on its territory. Poverty, stagnation, and hopelessness prevail. Emigration by Russians to Europe and the U.S. is seen as the only possibility of salvation.

Scenario five (one percent probability): The CIS was abandoned totally in the late 1990s. After a bitter winter and with the help of the Europeans and Americans, the economy stabilized and began to grow. No longer threatened by economic chaos, the political institutions established during the Yeltsin era prospered and liberal democracy prevailed. Russia, Belarus, Ukraine, and Moldava joined NATO and the European Community. Cooperation with the U.S. and its friends and allies has led to an era of peace and economic progress. The Cold War truly has come to an end.

WHAT NEW WORLD ORDER?[6]

The 1991 Persian Gulf War was, according to President Bush, about "more than one small country; it is a big idea; a new world order," with "new ways of working with other nations . . . peaceful settlement of disputes, solidarity against aggression, reduced and controlled arsenals and just treatment of all peoples." Not long after the war, however, the flow of White House words about a new world order slowed to a trickle.

Like Woodrow Wilson's fourteen points or Franklin Roosevelt's four freedoms, George Bush's grand rhetoric expressed the larger goals important for public support when a liberal democratic state goes to war. But after the war, when reality intruded, grand schemes turned into a liability. People were led to compare the war's imperfect outcome with an impossible ideal. The proper standard for judgment should have been what the world would look like if Saddam Hussein had been left in possession of Kuwait. The victory lost its lustre because of an unfair comparison that the president inadvertently encouraged, and recession shifted the political agenda to the domestic economy. The White House thus decided to lower the rhetorical volume.

The administration faces a deeper problem than mere political tactics. The world has changed more rapidly in the past two years than at any time since 1945. It is difficult to keep one's conceptual footing within such fundamental shifts in politics. Familiar concepts fail to fit a new reality. It is worth recalling that it took Americans several years to adjust to the last great shift in the late 1940s. But the Bush administration, famous for eschewing "the vision thing," added to the confusion because it had never really thought through what it meant by the concept it launched. Neither the administration nor its critics were clear about the fact

[6]Article by Joseph S. Nye, Jr., author and director of the Harvard Center for International Affairs, from *Foreign Affairs* 71:83–96 Spring '92. Copyright © 1992 by the Council on Foreign Relations, Inc. Reprinted with permission.

that the term "world order" is used in two very different ways in discussions of world politics.

Realists, in the tradition of Richard Nixon and Henry Kissinger, see international politics occurring among sovereign states balancing each others' power. World order is the product of a stable distribution of power among the major states. Liberals, in the tradition of Woodrow Wilson and Jimmy Carter, look at relations among peoples as well as states. They see order arising from broad values like democracy and human rights, as well as from international law and institutions such as the United Nations.

The problem for the Bush administration was that it thought and acted like Nixon, but borrowed the rhetoric of Wilson and Carter. Both aspects of order are relevant to the current world situation, but the administration has not sorted out the relation between them.

From the realist perspective there is definitely a new world order, but it did not begin with the Gulf War. Since order has little to do with justice, but a lot to do with the distribution of power among states, realists date the new world order from the collapse of the Soviet empire in eastern Europe in the autumn of 1989. The rapid decline of the Soviet Union caused the end of the old bipolar order that had persisted for nearly half a century.

The old world order provided a stability of sorts. The Cold War exacerbated a number of Third World conflicts, but economic conflicts among the United States, Europe and Japan were dampened by common concerns about the Soviet military threat. Bitter ethnic divisions were kept under a tight lid by the Soviet presence in eastern Europe. A number of Third World conflicts were averted or shortened when the superpowers feared that their clients might drag them too close to the nuclear abyss. The various Arab-Israeli wars, for example, were brief. In fact some experts believe that a stronger Soviet Union would never have allowed its Iraqi client to invade Kuwait. If so Kuwait can be counted as the victim rather than the cause of the new world order.

Some analysts see the collapse of the Cold War as the victory of liberal capitalism and the end of the large ideological cleavages that drove the great international conflicts of this century. There is no single competitor to liberal capitalism as an overarching ideology. Rather than the end of history, the post-Cold War world is witnessing a return of history in the diversity of sources of international conflict. Liberal capitalism has many competitors, albeit fragmented ones. Examples include the indigenous neo-Maoism of Peru's Shining Path guerrilla movement, the many variants of Islamic fundamentalism and the rise of ethnic nationalism.

This does not mean that the new world politics will be "back to the future." There is an enormous difference between the democratically tamed and institutionally harnessed nationalisms of western Europe and the revival in eastern Europe of untamed nationalisms whose ancient animosities were never resolved in the institutional structure of state communism and the Soviet empire.

Moreover national boundaries will be more permeable than in the past. Nationalism and transnationalism will be contending forces in the new world politics. Large transnational corporations distribute economic production according to global strategies. Transnational technological changes in communications and transportation are making the world smaller. Diplomacy occurs in real time; both George Bush and Saddam Hussein watched Cable News Network for the latest reports. Human rights violations and mass suffering in distant parts of the globe are brought home by television. Although Marshall McLuhan argued that modern communications would produce a "global village," his metaphor was misleading because a global political identity remains feeble. In fact nationalism is becoming stronger in most of the world, not weaker. Instead of one global village there are villages around the globe more aware of each other. That, in turn, increases the opportunities for conflict.

Not all transnational forces are benign any more than all nationalisms are malign. Transnational drug trade, terrorism, the spread of AIDS and global warming are cases in point. With time, technology spreads across borders, and the technologies of weapons of mass destruction are now more than a half century old. The collapse of the Soviet Union removes two of the factors that slowed the spread of nuclear weapons in the old world order: tight Soviet technological controls and influence over its client states. The United States cannot escape from these transnational problems and few of them are susceptible to unilateral solutions. Like other countries in the new world order, the United States will be caught in the dialogue between the national and the transnational.

The United States will need power to influence others in regard to both transnational and traditional concerns. If the old world order has collapsed, what will be the new distribution of power? Over the past few years of dramatic change, different observers have claimed to discern five alternatives.

Return to bipolarity. Before the failure of the August coup and the final collapse of the Soviet Union, some argued that a newly repressive Soviet or Russian regime would create a harsh international climate and a return to the Cold War. But even if the coup had succeeded, it would not have restored bipolarity. The decline of the Soviet Union stemmed in large part from overcentralization. Stalin's system was unable to cope with the Third Industrial Revolution, in which flexible use of information is the key to successful economic growth. The return of the centralizers might have created a nasty international climate, but rather than restoring Soviet strength, recentralization would have continued the long-term decline of the Soviet economy. The same would be true for a centralizing Russian dictatorship.

Multipolarity. This is a popular cliché that drips easily from the pens of editorialists, but if used to imply an historical analogy with the nineteenth century it is highly misleading, for the old order rested on a balance of five roughly equal great powers while today's great powers are far from equally balanced. Russia will continue to suffer from economic weakness, and its reform is a question of decades, not years. China is a developing country and, despite favorable growth, will remain so well into the next century. Europe is the equal of the United States in population, economy and human resources. Even after the December 1991 summit at Maastricht, however, Europe lacks the political unity necessary to act as a single global power.

Japan is well endowed with economic and technological strength, but its portfolio of power resources is limited in the hard military area as well as in the cultural and ideological appeal that provides soft power. Japan would have to make major changes in its attitudes toward military power as well as in its ethnocentricity before it would be a challenger on the scale of the United States.

Three economic blocs. Those who devalue military power argue that Europe and Japan will be superpowers in a world of restrictive economic blocs. An Asian bloc will form around the yen, a western hemisphere bloc around the dollar and a European bloc (including remnants of the former Soviet Union) will cluster around the European Currency Unit (according to optimists) or the deutsche mark (in the view of pessimists). Others foresee a European versus a Pacific bloc.

There are three problems with this vision. First, it runs counter to the thrust of global technological trends. While regional trade will certainly grow, many firms would not want to be limited to one-third of the global market and would resist restrictive regionalism. Second, restrictive regional blocs run against nationalistic concerns of some of the lesser states that need a global system to protect themselves against domination by their large neighbors. Japan's Asian neighbors do not want to be locked up in a yen bloc with Japan. There will continue to be a constituency for a broader international trade system.

Most important, however, this vision is too dismissive of security concerns. With large nuclear neighbors in turmoil, both Europe and Japan want to keep their American insurance policies against uncertainty. The second Russian revolution is still in its early years, and China faces a generational transition. It is difficult to imagine the United States continuing its security guarantees in the context of trade wars. The end of the Cold War was not marked by European and Japanese calls for withdrawal of American troops. European and Japanese security concerns are likely to set limits on how restrictive the economic blocs become.

Unipolar hegemony. According to Charles Krauthammer, the Gulf War marked the beginning of a Pax Americana in which the world will acquiesce in a benign American hegemony. The premise is correct that the collapse of the Soviet Union left the world with only one superpower, but the hegemonic conclusion does not follow. For one thing the world economy is tripolar and has been since the 1970s. Europe, Japan and the United States account for two-thirds of the world's product. In economics, at least, the United States cannot exercise hegemony.

Hegemony is also unlikely because of the diffusion of power through transnational interdependence. To cite a few examples: private actors in global capital markets constrain the way interest rates can be used to manage the American economy; the transnational spread of technology increases the destructive capacities of otherwise poor and weak states; and a number of issues on the international agenda—drug trade, AIDS, migration, global warming—have deep societal roots in more than one country and flow across borders largely outside of governmental control. Since military means are not very effective in coping with such problems, no great power, the United States included, will be able to solve them alone.

Multilevel interdependence. No single hierarchy describes adequately a world politics with multiple structures. The distribution of power in world politics has become like a layer cake. The top military layer is largely unipolar, for there is no other military power comparable to the United States. The economic middle layer is tripolar and has been for two decades. The bottom layer of transnational interdependence shows a diffusion of power.

None of this complexity would matter if military power were as fungible as money and could determine the outcomes in all areas. In describing Europe before 1914, the British historian A.J.P. Taylor wrote that the test of a great power was the ability to prevail in war. But military prowess is a poor predictor of the outcomes in the economic and transnational layers of current world politics. The United States is better placed with a more diversified portfolio of power resources than any other country, but the new world order will not be an era of American hegemony. We must be wary of the prison of old concepts.

The world order after the Cold War is sui generis, and we overly constrain our understanding by trying to force it into the procrustean bed of traditional metaphors with their mechanical polarities. Power is becoming more multidimensional, structures more complex and states themselves more permeable. This added complexity means that world order must rest on more than the traditional military balance of power alone. The problems encountered by the Bush administration at the end of the Gulf War are illustrative. The traditional approach of balancing Iran and Iraq was clearly not enough, and U.N. resolutions 687 and 688 (which dealt with Iraq's weapons and refugees) went deep into areas of national sovereignty.

The realist view of world order, resting on a balance of military power, is necessary but not sufficient, because it does not take into account the long-term societal changes that have been slowly moving the world away from the Westphalian system. In 1648, after thirty years of tearing each other apart over religion, the European states agreed in the Treaty of Westphalia that the ruler, in effect, would determine the religion of a state regardless of popular preference. Order was based on the sovereignty of states, not the sovereignty of peoples.

The mechanical balance of states was slowly eroded over the ensuing centuries by the growth of nationalism and democratic participation, but the norms of state sovereignty persist. Now the rapid growth in transnational communications, migration and economic interdependence is accelerating the erosion of that classical conception and increasing the gap between norm and reality.

This evolution makes more relevant the liberal conception of a world society of peoples as well as states, and of order resting on values and institutions as well as military power. Liberal views that were once regarded as hopelessly utopian, such as Immanuel Kant's plea for a peaceful league of democracies, seem less far-fetched now that political scientists report virtually no cases of democracies going to war with each other. Current debates over the effects of German reunification, for example, pit against each other realists who see western Europe going back to the troubled balance of power, and liberals who fault such analysis for neglecting the fact that unlike 1870, 1914 or 1939, the new Germany is democratic and deeply enmeshed with its western neighbors through the institutions of the European Community. Moreover the interactions between democratic politics and international institutions reinforce each other.

Of course the game is still open in post-Cold War Europe, and Europe is very different from other parts of the world such as the Middle East, where traditional views of the balance of military power are still the core of wisdom. But the experience of Europe (and the democratic market economies more generally) suggests that in at least parts of this hybrid world, conceptions of divisible and transferable sovereignty may play an increasing part in a new world order. The complex practices of the European Community are a case in point.

These liberal conceptions of order are not entirely new. The Cold War order had norms and institutions, but they played a limited role. During World War II Roosevelt, Stalin and Churchill agreed to a United Nations that assumed a multipolar distribution of power. The U.N. Security Council would enforce the doctrine of collective security and nonaggression against smaller states while the five great powers were protected by their vetos.

Even this abbreviated version of Woodrow Wilson's institutional approach to order was hobbled, however, by the rise of bipolarity. The superpowers vetoed each other's initiatives, and the organization was reduced to the more modest role of stationing peacekeepers to observe ceasefires rather than repelling aggressors. The one exception, the U.N. role in the Korean War, proved the rule; it was made possible only by a temporary Soviet boycott of the Security Council in June 1950. When the decline of

Soviet power led to Moscow's new policy of cooperation with Washington in applying the U.N. doctrine of collective security against Baghdad, it was less the arrival of a new world order than the reappearance of an aspect of the liberal institutional order that was supposed to have come into effect in 1945.

But just as the Gulf War resurrected one aspect of the liberal approach to world order, it also exposed an important weakness in the liberal conception. The doctrine of collective security enshrined in the U.N. Charter is state-centric, applicable when borders are crossed but not when force is used against peoples within a state.

Liberals try to escape this problem by appealing to the principles of democracy and self-determination. Let peoples within states vote on whether they want to be protected behind borders of their own. But self-determination is not as simple as it sounds. Who decides what self will determine? Take Ireland, for example. If Irish people voted within the existing political boundaries, Ulster would have a Protestant majority, but if the Irish voted within the geographical boundaries of the island, Ulster would be encompassed within a Catholic majority. Whoever has the power to determine the boundaries of the vote has the power to determine the outcome.

A similar problem plagues Yugoslavia. It seemed clear that relatively homogeneous Slovenia should be allowed to vote on self-determination, but a similar vote in Croatia turns Serbs in some districts into a minority who then demand a vote on secession from an independent Croatia. It is not surprising that issues of secession are more often determined by bullets than ballots.

Nor are these rare examples. Less than ten percent of the 170 states in today's world are ethnically homogeneous. Only half have one ethnic group that accounts for as much as 75 percent of their population. Most of the republics of the former Soviet Union have significant minorities and many have disputed borders. Africa is a continent of a thousand ethnic and linguistic peoples squeezed within and across some forty-odd states. Once such states are called into question, it is difficult to see where the process ends. In such a world, federalism, local autonomy and international surveillance of minority rights hold some promise, but a policy of unqualified support for national self-determination would turn into a principle of enormous world disorder.

How then is it possible to preserve some order in traditional terms of the balance of power among sovereign states, while also moving toward international institutions that promote "justice among peoples?"

International institutions are gradually evolving in just such a post-Westphalian direction. Already in 1945, articles 55 and 56 of the U.N. Charter pledged states to collective responsibility for observance of human rights and fundamental freedoms. Even before the recent Security Council resolutions authorizing post-war interventions in Iraq. U.N. recommendations of sanctions against apartheid in South Africa set a precedent for not being strictly limited by the charter's statements about sovereignty. In Europe the 1975 Helsinki Accords codified human rights. Violations can be referred to the European Conference on Security and Cooperation or the Council of Europe. International law is gradually evolving. In 1965 the American Law Institute defined international law as "rules and principles . . . dealing with the conduct of states and international organizations." More recently the institute's lawyers added the revealing words, "as well as some of their relations with persons." Individual and minority rights are increasingly treated as more than just national concerns.

Of course in many, perhaps most, parts of the world such principles are flouted and violations go unpunished. To mount an armed multilateral intervention to right all such wrongs would be another source of enormous disorder. But we should not think of intervention solely in military terms. Intervention is a matter of degree, with actions ranging from statements and limited economic measures at the low end of the spectrum to full-fledged invasions at the high end. The U.N. Security Council and regional organizations may decide on limited nonmilitary interventions. Multilateral infringements of sovereignty will gradually increase without suddenly disrupting the distribution of power among states.

On a larger scale the Security Council can act under chapter seven of the U.N. Charter if it determines that internal violence of development of weapons of mass destruction are likely to spill over into a more general threat to the peace in a region. Such definitions are somewhat elastic—witness the imposition of sanctions against Rhodesia in the 1960s. The reasons for multilateral intervention will gradually expand over time. Although Iraq was a special case because of its blatant aggression. Security Council resolutions 687 and 688 may create a precedent for other situations where mistreatment of minorities threatens relations with neighbors or where a country is developing weapons of mass destruction in violation of its obligations under the Nonproliferation Treaty.

In other instances groups of states may act on a regional basis to deal with internal fighting, as Nigeria and others did by sending troops to Liberia under the framework of the Economic Community of West African States. In Yugoslavia the European Community employed the threat of economic sanctions as well as observer missions in an effort to limit the violence. In Haiti members of the Organization of American States imposed economic sanctions in response to the overthrow of a democratically elected government. None of the efforts was fully successful, but each involved intervention in what are usually considered domestic affairs.

It may also be possible to enhance U.N. capabilities for independent actions in cases where the permanent members do not have a direct interest. The gains for collective security from the Gulf War would be squandered, for example, if there were no international response to a Rwandan invasion of Uganda or a Libyan incursion into Chad. A U.N. rapid deployment force of 60,000 troops formed from earmarked brigades from a dozen countries could cope with a number of such contingencies as determined by the Security Council.

Such a fighting force, as contrasted to traditional peacekeeping forces, could be formed around a professional core of 5,000 U.N. soldiers. They would need frequent joint exercises to develop common command and operational procedures. The U.S. involvement could be limited to logistical and air support and, of course, the right to help control its activities through the Security Council and the military staff committee. Many details need to be worked out, but an idea that would have been silly or utopian during the Cold War suddenly becomes worth detailed practical examination in the aftermath of the Cold War and Gulf War.

Such imperfect principles and institutions will leave much room for domestic violence and injustice among peoples. Yugoslavia is an immediate example, and it will not be alone. But the moral horrors will be less than if policymakers were to try either to right all wrongs by force or, alternatively, to return to the unmodified Westphalian system. Among the staunchest defenders of the old system are the poorly integrated postcolonial states whose elites fear that new doctrines of multilateral intervention by the United Nations will infringe their sovereignty. The transition to a liberal vision of a new world order is occurring, but not smoothly. Liberals must realize that the evolution beyond Westphalia is a matter of decades and centuries, while realists must recognize that the traditional definitions of power and order in purely military terms miss the changes that are occurring in a world of transnational communications and instant information.

What is the American national interest in promoting a new world order? As [1992] election-year rhetoric asks, why not put America first? The country faces a number of serious domestic problems. The net savings rate has dropped from about 7.5 percent of gross national product in the 1970s to about 4.5 percent [in the Spring of 1992.] The federal budget deficit eats up about half of net private savings. The educational system is not producing a high enough level of skills for continuing progress in an information-age economy. In terms of high school dropouts the United States is wasting a quarter of its human resources compared to five percent for Japan. There is a need for investment in public infrastructure. Clearly we need to do more at home.

But Americans should beware of a false debate between domestic and foreign needs. In a world of transnational interdependence the distinction between domestic and foreign policy becomes blurred. The real choice that Americans face is not between domestic and foreign policy, but between consumption and investment. President Bush has said that the United States has the will but not the wallet. The opposite is closer to the mark. The United States spends about 31 percent of gross national product on government at all levels, while most European countries spend closer to 40 percent. The United States is a rich country that acts poor. America's U.N. dues are a relative pittance, and many countries see our failure to pay them as proof of our hypocrisy about a new world order. Similarly Europeans cite our low levels of aid and question our seriousness and relevance to stability in postcommunist eastern Europe. The American economy could support a few more percentage points of gross national product to invest at home while helping to maintain international order.

But why spend anything on international order? The simple answer is that in a world of transnational interdependence, international disorder can hurt, influence or disturb the majority of people living in the United States. A nuclear weapon sold or stolen from a former Soviet republic could be brought into the United States in the hold of a freighter or the cargo bay of a commercial airliner. Chaos in a Middle Eastern country can sustain terrorists who threaten American travelers abroad. A Caribbean country's inability to control drugs or disease could mean larger flows of both across our borders. Release of ozone-depleting chemicals overseas can contribute to a rise in skin cancer in the United States. With more than ten percent of U.S. gross national product exported, American jobs depend upon international economic conditions. And even though not a direct threat to U.S. security, the human rights violations brought home to Americans by transnational communications are discomforting. If the rest of the world is mired in chaos, and governments are too weak to deal with their parts of a transnational problem, the U.S. government will not be able to solve such problems alone or influence them to reduce the damage done to Americans.

In addition, even after the Cold War the United States has geopolitical interests in international stability. The United States has a continuing interest that no hostile power control the continent of Europe or that European turmoil draw us in under adverse circumstances, as happened twice before in this century. While such events now have a much lower probability and thus can be met with a much reduced investment, a wise foreign policy still takes out insurance against low probability events. Given the uncertainties in the aftermath of the Soviet collapse, an American security presence, even at greatly reduced troop levels, has a reassuring effect as European integration proceeds. The United States has an interest in a stable and prosperous western Europe that gradually draws the eastern part of the continent toward pluralism and democracy. The primary role will rest with the Europeans, but if the United States were to divorce itself from the process, we might find the future geopolitical situation far less stable.

The United States also has geopolitical and economic interests in the Pacific. The United States is the only country with both economic and military power resources in the region, and its continued presence is desired by Asian powers who do not want Japan to remilitarize. Japan's current political consensus is opposed to such a military role, and Japanese leaders realize it would be destabilizing in the region. With a relatively small but symbolically important military presence in the United States can help to provide reassurance in the region, while encouraging Japan to invest its economic power not in military force but in international institutions and to help share the lead in dealing with transnational issues.

In realist terms the United States will remain the world's largest power well into the next century. Economists have long noted that if the largest consumer of a collective good, such as order, does not take the lead in organizing its production, there is little likelihood that the good will be produced by others. That was the situation in the 1920s when the United States refused to join the League of Nations or cooperate in preserving the stability of the international economy. Isolationism in the 1920s came back to haunt and hurt Americans a decade later. There is even less room for neo-isolationism today.

Why not simply leave the task of world order to the United Nations? Because the United Nations is the sum of its member nations and the United States is by far the largest member. Large scale U.N. efforts like the repulse of Iraq will continue to require the participation of the world's largest power.

The United States correctly wants to avoid the role of world policeman. The way to steer a middle path between bearing too much and too little of the international burden is to renew the American commitment to multilateral institutions that fell into abeyance in the 1980s. The use of multilateral institutions, while sometimes constraining, also helps share the burden that the American people do not want to bear alone. Multilateralism also limits the resentments and balances the behavior of other nations that can lead them to resist American wishes and make it harder for Americans to achieve national interests.

While the Bush administration failed in its policies toward Iraq before and at the end of the Gulf War, its actions in organizing the multilateral coalition that expelled Iraq from Kuwait fit the national interest in a new world order. The administration combined both the hard power of military might and the soft power of using institutions to co-opt others to share the burden. Without the U.N. resolutions it might have been impossible for the Saudis to accept troops and for others to send troops. Nor is it likely that the United States could have persuaded others to foot nearly the entire bill for the war. Had there been no response to Iraq's aggression and violation of its obligations under the Non-proliferation Treaty, the post-Cold War order would be far more dangerous.

In short the new world order has begun. It is messy, evolving and not susceptible to simple formulation or manipulation. Russia and China face uncertain futures. Regional bullies will seek weapons of mass destruction. Protectionist pressure may increase. The United States will have to combine both traditional power and liberal institutional approaches if it is to pursue effectively its national interest. We want to promote liberal democracy and human rights where we can do so without causing chaos. The reason is obvious: liberal democratic governments are less likely to threaten us over time. We will need to maintain our alliances and a balance of power in the short run, while simultaneously working to promote democratic values, human rights and institutions for the long run. To do less is to have only a fraction of a foreign policy.

BIBLIOGRAPHY

An asterisk (*) preceding a reference indicates an excerpt from the work has been reprinted in this book.

BOOKS AND PAMPHLETS

Abel, Elie. The shattered bloc: Behind the upheaval in Eastern Europe. Houghton Mifflin Company. '90.

Akchurin, Marat. Red odyssey: A journey through the Soviet republics. HarperCollins. '92.

Billington, James H. Russia transformed: Breakthrough to hope. The Free Press. '92.

Bloom, William. Personal identity, national identity, and international relations. Cambridge University Press. '90.

Breslauer, George, ed. Dilemmas of transition in the Soviet Union and Eastern Europe. Berkeley-Stanford Program in Soviet Studies. '91.

Bultman, Bud. Revolution by candlelight: The real story behind the changes in Eastern Europe. '91.

Challenger, Richard D., ed. The Cold War: From Iron Curtain to Perestroika. (15 vols.) Meckler Corp. '92.

Conquest, Robert. The harvest of sorrow: Soviet collectivization and the terrorfamine. Oxford University Press. '86.

Cullen, Robert. Twilight of empire: Inside the crumbling Soviet bloc. Atlantic Monthly Press. '91.

Doder, Dusko, & Branson, Louise. Gorbachev: Heretic in the Kremlin. Viking Penguin. '90.

Gaddis, John Lewis. The long peace: Inquiries into the history of the Cold War. Oxford University Press. '89.

Gorbachev, Mikhail. The August coup: The truth and the lessons. HarperCollins. '91.

Gorbachev, Mikhail. Perestroika: New thinking for our country and the world. Harper & Row, Publishers. '87.

Hirsch, Steve, ed. MEMO 3: In search of answers in the post-Soviet era. BNA Books. '92.

Jowitt, Ken. New world disorder: The Leninist extinction. University of California Press. '92.

Katsenelinboigen, Aron. The Soviet Union: Empire, nation, and system. Transaction Publications. '90.

Kimball, John C. U.S.S.R. and Eastern Europe: The shattered heartland. Foreign Policy Association. '91.

Kirkpatrick, Jeanne J. The withering away of the totalitarian state—and other surprises. American Enterprise Institute for Public Policy Research. '90.

Kronenwetter, Michael. The new Eastern Europe. Franklin Watts. '91.

Kull, Steven. Burying Lenin. Westview Press. '92.

Lynch, Allen. The Cold War is over—again. Westview Press. '92.

Lynch, Allen. The Soviet breakup and U.S. foreign policy. Foreign Policy Association. '92.

Mandelbaum, Michael, ed. The rise of nations in the Soviet Union: American foreign policy & the disintegration of the USSR. Council on Foreign Relations Press. '91.

MccGwire, Michael K. Perestroika & Soviet national security. Brookings Institution. '91.

Morrison, John. Boris Yeltsin: From Bolshevik to Democrat. Dutton. '91.

Murphy, Kenneth. Retreat from the Finland station: Moral odysseys in the breakdown of Communism. The Free Press. '92.

Nielsen, Niels Christian. Revolutions in Eastern Europe: Religious roots. Orbis Books. '91.

Peukert, Detlev J. K. The Weimar Republic: The crisis of classical modernity. Hill & Wang. '92.

Pipes, Richard. The formation of the Soviet Union: Communism and nationalism 1917–1923. Harvard University Press. '64.

Reisinger, William M. Energy & the Soviet bloc: Alliance politics after Stalin. Cornell University Press. '92.

Roberts, Paul Craig & LaFollette, Karen. Meltdown: Inside the Soviet economy. Cato Institute. '90.

Rothschild, Joseph. Ethnopolitics: A conceptual framework. Columbia University Press. '81.

Rowen, Henry S. & Wolf, Charles, eds. The impoverished superpower: Perestroika and the Soviet military burden. ICS Press. '90.

Roxburgh, Angus. The second Russian Revolution: The struggle for power in the Kremlin. BBC Books. '91.

Serfaty, Simon. Taking Europe seriously. St. Martin's Press. '92.

Shevardnadze, Eduard A. The future belongs to freedom. The Free Press. '91.

Smith, Graham, ed. The nationalities question in the Soviet Union. Longman. '90.

Smith, Hedrick. The new Russians. Random House. '90.

Sobchak, Anatoli. For a new Russia: The mayor of St. Petersburg's own story of the struggle for justice and democracy. The Free Press. '91.

Solovyov, Vladimir & Klepikova, Elena. Boris Yeltsin: A political biography. Putnam. '92.

Solzhenitsyn, Aleksandr. (trans. Alexis Klimoff) Rebuilding Russia: Reflections and tentative proposals. Farrar, Straus & Giroux. '91.

Sommer, Mark. Living in freedom: The exhilaration and anguish of Prague's second spring. Mercury House. '92.

Soros, George. Underwriting democracy. The Free Press. '91.

Tismaneanu, Vladimir. Reinventing politics: Eastern Europe from Stalin to Havel. The Free Press. '92.

Treverton, Gregory F., ed. The shape of the new Europe. Council on Foreign Relations Press. '92.

Tucker, Robert W. & Hendrickson, David C. The imperial temptation: The new world order and America's purpose. Council on Foreign Relations Press. '92.

Urban, Joan Barth, ed. Moscow and the global left in the Gorbachev era. Cornell University Press. '92.

Wedel, Janine R., ed. The unplanned society. Columbia University Press. '92.

Yeltsin, Boris. Against the grain. Summit Books. '90.

Yevtushenko, Yevgeny Aleksandrovich. (trans. & ed. Antonina W. Bouis) Fatal half measures: The culture of democracy in the Soviet Union. Little, Brown. '91.

ADDITIONAL PERIODICAL ARTICLES WITH ABSTRACTS

For those who wish to read more widely on the subject of the breakup of Communism: the Soviet Union and Eastern Europe, this section contains abstracts of additional articles that bear on the topic. Readers who require a comprehensive list of materials are advised to consult the *Readers' Guide to Periodical Literature* and other Wilson indexes.

The Baltics go it alone. F. Lazare. *World Press Review* 39:44 F '92

An article excerpted from *Le Monde* of Paris. Lithuania, Latvia, and Estonia have gained political independence from the Soviet Union, but economic freedom remains a distant goal. Since their annexation in 1940 by the Soviets, the Baltic States have been closely integrated into the Soviet economy, on which the republics depend both for raw materials and as a market. This situation continues today, despite the republics' stated intention of gaining economic independence. The Baltic States have all established central banks and ministries of external trade and are planning new currencies, yet none has devised a specific economic reform program or found the key to future relations with the other republics. Moreover, given their combined population of only 8 million, the Baltics have scant hope of attracting much foreign investment. As a result, the

Soviet Union will likely continue to be their main training partner for
another year.

The free Baltic republics—a victory of self-liberation. D. Quayle. *US Department of State Dispatch* 2:813–14 N 4 '91

In an address delivered before the Hudson Institute's Conference on the
Baltics in Indianapolis, U.S. vice-president Dan Quayle discusses the tasks
facing the residents of the Baltic States: The people of the Baltic nations
have triumphed over oppression. To succeed as democratic nations, they
must integrate themselves into the international community, resolve the
issues surrounding the continued presence of soviet troops on their soil,
look to the West for their security, and take all possible steps to protect the
rights of ethnic minorities within their borders. In addition, they must
establish the reforms necessary to make the move to free-market economies. Membership in the International Monetary Fund and World Bank
will help them make that move, but the Baltics should also engage in a
wide-ranging dialogue with the United States. Ultimately, they must look
beyond assistance and aid and unleash the creativity and enterprise of
their people.

Europe's scrambled egg. J. A. Broun. *Commonweal* 119:5–6 My 8 '92

The civil war in Bosnia and Hercegovina, the only former Yugoslavian
republic where no single ethnic group dominates, is even more tragic than
the recent war in Croatia. Bosnia's population of 4.3 million is 44 percent
Muslim Slav, 31 percent Orthodox Serbian, and 17 percent Catholic Croatian. Much publicity has been focused on the strife between Serbians and
Croatians, but now that the Muslims have been drawn into the fray, outsiders must understand their predicament as well. Traditionally, Bosnian
Muslims have been flexible pragmatists who prefer negotiation to armed
conflict. Enlightened Muslim leaders deny Serbian allegations that they
intend to undermine the secular state, but many imams are now demanding the reintroduction of traditional Islamic codes regarding schools and
the role of women. The Muslims are currently allied with the Croatians
but fear that the Croatians and Serbians may seek to divide Bosnia between themselves.

Fishy rhetoric, stinking reality. *America* 166:375 My 2 '92

The aggression of the Serbian government must not be seen as some kind
of fratricidal struggle against Croatia and now Bosnia and Hercegovina.
Instead, it should be viewed as a naked attempt to take territory by force
and at the expense of others. It has been difficult to sort out who is to
blame in Yugoslavia's bloody civil war, because it has been portrayed in the
press as a mutual hatred that makes no sense and therefore has no rational solution. The reality, however, is that Serbia is governed by one of the

last Communist regimes in Eastern Europe and that Croatians and Bosnians were forced to defend themselves against the Serbian-controlled Yugoslavian army, which essentially invaded their countries. The UN must work to restore the territorial integrity of the former Yugoslavian republics, protect the rights of minorities in those republics, and evict the Yugoslavian army from Croatia and Bosnia.

Balkan brew. A. Borden. *The Nation* 254:545+ Ap 27 '92

The recent formal recognition of Bosnia and Hercegovina, the former Yugoslavian republic, by the European Community (EC) and the United States has fueled tensions among the country's Serbians, Muslims, and Croatians. The EC's recognition of Croatia and Slovenia severely damaged its credibility and forced Bosnia to take up the question of independence before it had resolved its ethnic groups' relations. As independence day for Bosnia approached, the EC and the United States withheld comment on their likely response, encouraging Serbian paramilitary attacks intended to destabilize Yugoslavia. The EC has given its blessing to an unworkable cantonization plan to divide Bosnia into ethnically determined administrative zones. Moreover, the EC and other organizations have ignored moderate and pluralistic voices that call for building an alternative politics in the south Slav region.

The great game, chapter two. T. Post. *Newsweek* 119:28–9 F 3 '92

A regional battle is brewing over the 5 Central Asian republics of the former Soviet Union. Turkey, Iran, and Saudi Arabia are the chief rivals for influence in the area, which contains more than 50 million Muslims. Turkey already has a head start on its rivals, having begun to develop relations in 1989 with the republics. Turkey's current projects include the formation of a Black Sea Economic Cooperation Zone that includes Azerbaijan, a $7 million tannery in Kyrgyzstan, a cooperative banking arrangement in Tajikistan, and air links between Istanbul and most Central Asian capitals. A close second in the race for influence is Iran, which has been courting the Muslim republics with diplomatic and trade overtures. To promote a conservative religious revival, Saudi Arabia has put almost $1 billion into the region and pledged 1 million Korans. Russia, which is deeply preoccupied with its own mounting economic troubles, is adopting a wait-and-see strategy toward the region.

Another Islamic revolution. V. Pope. *U.S. News & World Report* 111:65–7 D 16 '91

The collapse of the Soviet Union has fueled a Muslim revival in the Central Asian republics. Tribal and religious loyalties that predate communism are filling the political void left by the dissolution of the Soviet empire. Some 60 million to 70 million Muslims live in the Soviet Union, mostly in Central Asia and the Caucasus. Stalinist repression led to the deaths of many Muslim religious leaders and the destruction of most mosques, but today, in swelling numbers, Muslims are learning Arabic, studying the Koran, and praying at mosques. The leaders of the Soviet Union and Russia have applauded the religious revival, but they are also leery of militant Islamic politics. The 6 central Asian republics are also forging new alliances with their Muslim neighbors—Turkey, Iran, and the Middle East.

Shedding the past. M. Gray. *Maclean's* 104:34–5 N 25 '91

Soviet Central Asia, a vast, arid region that touches Russia, China, Iran, and Afghanistan, is home to a growing number of democratic reformers and Islamic activists who are beginning to challenge Communist rule. The area, which is composed of the republics of Tadzhikistan, Kazakstan, Uzbekistan, Turkmenistan, and Kyrgyzstan, is struggling with potentially explosive problems stemming from Communist rule. In Izbekistan and Tadzhikistan, for example, agricultural policies made by Soviets converted the republics' most productive vegetable and fruit land to the cultivation of cotton. The massive amount of water that was diverted from rivers to irrigate the cotton fields has helped shrink the Aral Sea by some 40 percent over the past 30 years. The republics have since abolished the Soviet ministry that monitored distribution of the water, thus increasing the possibility of water wars breaking out among the region's competing users.

Choosing sides in the Asian republics. A. Zein. *World Press Review* 38:21 N '91

An article excerpted from *Al-Hawadeth* of London. Conspicuously absent from the Soviet republics' call for independence in the wake of the August coup attempt are the central and southern Asian states that lie adjacent to the Muslim world. The republics of Azerbaijan, Kazakhstan, and Uzbekistan declared their independence in 1990, at least in theory, but they have not begun dispatching envoys or establishing institutions that would practice self rule. It is unclear whether this silence reflects a genuine desire to remain a part of the Soviet Union or an awareness of the ambitious desires of the major regional countries, primarily Iran and Turkey. The Asian republics, which hold a large proportion of the Soviet Union's oil and natural gas reserves and support a number of ethnic groups, are also well aware of their strategic and economic importance. Before long, they will be playing Turkey against Iran.

Five new nations ask who are we? J. Kohan. *Time* 139:44–6 Ap 27 '92

Since the Soviet Union's collapse 5 months ago, the Muslim republics have been searching for an identity. After serving as passive but powerful props for the Communist regime, the republics of Uzbekistan, Turkmenistan, Tajikistan, Kyrgyzstan, and Kazakhstan had little choice but to join the exodus toward independence when the centralized Soviet control began splitting apart. Since then, Washington has established formal diplomatic ties with Kyrgyzstan and Kazakhstan, neighboring Turkey and Iran have vied for influence in the region. China has proposed joint-venture projects, and the South Koreans have offered a sample of free enterprise. However, the newly independent states—home to 50 million predominantly Muslim, Turkic-speaking people—have been wary of making any geopolitical commitments. The article discusses the pressure on these countries to pursue either radical Islam or Western secularism.

Report from Turkestan. R. Wright. *The New Yorker* 68:53–8+ Ap 6 '92

Despite their common heritage and their agreement on the need for regional unity, the 5 Central Asian republics of the Commonwealth of Independent States are emerging from Soviet rule in their own ways. All the republics are focusing on economic reforms, but they are either unwilling or unable to deal with political change. In all but Kyrgyzstan, Communist or 1-party rule is still entrenched, and democratic movements are tightly monitored, denied media exposure, or banned. Frustration, tension, and nationalist rivalries are likely to deepen. With Islam offering the only strong and unifying factor, a new and vibrant Islamic Turkestan could take shape. The writer discusses the revival of Islam and traditional cultures and languages in the Central Asian republics; the reduction to second class status of Russians; ecological, health, and economic problems caused by the region's cotton monoculture; and the creation of Central Asian and Islamic common markets.

Shatter zone. R. D. Kaplan. *The Atlantic* 269:24–5+ Ap '92

The division of Central Asia into various nations masks the fact that the region stretching from the Middle East to western China is largely a single cultural world based on the Turkic languages. Experts note that the creation of Uzbekistan, Kazakhstan, Kyrgyzstan, Turkmenistan, Azerbaijan, and the "autonomous regions" of the Karakalpaks and the Crimean Tatars resulted from the Stalinist method of divide-and-rule, whereby "nationalities" were ordained out of tribal and linguistic subgroups of the same Turkic people. With the recent political dislocations throughout Eurasia, this Turkic world is beginning to reemerge. The writer discusses the Turkic people's history, similarities between the collapse of Soviet communism and the demise of the Ottoman Empire, the role of Islam as a unifying factor, and the way that the reappearance of the Turkic peoples as political forces will affect Russia, Turkey, Iran, Afghanistan, Pakistan, and China.

Now the new new Europe. S. Tully. *Fortune* 124:136–8+ D 2 '91

Part of a special section on Europe. The fall of communism and the movement toward a unified market have made Europe a larger and more competitive place to do business. The European Community (EC) is pursuing agreements with the European Free Trade Association (EFTA)—a long-standing confederation consisting of Austria, Finland, Iceland, Lichtenstein, Norway, Sweden, and Switzerland—and with Hungary, Czechoslovakia, and Poland, which are Central Europe's strongest economies. The deals with Central Europe promise to be more significant than those with EFTA because Central Europe now consumes only minuscule amounts of Western goods and thus offers greater opportunities for new business. Europe's prosperity could be undermined if a credit crunch develops or if chaos in the Soviet Union sends a flood of refugees West, but the new trade pacts should spread prosperity in Central Europe and reduce the danger of both migration and a shortage of credit.

Watching rights. A. Neier. *The Nation* 254:440 Ap 6 '92

Around the world, advocates of racial, religious, and political purification seem to be shaping public policy. Romanian authorities tolerate pogroms against gypsies, authorities in eastern Germany allow skinhead attacks on foreigners, many Latvian residents who are not ethnic Latvians have been stripped of their citizenship, and many Czechoslovakians and Germans linked to former Communist regimes are barred from responsible jobs. Wars are being fought along tribal lines in Yugoslavia and the former Soviet Union, campaigns against alleged infidels and apostates are taking place in Islamic countries, and Israel is trying to drive Palestinians out of Jerusalem and the territories. In Western Europe, attacks on foreigners are increasing, and French politician Jean-Marie Le Pen is gaining power. In the United States, there is the phenomenon of David Duke and Patrick Buchanan. In every case, those who allegedly sully the purity of society are blamed for every ill.

Rumblings in the 'Red Army'. M. Hopkins. *The New Leader* 75:10–11 Mr 23 '92

The demoralized, directionless, and divided Red Army of the former Soviet Union is a ticking bomb. The once-glorified Red Army has been battered and humiliated since the collapse of the Soviet Union, an event that its members deplore. As 300,000 professional officers struggle to find housing for their families, they see their troops being fired upon as they defend weapons depots from marauding ethnic groups in the Caucasus and Moldova. They also see the military being abused in political maneuvers between the republics. The Moscow government has pledged to fund the mostly Russian forces of the Commonwealth of Independent States, but Russia's defense budget is being drastically cut because of the economic recession. Few analysts would be surprised if the military endorsed a hard line conservative government before the end of 1992.

Sailing into the sunset: the Soviet military's collapse is danger-ous. D. Stanglin and R. Knight. *U.S. News & World Report* 112:31–2+ F 17 '92

The collapse of the Soviet military signals great danger. In less than 5 years, the military has assumed a defensive position, cut 500,000 troops, withdrawn from most of Eastern Europe, dismantled much of its tactical nuclear force, and watched its country disintegrate. The result is tens of thousands of angry ex-soldiers who are returning to Russia with few prospects for the future, and the soldiers who are still employed are living in squalid conditions with no guarantees of food or income. The troops are unlikely to turn against the West or their former satellite countries, but they do threaten the former Soviet republics because the military could choose to rally to the cause of authoritarian Russian nationalism. Meanwhile, attempts by the republics to form a unified defense structure have been unsuccessful thus far. Russia wants a commonwealth defense force under a unified command, and Ukraine wants to form its own independent army.

The fight for Red October. R. Watson. *Newsweek* 109:38–9 Ja 20 '92

The Black Sea fleet and other elements of the Soviet armed forces are pawns in the political battle between Russia and Ukraine, the 2 most important members of the new Commonwealth of Independent States. Ukraine wants the commonwealth to be as loose as possible, in part to minimize the dominance of Russia over the other 10 members, while Russian president Boris Yeltsin, who sees Russia as the logical heir to Soviet power, seems to want more central coordination. In a recent surprise move, Russia agreed to concede part of the Black Sea fleet to Ukrainian control. Earlier, Moscow had moved its newest aircraft carrier, the *Admiral Kuznetsov*, from the Black Sea port of Sevastopol to Arctic Murmansk, far beyond Ukraine's control. Ukrainians retaliated by disconnecting the system that enables Moscow to communicate with some of its ground forces in Ukraine, including units armed with tactical nuclear weapons. To date, the link has not been restored.

An economy in trauma. J. Brimelow. *Forbes* 149:181 F 17 '92

Events in the territories of the former Soviet Union could trigger a powerful commodity price boom. These territories are in extreme economic trauma, with barter, hoarding, massive intensification of extralegal economic activity, and loss of respect for local currency all in evidence. The desire of people in these territories to acquire foreign currency has been the immediate cause of the unprecedented flood of commodity shipments from the Soviet Union during the past 2 years, which is expected to continue. The example of other economies that have suffered extreme trauma suggests that the economy of the former Soviet Union will recover, and the magnitude of that recovery could be enormous. Ultimately, changes in the former Soviet territories could boost world commodity prices and accelerate world inflation.

The Commonwealth's best chance is competition. G. S. Becker. *Business Week* p14 F 3 '92

Competition will give the Commonwealth of Independent States (C.I.S.) a great opportunity for economic progress and political freedom. The free movement of goods, capital, and people among the republics of the former Soviet Union would encourage each one to adopt the most effective political and economic policies because both people and capital would gravitate toward the best policies. Freedom to migrate would also help protect minorities from the most flagrant forms of discrimination because states that were too restrictive of individual liberties would lose people. It would also be better if the former Soviet republics issued their own currencies. Competition among currencies would also pressure governments to behave more responsibly. One area in which competition would be inappropriate would be nuclear weapons. It is essential that the C.I.S. establish control and safeguards over its nuclear warheads.

How long can Yeltsin hold it all together? D. Stead and others. *Business Week* p49 Ja 13 '92

The new Commonwealth of Independent States faces such deep problems that some people doubt it will hold together longer than a few months. Both the West and people in the former Soviet Union would benefit if the commonwealth did succeed, because the confederation could be a useful vehicle for smoothing economic reform and dealing with nuclear and diplomatic issues. It will be difficult, however, to reconcile the disparate nationalities and unequal economic clout of its 11 members. The key to the commonwealth's success lies with Russian president Boris Yeltsin, who faces the double challenge of improving living standards quickly and overcoming the other republics' suspicion of his large, powerful, disproportionately wealthy state. Unfortunately, his blunt manner and his haste in seizing control of the former Soviet apparatus are already undermining whatever trust he once enjoyed.

New year, old fears. R. Knight. *U.S. News & World Report* 112:34–6 Ja 13 '92

The newly created Commonwealth of Independent States may already be suffering its death throes. The group of 11 former Soviet republics has been unable to agree on its purpose or resolve 3 major issues—the fate of the former Soviet military and its nuclear weapons; the prevention of further civil wars such as the one now raging in Georgia; and most critically, the coordination of economic policies. Inflation in the former Soviet Union is at 450 percent and climbing, the ruble has lost 90 percent of its hard currency value, tax revenues have collapsed, and industrial production and farm output are plummeting. The commonwealth's inherent problem is that Russia wants to move away from its Communist past as quickly as possible, while the other republics want first to establish their own identities.

Forget the Soviet Union. P. A. Goble. *Foreign Policy* 86:56–65 Spr '92

The Soviet Union has been decisively replaced by 15 independent states, but U.S. policymakers have yet to accept the full implications of that fact. While the Commonwealth of Independent States performs important temporary and permanent functions, it is not a successor state to the USSR. The United States must therefore shift its focus to the specific problems of the 15 republics. These problems fall into 3 broad categories: challenges shared by all the successor states, such as democratization and transition to a market economy, emerging interstate regional problems, including migration, border changes, and the potential for violence between republics, and issues concerning the new states at the individual level. So far, the West has largely ignored this third class of problems, which are precisely the ones that deserve the most attention. Experts must learn local languages and histories in order to deal with these issues.

What's really happening in Russia? *The Nation* 254:259–64+ Mr 2 '92

Stephen F. Cohen, a professor of politics and the director of Russian studies at Princeton University, recently returned from a trip to Russia. In an interview, he discusses the new stereotypes, myths, and misconceptions about Russia that are emerging in the U.S. mass media, the American habit of interpreting Russia through the prism of its own ideology; the struggle among elites in the Commonwealth of Independent States (C.I.S.) to appropriate Soviet property, the migration of power from Moscow to the provinces, where large state factories and farms are located; the difficulty in assessing what has and has not changed irrevocably in the former Soviet Union; the slim chance that the C.I.S. will survive, former Soviet president Mikhail Gorbachev's reforms; the prospects for democracy in Russia; Russian president Boris Yeltsin's economic reforms; and the need for a more generous but less conditional and intrusive U.S. policy toward the C.I.S.

The new Russian question: U.S. policy must seek to prevent the return of aggressive nationalism. H. Kissinger *Newsweek* 119:34–5 F 10 '92

In its relations with the new Commonwealth of Independent States, the United States must take care not to encourage the Russian Republic's historic tendencies toward domination. No peoples have been systematically more abused by their government than those of the Russian Empire, and many Ukrainians, as well as the leaders of several other republics, are concerned about the threat of Russian imperialism. The United States has been remarkably slow in dealing with the new republics, and it treats Yeltsin as the linear descendant of Gorbachev and the commonwealth as if it were the old Soviet Union with a different name. It should be made clear that the United States considers Russia an appropriate partner in world affairs, but Russia must also know that new expansionism will exact a heavy price. If Russia respects the new situation, a significant Western aid program should be initiated. The United States should also rapidly expand its contacts with other republics.

The Yeltsin revolution. M. Malia. *The New Republic* 206:21–5 F 10 '92

Russian president Boris Yeltsin is leading a struggle to build a democratic post-Communist order out of the rubble of the former Soviet Union. Because the Soviet Union was a totalitarian society, its dissolution has involved the collapse of all its components—the economy, the administrative system, and the state structure. Yeltsin and the Russian democrats, who seek a radical change from the Communist legacy, thus face a task that is more difficult than any that the West has ever known. Rather than judging Yeltsin's project through the prism of Jeffersonian democracy, Western leaders should remember that the conditions in the Commonwealth of Independent States would lead any government to impose emergency measures. Yeltsin and the Russians must concentrate above all on building a market economy. If that effort succeeds, the higher refinements of democracy can follow, but Yeltsin should be given some leeway in the meantime.

New Commonwealth prospects. *America* 166:51 F 1 '92

There are signs of hope and trouble for the 11 former Soviet republics that have organized themselves into the Commonwealth of Independent States. Freed from an arbitrary, tyrannical government, the people of the 11 republics now have prospects for political, economic, and religious liberty. Marxists communism, however, could regain its appeal if capitalism fails to satisfy human needs. The republics have yet to devise constitutional structures for viable democracies, passionate ethnic tensions abound, and unemployment, consumer resistance to shortages, high prices, and black marketing could weaken the commonwealth's potential for political endurance. The rest of the world should be generous with aid and support, and the new confederation should be patient.

The former Soviet Union. *World Press Review* 39:18–21 F '92

A special section examines the collapse of the Soviet Union. Articles discuss the real reason for the demise of the Soviet Union, the need for a collective security system to guarantee the vital interests of all parties in the Commonwealth of Independent States, and the choice that Russians must make between parliamentary democracy and authoritarianism. Excerpts from several newspapers comment on Mikhail Gorbachev's resignation and the growing power of Russian president Boris Yeltsin.

From Maastricht to Minsk. *The New Republic* 206:7–8 Ja 6–13 '92

Most commentators have failed to realize that the European Community (EC) and the Commonwealth of Independent States are more a sign of the resilience of the nation-state than a sign of its decay. The commonwealth was born of desperate self interest, and the realism from which it arose gives the lie to those who equate nationalism with irrationality or suicidalism. When the central government in Moscow became intolerable, the former Soviet republics responsibly established a new center in Minsk. The unity deal made at the EC conference in Maastricht was founded on the same sensible blend of pragmatism and nationalism. The EC has long been adept at cloaking national self interest in the mantle of collective will, but self interest is clearly what motivates its members.

The late U.S.S.R. *The Nation* 254:3–4 Ja 6–13 '92

Mikhail Gorbachev's fall from power and the breakup of the Soviet Union will not necessarily be good for formerly Soviet citizens. However cruelly it came together and developed, the Soviet Union had the potential to improve the lives of millions of people, as a confederacy of sovereign and unequal states cannot. The Commonwealth of Independent States will probably not last long. Dominated by Russia in politics and by Slavs in culture, it will not express the identity and aspirations of the other republics. In addition, there isn't even the slightest element of democracy in the new arrangement. In Russia, Boris Yeltsin rules by decree in growing similarity to czarist and Stalinist methods, and in the provinces, renamed but unreconstructed Communist Party functionaries hold sway. The ruling elites are concerned about power struggles, privileges, and property, not the well-being of the people.

The ash heap of history. A. Meyerson. *Policy Review* no58:4–5 Fall '91

The collapse of Soviet communism occurred because large parts of the Soviet Communist Party, the KGB, and the military lost faith in communism as an idea worth killing for and because Western political, economic, and religious institutions offered a more attractive alternative. Communism was well suited for military strength, intimidation, and certain other fields of human endeavor, but it stunted human creativity and prosperity. It failed because it misunderstood human nature, ignoring man's universal capacity for reason, justice, generosity, corruption, and cruelty and rejecting man's desire for freedom, love, friendship, community, and religion.

Eastern reproaches. N. Beloff. *National Review* 44:44–5 Ap 13 '92

In its call for independence for Croatia and Slovenia, *National Review* seems to harbor the mistaken belief that if self determination were allowed, Yugoslavia would separate neatly into several democracies that would coexist harmoniously with each other. The ethnic map of Yugoslavia, however, shows so many nationalities and groups that self determination is a delusion. It also shows that one-third of Croatian territory is inhabited by Serbians or "Yugoslavs" of mixed parentage. Centuries of migrations in Croatia and Bosnia have intermingled the Catholic and Orthodox populations to such an extent that it is impossible to draw a clear line between them. The writer discusses the history of Croatia, the atrocities that Yugoslavia suffered during World War II, the current violence, and the outside world's obligation to forgo military support for any faction.

Yugoblunder. P. Glynn. *The New Republic* 206:15–17 F 24 '92

U.S. handling of the Yugoslavia crisis has been disastrous. The main problem was the Bush administration's devotion to geopolitical "stability" at the expense of democratic values and human rights. The administration attempted to prop up a declining Communist central government at the expense of the democratically minded republics of Slovenia and Croatia, which desire independence. This failed effort may have contributed to the country's violent civil war. After the war began, the United States argued that recognition of Croatia and Slovenia would only escalate hostilities, but Germany's decision to break with the United States and recognize the 2 republics brought the first enduring cease-fire. Now, 39 nations have recognized the republics, while the United States, still resisting recognition, remains isolated. America's influence and prestige in Europe have clearly been undermined by its Yugoslavia policy.

NATO slowly opens its door to East Europe. R. Knight. *U.S. News & World Report* 111:68 N 18 '91

The compromise reached between the North Atlantic Treaty Organization (NATO) and Eastern European countries at the recent summit in Rome is unlikely to be the last word. The agreement provides for alliance experts to give advice on defense planning and procurement policies to Czechoslovakia, Poland, and Hungary, but according to Hungarian leader Jozsef Antall, the East Europeans also want NATO's guarantee that it will defend Eastern Europe's borders against future aggression. As much as NATO would like to anchor Eastern Europe on the West's side, however, it is fearful of doing anything to upset Russia's democratic leadership, discourage the Russians from cutting defense, or antagonize Communist reactionaries. The Rome agreement also widens the breach between NATO members who support expanding the alliance and those who believe that such a move will ultimately discredit the principle that has guided the alliance since 1950—an attack on one member is an attack on all.

The 'other' Europe at century's end. J. Lukacs. *The Wilson Quarterly* 15:116–22 Aut '91

The West is mistaken in its prevailing belief that a deep economic crisis in Eastern Europe is stimulating uneven progress toward liberal democracy. Eastern Europe's economic problems are serious, but they are not vastly different from those confronting the West. The region's great, enduring, and distinctive problems are not economic but political. Nationalism, especially in its modern populist form, is the main political reality in Eastern Europe today. Fortunately, the prestige of the West and the middle class aspirations of the East European masses will probably limit the appeals of demogoguery and prevent great national uprisings from taking place. At the same time, however, parliamentary liberalism will not become the dominant political reality in the region. That system, like capitalism, belonged to a bourgeois society that was specific to the 19th century.

Pink tanks and red ink. R. Knight. *U.S. News & World Report* 112:46+ Mr 23 '92

Two years after communism's collapse, Eastern Europe's transition to democracy is proving even more complex and protracted than expected. Poland's gross national product dropped 10 percent in 1991, its unemployment rate is nearing 12 percent, and its leaders contend that the West is indifferent to their country's problems. Polish president, Lech Wałęsa recently hinted of possible coups, and Czechoslovakian president Václav Havel warned that political polarization and paralysis are threatening his country's unity. Other signs of tension include increasing nationalism, anti-German xenophobia, anger over the old Communist elite's staying power, and the growing temptation to resort to authoritarian means to speed the pace of reform. Democracy's cacophony of competing views only adds to Eastern Europeans' confusion. There are, nevertheless, some signs of a turnaround, including a massive upsurge in entrepreneurship and the emergence of new ideas and new politicians.

Shock of reform. G. J. Church. *Time* 139:38–40 F 17 '92

Many analysts had predicted that Eastern Europe could move swiftly from Communist stagnation to free-market prosperity, but it isn't working out that way. Critics point out that East European nations lacked essential preconditions to make an overnight change successful, such as a well-developed banking system. Now the slump in production and the rise in prices and joblessness are breeding dangerous discontent, although small signs of economic revival are also appearing. Western advisers and East European free-marketers advocate charging ahead with reform, but some populist politicians in the East now want to slow down. They advocate government action to keep afloat giant state enterprises, such as steel and textile mills. Renewed subsidies, however, would only prolong the economic agony. The economic situation in Russia, Poland, Czechoslovakia, Hungary, Romania, Bulgaria, and Albania is discussed.

The lessons Russia can learn from Eastern Europe. G. E. Schares. *Business Week* p45+ Ja 20 '92

Part of a special section on the Commonwealth of Independent States. Eastern Europe serves as a model for the period of transition that lies ahead for Russia and the other former Soviet republics as they move toward a market economy. Eastern Europeans appear to be well on their way to reshaping their economies in the Western mold, though the gains they have made have been costly. The former Soviet republics should realize that the critical framework for reform in Eastern Europe resulted from freeing prices, lifting trade restraints, and keeping a tight rein on the money supply. Many state enterprises went under in the face of increased competition, but the survivors are now pumping hard currency into the East European economies. Foreign investment has been a key ingredient in Eastern Europe's successful transition, and it offers the best hope for the former Soviet republics as well.

The red tide ebbs. M. M. Wooster. *Reason* 23:42-3 Ja '92

Economic conditions had much to do with the collapse of the Soviet Union. In particular, as Stephen S. Moody pointed out in the September 9, 1991, issue of the *New Republic,* the decontrol of oil prices under Ronald Reagan deprived the Soviets of the hard currency that they needed to support their military policy and to prop up their failing agricultural system. The budget deficit grew, inflation mounted, and black markets flourished, undermining the foundations of the command-and-control economy. The Soviet economy can only worsen in the coming months, but there is hope for Central and Eastern Europe. Americans who want to help that region move toward democracy should stop worrying about nationalism and concentrate on keeping the price of oil low, which will help Poland, Czechoslovakia, and Hungary free themselves from dependence on Soviet oil.

Eastern Europe after the revolutions. R. A. Remington. bibl f *Current History* 90:379–83 N '91

Part of a special issue on changes in Europe. The success of democracy and economic development in post-Communist Eastern Europe will depend largely on whether the West helps out. As the new governments of Eastern Europe search for identity and security, they face problems of economic reform, ethnic hostility, and territorial conflicts. Political pressures for fragmentation counter economic pressures for the cohesion that will allow post-Communist Europe to join in the European Community's move toward European integration. The transition to market economies will involve hardships, and unless the West is willing to help Eastern Europe's fragile democratic coalitions with a solid foundation of economic development, the region's multiparty systems will fail to develop into stable democracies. The United States and the European Community should help Eastern Europe by granting debt-servicing moratoriums of 3 to 5 years.

Ghoulish Hungary. *The American Spectator* 24:8–9 N '91

An article adapted from a *Washington Times* column. The cities of Eastern Europe are full of idealistic young and middle aged people who have spent years protesting the Soviet presence in their countries and the totalitarian nature of their repressive Communist governments. These ex-protesters look like the leftwing American protesters of years past, but their politics could not be more different. Advocates of free markets and immediate privatization, they greet American conservatives as kindred spirits and want to rebuild their countries on the model of Reagan's America.

Culture, high and low, in chaos. M. Batki and others. *U.S. News & World Report* 112:50–1 Mr 23 '92

Changes in the Eastern European arts community reflect the region's adjustment to democracy and market economics. With freedom, writers have lost much of their moral authority, and Poles no longer attend a film or play in order "to touch the truth." Communism coddled culture, as long as it followed the dictates of the state, but since the collapse of communism, the Polish government has slashed spending on the arts 30 percent, theaters and publishers throughout Eastern Europe have gone bankrupt, actors have grown accustomed to unemployment, and culture "houses" have become strip joints. Despite these problems, artistic freedom and the market economy are starting to reach an equilibrium. According to Arpad Goncz, Hungary's playwright president, private foundations and banks are assuming much of the burden of arts sponsorship.

Focus on the emerging democracies. *US Department of State Dispatch* 3:186–8 Mr 2 '92

A report is provided on economic and political assistance for the Commonwealth of Independent States and other emerging democracies in Central and Eastern Europe. Discussed are the United States' role in Operation Provide Hope, a multinational effort to send 2,200 tons of supplies to selected cities in the commonwealth; the Coordinating Conference on Assistance to the New Independent States; the Citizens Democracy Corps' Conference on Private Sector Assistance to the Commonwealth of Independent States and that conference's 5 working groups; proposed and existing U.S. aid commitments to the independent states; and Vice-

President Quayle's visit to Estonia, Latvia, and Lithuania. A phone number is provided for groups or individuals who wish to offer their assistance to the independent states.

Focus on Central and Eastern Europe. *US Department of State Dispatch* 2:876–8 D 2 '91

An update on U.S. relations with Central and Eastern Europe. Plans for free markets in the Baltic States, activities of the Central and East European Law Initiative of the American Bar Association, and developments in Albania, Bulgaria, Czechoslovakia, Hungary, Poland, Romania, and Yugoslavia are discussed.

Prodding Russia to step up economic shock therapy. J. Corwin. *U.S. News & World Report* 112:46–7 My 11 '92

The $24 billion bailout of Russia could be a huge gamble for the International Monetary Fund (IMF). The bailout could fuel hyperinflation, throw millions of Russians out of work, and undermine Russian president Boris Yeltsin's fragile government. Yeltsin's government has not imposed the kind of unpopular reforms that the IMF has been demanding, and Russian politics no longer favors reform. The ad hoc coalition of commercial bankers, commodity exchange brokers, and managers of large state-owned enterprises that made *perestroika* possible has collapsed, and each group now opposes further change when its new interests are threatened. Because of political pressure on the IMF and its members, however, some kind of IMF adjustment program seems certain to be adopted this spring, even if the Russian government fails to adopt the tough reform policies.

Just how much will be enough for the republics? B. Bremner. *Business Week* p55 My 4 '92

According to U.S. officials, disagreements are increasing between Western governments and aid officials over the cost of rebuilding the republics of the former Soviet Union. Michel Camdessus, executive director of the International Monetary Fund (IMF), and other officials who have the task of overhauling the former Soviet bloc are painting a dire economic picture of the region in hopes of obtaining as much funding as possible. The IMF calculates that the cost of the overhaul could total $145 billion over 4 years, a figure that far exceeds the Group of Seven's $24 billion aid and loan package. Camdessus also wants the West to help all 15 former Soviet republics, but Western leaders are reluctant to do so; thus far, only Russia has an acceptable reform program in place, and even that program is shaky.

Ruble-shooters. A. Åslund. *The New Republic* 206:13–14 My 4 '92

On April 1, Helmut Kohl and George Bush announced that the West would give Russia $24 billion of assistance this year in support of Russia's reform program. The main purpose of the package is to instill confidence in the ruble and thus facilitate trade. By guaranteeing credit lines as extra currency reserves, the West will give credence to the currency and make it possible to raise the currency's exchange rate and check inflation. Although it has been argued that Russia should not be given aid unless all the republics, or at least Ukraine, obtain equal treatment, it is important for each republic to be judged on its own merits; only those that institute serious reforms should attract serious government funding. The writer outlines the benefits of the aid package and discusses the way that the Congress of People's Deputies, which is packed with Communists, tried to jeopardize the government's economic strategy.

The rubles just don't add up. M. B. Zuckerman. *U.S. News & World Report* 112:80 Ap 27 '92

Much of the $24 billion aid program for Russia announced by President Bush is foolish. The dollar amount is too small to address the large scale of need in Russia and the other republics. In addition, the West's proposal of a $6 billion fund to help stabilize money and credit is laudable but hopeless right now, and the Bush administration's proposal to contribute more than $12 billion to the International Monetary Fund to make loans to the republics is folly because most of the money would be used to repay bad loans made by Western banks to the old Soviet Union. What is needed is a focus on realistic short term goals. To this end, the United States should offer management skills and concentrate on transportation, agricultural distribution, and energy development.

Is this too much austerity? Aid to Russia means tough scrutiny from the IMF. R. Watson. *Newsweek* 119:44 Ap 13 '92

The G-7 nations—Germany, Japan, France, Great Britain, Canada, Italy, and the United States—have pledged $24 million in aid to Russia. The terms of the agreement will be enforced by the International Monetary Fund (IMF). Russian president Boris Yeltsin may have to keep taxes and prices high, tighten credit, reduce imports, and slash social programs in order to present a respectable balance sheet to his creditors. Some experts believe that the IMF will demand too much austerity from Russia. Chief economist Alan Reynolds of the Hudson Institute says that the IMF's traditional emphasis on reduced budget deficits and currency devaluation, usually through higher taxes, promotes inflation and hinders growth. The IMF's monitoring of aid to Russia, however, could be a signal to Russians and foreign investors that economic reform now has a chance to take hold.

To Russia with trepidation: the West takes a gamble. R. Brady and others. *Business Week* p57 Ap 13 '92

Western countries have agreed to buttress Russia and the other republics of the former Soviet Union with a $24 billion package of loans and aid as the new states move haltingly toward a market economy. The assistance will include balance-of-payment loans, debt deferrals, short term credits, membership in the International Monetary Fund, and a fund to stabilize the ruble. These measures should bolster confidence, help make the republics' currencies convertible, enable farms and factories to import spare parts and other supplies, and open the way for more foreign investment. Their success will depend, however, on the resolve of Russian president Boris Yeltsin, who is under heavy internal pressure to abandon his economic reforms.

Is the West losing Russia? B. W. Nelan. *Time* 139:34–7 Mr 16 '92

The West must do more to assist Russia with its transition to democracy and a free economy. U.S. ambassador in Moscow Robert Strauss predicts a traumatic year for Russia and urges Western governments and corporations to increase their investment and technical assistance. Students of Russian affairs in several countries have warned of Russian fascists and militarists taking advantage of anger and hunger to seize power from Russian president Boris Yeltsin and his fellow reformers. An anti-Western, nationalistic regime might refurbish Russia's nuclear arsenal and recharge its military-industrial complex. By failing to spend a few tens of billions of dollars in aid over the next few years, the West could be forced to increase defense spending again to meet a renewed threat from Russia, says a Western diplomat in Moscow. Yeltsin's plan to stabilize the Russian economy and the politics of U.S. aid in an election year are discussed.

The promise of peace. R. M. Nixon. *Vital Speeches of the Day* 58:450–3 My 15 '92

In a speech delivered at the Nixon Library Conference in Washington, D.C., former U.S. president Richard Nixon outlines the role of foreign policy in American politics and calls for U.S.-led Western aid to Eastern Europe. He discusses the positive and negative factors in Russia's attempt to establish economic and political freedom; the physical and political courage of Russia's President Boris Yeltsin, who is the most pro-Western Russian leader in history and thus deserving of help; the monetary, organizational, and humanitarian aid that Russia needs; the nations that should assume the burden of aid for the emerging democracies, newly independent states, and free-market economies in the former Soviet Union and Eastern Europe; and how an international victory for freedom can be realized by a Republican president and a Democratic Congress if they can come together to provide aid to Russia.

A strategy for foreign policy. B. Clinton. *Vital Speeches of the Day* 58:421–5 My 1 '92

In an address before the Foreign Policy Association in New York City, Arkansas governor Bill Clinton discusses his foreign policy strategy: With the end of the cold war and the collapse of the Soviet empire, the United States faces an unprecedented opportunity to ensure a more prosperous and secure future. America should lead a global alliance for democracy that is as united and steadfast as the global alliance that defeated communism. So far, the Bush administration has failed to offer a compelling rationale for America's continued engagement in the world, thereby inviting a rebirth of isolationism on the Left and the Right. The United States must help the people of the former Soviet bloc to demilitarize their societies and to build free political and economic institutions.

The Nixon doctrine. R. E. Tyrrell. *The American Spectator* 25:14+ My '92

An article adapted from the *Washington Times*. Virtually alone among America's political leaders, Richard Nixon has called for a dramatic response to the changes occurring in Russia. In a recent memo to friends and associates, he urged Washington politicians to help Russian president Boris Yeltsin by sending his country temporary humanitarian aid. Nixon also prescribes rescheduling the debt incurred by Gorbachev, deferring interest payments, opening Western markets to Russian exports, stabilizing the ruble, creating a "Western-led organization to assess Soviet needs and coordinate wide-ranging governmental and private aid projects," and creating a "free enterprise corps" to send thousands of Western managers to Russia to provide "free-market know-how."

Packages with strings. *The Nation* 254:505 Ap 20 '92

The West should provide generous financial aid to Russia without making the money conditional on a quickly imposed free-market system: Both President George Bush and Democratic presidential candidate Bill Clinton have proposed aid packages that favor working through the IMF. No one appears to be concerned, however, about a possible backlash to such rapid change, which could eliminate Russia's new class of democrats and entrepreneurs. If the Russian people undergo a lengthy period of pain for a program imposed by the West, the future relationship between Russia and the United States would be uncertain. Neither the United States nor the IMF wants to fund industries that are owned by the state, but it will take a generation for private enterprises to replace those crumbling "socialist" remnants. The West should recognize that Russia knows better than the IMF how to move toward democracy and a pluralistic economy.

Aid to the new Independent State: a peace we must not lose. G. Bush. *US Department of State Dispatch* 3:281–3 Ap 13 '92

In an article excerpted from remarks made before the American Society of Newspaper Editors in Washington, D.C., President Bush discusses the importance of aid to the Commonwealth of Independent States: Securing a democratic peace in Europe and the former Soviet Union will ensure a lasting peace for the United States. The end of the cold war presents the United States with new dangers and opportunities alike. On the one hand, failure of the democratic experiment in Russia could trigger a return to authoritarianism or a descent into anarchy, threatening U.S. peace, prosperity, and security. On the other, the success of democracy in the former Soviet Union can produce a genuine peace dividend for America, a new international landscape, and extensive opportunities for global trade and economic growth.

Cold shoulder. E. V. Rostow. *The New Republic* 206:12+ Ap 13 '92

The Bush administration, which has been hesitant and equivocal on the question of aid to the former Soviet Union, should act decisively. One reason for George Bush to act now is that the failure of the provisional regimes now in place could lead to catastrophes like those that engulfed world politics after the Western allies failed in 1917–18 to rescue the Russian Republic under Aleksandr Kerensky from Vladimir Lenin's coup d'état. Another reason is that America now has a chance to do for Eastern Europe and Russia what it did for Western Europe, Germany, and Japan after World War II. Such action could greatly increase stability in world politics and make genuine peace a practical goal for the first time since 1914. The writer states that the funds needed to surmount the crisis should be provided by private investment and discusses the need for reforms of Eastern and Central European and Russian legal systems to establish environments favorable to such investment.

Imagine peacetime. R. Borosage. *Mother Jones* 17:20–3 Ja/F '92

Now that the cold war is over, America should shift money away from defense to domestic programs. Former defense secretaries and planners agree that the military budget could be cut by $150 billion a year, largely by eliminating weapons that have no current mission and by reducing unnecessary aid to allies. Even with these cuts, the United States could still maintain the strongest military in the world. America should use the money saved to rebuild the country, educate the young, clean up the environment, and boost the competitiveness of its economy. Although dramatic transformations usually occur after wars, making a dramatic change now will be much more difficult because the military has been woven into the national fabric over the course of the cold war and because the national security establishment has mobilized against the threat of peace.

Defense conversion: bulldozing the management. K. L. Adelman and N. R. Augustine. bibl f *Foreign Affairs* 71:26–47 Spr '92

Efforts to convert defense facilities to civilian production in the former Warsaw Pact countries face staggering obstacles, but the critical step of privatization is occurring in Eastern Europe. Eastern European governments should shed defense assets and encourage the absorption of such labor and capital by newly created companies. Western firms could take advantage of Eastern Europe's well-educated and fairly well-motivated work force and low labor costs by building new facilities or modifying existing ones for low cost production. A successful conversion process will require political stability, a business-friendly infrastructure, a generous approach to foreign ownership, a need-driven approach to conversion, the development of sources of hard currency, and Western efforts to inhibit top former Soviet scientists and engineers from selling their expertise elsewhere.

Disarming developments. E. Cocoran. *Scientific American* 266:110 Mr '92

The United States and the Commonwealth of Independent States are both moving to convert arms industries into civilian industries, but the commonwealth faces a more difficult challenge. Whereas weapons manufacturers of both powers once had the luxury of a single buyer with bottomless pockets, they must now contend with a market that changes with the whims and needs of consumers. In addition, the former Soviet military-industrial complex must confront confusion over who will make the decisions on military cutbacks; citizens who are psychologically unprepared for the concept of factory closings, top scientists and engineers who are leaving the country, and research and development program funding that is in disarray. Working in favor of the former Soviet republics are the beginnings of foreign investment, a host of barter exchanges, and workers in the military infrastructure, who have long been the best trained and highest paid in the Soviet work force.

Beating swords into . . . refrigerators? B. Z. Rumer. *World Monitor* 5:36–40 Ja '92

Until the military-industrial complex of the former Soviet Union is successfully converted to civilian production, the survival and recovery of the Soviet economy will be in doubt. The Soviet military-industrial sector has been dealt a mortal blow by the victory of the democratic revolution, yet thousands of enterprises and research centers remain for potential civilian use. If the West does not aid in this conversion, it would forgo a significant opportunity to tap Soviet resources and thus bolster its own economic potential. Unfortunately, shortcomings in Soviet military technology complicate the conversion economics.

The ghosts of nationalism. D. Singer. *The Nation* 254:372+ Mr 23 '92

The specter of 19th-century nationalism is haunting both Eastern and Western Europe. In the east, the collapse of the Soviet empire has enabled local nationalisms to resurface in a way that is likely to cause great disruption. As economic discontent rises in these newly independent countries,

governments are blaming Communists and "aliens." In the west, where
national boundaries are being blurred, an economic crisis has triggered a
search for foreign scapegoats, resulting in a boost for xenophobic parties
in Austria, Belgium, Italy, and Switzerland; attacks against immigrants
in Germany; and a probable advance for the racist National Front
in France's upcoming regional elections. The revival of nationalism
throughout Europe can be traced to the disappearance of the socialist
alternative. Socialism was the heir to the more rationalist and universalist
form of 19th-century nationalism. The other form, based on blood, kith,
and kin, is now dominant.

Europe's new flags. *U.S. News & World Report* 112:44–5+ F 24 '92

A special section discusses the spread of nationalism throughout Europe.
The demands for autonomy that followed the liberalization of Eastern
Europe have spread to Western Europe. Nationalist tendencies can be
attributed not only to the fall of communism but also the absence of any
new threat to European security. Paradoxically, separatism is appearing at
the same time that existing European countries are uniting as never before. The 12-nation European Community, for example, is on the verge
of creating a single, tariff-free market and may soon expand to 20 or
more members. These trends toward secession and unification have both
global and local implications. As Rutgers University professor Benjamin
Barber noted in the *Atlantic,* separatism is reappearing at a time when
economies, ecology, technology, and communications are demanding
worldwide integration and unification. Articles discuss separatist movements in Scotland, Tatarstan, and Slovakia.

In search of Europe. M. J. Rodríguez-Salgado. *History Today*
42:11–15 F '92

The meaning of the word *Europe* has changed dramatically over time. For
centuries, its meaning was strictly geographical, with Christianity giving rise
to the development of a European identity. During the enlightenment, a
time of reaction against the fusion of religion and politics, Europe became a
secular concept associated with certain cultural and political ideals. Since the
1950s, the word has been associated with the union of countries under the
European Community. Supporters and opponents of greater unity within
the EC accuse one another of being anti-European. Antifederalists contend
that greater unification would undermine national sovereignty, which they
consider essential to the identity of European states, whereas proponents of
unification regard nationalism as a cause of devastation. In fact, separatism
and unity are both fundamental facets of European identity.

Fault lines and steeples. M. Beloff, Baron. *History Today* 42:11–
14 Ja '92

An article adapted from the Spring 1991 issue of the *National Interest.*
Europe is divided along linguistic, religious, class, economic, and

ideological lines. For centuries, population movements in Europe have either been encouraged by climatic changes and demographic pressure or blocked or diverted by political and military power. Because conditions for settlement and the ability of populations to fight off invaders have varied, Europe's ethnic and linguistic map is checkered, with many unexpected anomalies. The shifting nature of the political map means that many nationalities in Eastern Europe may not be content merely with their new independence; several can look back at a past of great power. A history of persecution, discrimination, and violence in the Soviet Union and the Balkans has made residents of those areas seek to live only among their own kith and kin. The notion of a "common European home" must thus be viewed with skepticism.

The limits to self-determination. N. Gardels. *New Perspectives Quarterly* 9:50–3 Wint '92

Part of a special section on nationalism and other pitfalls for democracy following the collapse of the Soviet empire. In an interview, Spanish prime minister Felipe Gonzalez discusses the limits to self determination. He says that self determination as a principle ought to be a matter that is agreed to and regulated internationally, or there will be no end to the splintering that could occur. He believes that citizens of the member countries of the European Community (EC) should be citizens of both their own countries and Europe as a whole. He describes the effects of Soviet disintegration on European integration, and he asserts that the Eastern European countries should eventually become full members of the EC, although their present lack of competitiveness would make them unable to survive free trade with the EC.

Germany muscles in. D. Singer. *The Nation* 254:126–8 F 3 '92

The recent ascendancy of Germany reveals much about the evolution of the European Community over the past 15 years or so. Germany has seized a dominant position in Europe because of its industrial and monetary power and its championship of capitalist orthodoxy. Influenced by Germany, Western Europe has moved sharply to the right, rushing toward deregulation and privatization. Western Europe is still ahead of the United States in the areas of public health, education, and unemployment benefits, but it is moving backward. Economic growth has slowed since the mid 1970s, and unemployment has tripled. The new, unified Europe, which is being built with no real public participation, seems designed to ensure the profitability of private enterprise. In essence, the Western Left has been defeated, politically and ideologically. It must now reinvent and internationalize its mission to focus on the whole of Western Europe.

Order and disorder in the new world. L. Freedman. *Foreign Affairs* 71 Special Issue:20–37 ['92]

Part of a special issue on U.S. foreign policy. The Bush administration can be expected to argue for the continuing role of the United States at the center of the new world order, but that role may not be as central as supposed. The range of initiatives taken by the United States and its allies reflects the hope that the new world order can be managed from the top. The most probable scenarios, however, are far from global in scale, and the real policy test may be in responses to vicious but relatively limited conflicts or to evidence of economic and social breakdown that has yet to reach tragic proportions. In Europe at present, the intensive process of fragmentation undermines any attempt to produce a grand strategy for the whole area. The new world order will be created from the bottom up as states making the most progress in implementing effective post-Communist policies develop the most valuable relations with the West.

Surge to the right. G. J. Church. *Time* 139:22–4 Ja 13 '92

Throughout Europe, right wing politicians are inciting a virulent nationalism that is expressed primarily as hatred of immigrants and other foreigners. This shift to the right might seem paradoxical in light of the collapse of the Soviet empire and Western Europe's move toward economic and political unity. The decline of communism has lifted the lid on long suppressed nationalism in Eastern Europe, however, and prompted some people with no democratic traditions to seek an alternative form of strong government. In Western Europe, right wing movements have inherited some of the protest voters who used to support the Communist Party. In both East and West, economic distress has made it easy for demagogues to blame immigrants for taking jobs away from the native born. The extremists are not close to seizing power, but they are wielding considerable influence on mainstream politicians and parties in some countries.

The new Europe. G. F. Treverton. *Foreign Affairs* 71 Special Issue:94–112 ['92]

Part of a special issue on U.S. foreign policy. It has become clear that NATO is mismatched with Europe's future security problems and that the organization in its current form will not serve as the basis for anything like America's political role in Europe in the past 40 years. As the European Economic Community expands, it will find it difficult to cooperate, most acutely in the area of security. The challenge for Europe, and the concern for U.S. policy, is to ensure that Europe's center does not begin to disintegrate. NATO will remain as present reassurance and residual insurance, and the United States will have a diminished but still important political role. The events in Yugoslavia and Germany's pivotal role in widening the EC are discussed.